ANNA
and
BORIS

The Love Letters
(1944–1946)

TRANSLATED AND EDITED BY

Vera Kochanowsky

LUMINARE PRESS
WWW.LUMINAREPRESS.COM

Anna and Boris: The Love Letters
Copyright © 2022 by Vera Kochanowsky

All rights reserved. This book or any portion thereof may not be reproduced or used in any manner whatsoever without the express written permission of the publisher, except for the use of brief quotations in a book review.

Printed in the United States of America
Back cover photo by Gregory Hutton

Luminare Press
442 Charnelton St.
Eugene, OR 97401
www.luminarepress.com

LCCN: 2022911937
ISBN: 978-1-64388-991-7

For Anna

*Perhaps the mysteries of evolution
and the riddles of life that so puzzle us
are contained in the green of the earth,
among the trees and the flowers...*

—BORIS PASTERNAK, *Doctor Zhivago*

Table of Contents

Preface vii

Introduction xi

A Note to the Reader xxv

    1944 1

    1945 137

    1946 275

    Postscript 329

Epilogue 365

Afterword: Grandmother's Gift 369

Appendix A: Anna's Pearls of Wisdom 377

Appendix B: Remembrances of Anna 381

Preface

Imagine having the opportunity to better understand your parents' journey through life years after their deaths. Death seems so final and the barrier between life and death so utterly impenetrable, yet somehow that boundary has become less fixed for me after reading and translating these letters my parents exchanged during their courtship. How uncanny, yet marvelous it is to hear their voices again, describing their innermost thoughts, their fears, and their dreams, and to learn what guided them as they wrestled with the difficult decisions they faced.

When my father Boris Julius Kochanowsky (1905-1992) died, he left me a copy of his memoirs which I later edited and published under the title *Lenin, Hitler, and Me*. His dramatic story has now been shared with many. His driving ambition allowed him to realize most of his dreams despite the numerous setbacks he faced. After escaping the Soviet Union and the oppression of its Communist regime, he sought out and obtained a world-class education, established a successful career, found his "dream" girl with whom he started a family, and after many attempts, even his longest held dream came true: He finally made the United States his home.

My mother, Anna Rosa Stahel (1926-2000), had more modest ambitions. No doubt she wished to become a wife and mother. But none of the various short-term jobs she held during her life led to any career, something she never seemed to regret. When she died, I was dismayed by how few tangible reminders of her life remained behind. But among her belongings was a large cardboard box marked "for Vera." In it, at the top, was a folder full of letters, all carefully organized and labeled. They were the love letters my parents had exchanged between their first meeting in September 1944 and their wedding twenty-two months later.

After publishing *Lenin, Hitler, and Me* in 2016, I turned my attention to the letters. I was eager to learn what my mother had been like in her youth. I was also curious about my father's thoughts during the last months of World War II, and how he had come to the decision to take a job in Argentina. Finally, I wanted to see if I could uncover any hint of the irreconcilable differences that led my parents to divorce in 1970. Boris saw Anna as the woman of his dreams, the one for whom he had been searching all his life. What happened? In my discussions with readers of *Lenin, Hitler, and Me*, this question seemed to come up again and again. As the only child of their union and a witness to the dissolution of their marriage, I had always wanted to understand this aspect of their lives better. The letters revealed much that I did not know about my parents, including the nature of their early relationship, their respective expectations of marriage, and what it took for them to come together. Buried in these letters, too, are the seeds of what eventually pulled them apart.

Initially, I gave the letters only a cursory glance. There were so many, over 120, all in German, almost all of them handwritten. At first, I read only a few my mother had pulled out from the rest and clipped together.[1] On some of these she had later added explanatory headings such as "A change in thinking," and "Realization," and "Good thoughts about religion." I began by translating a few random passages from those letters she had set aside. But soon my curiosity was piqued, and I could not stop. I translated all her letters first, then continued with my father's. It became a labor of love that took nearly two years to complete.

Anna was more than twenty years younger than my father, and only eighteen when they met. In reading her letters I not only clearly recognized her personality, but I became fascinated with what she

---

1   The letters my mother had separated from the rest were A33, A34, A35, A36, A48, A57 and A58.

had been and how she changed because of my father's intervention. I was startled by the maturity she exhibited at such a young age, and by the seriousness with which she approached her life, her beliefs, and her future.

Because they resided in different locales and met in person only occasionally, my parents were forced to conduct most of their courtship through their correspondence. They shared many interests, including art, music, literature, and history. But their backgrounds, their ambitions, and their approach to life and to people could not have been more different. Their letters reveal the extent of those differences, particularly their views on some of life's most crucial questions: the nature of true love, the role of religion, the development of a personal philosophy, how to achieve emotional stability, how to get along with others, what a husband should be to his wife, and what a wife should be to her husband—issues that continue to challenge every human being. This book offers a detailed character study of two disparate, fascinating individuals during a brief but volatile period in their lives, a period that coincided with the last months of World War II and the beginning of reconstruction in Europe.

Translating the letters proved a formidable undertaking for me, partly because of the sheer quantity of letters, as well as the difficulties I faced deciphering some of the handwriting, but also because my German had suffered somewhat from thirty-five years of disuse. Happily, this project has allowed me to renew and strengthen my acquaintance with the language I spoke first as a child. For some of the most difficult passages I was fortunate to have the help of two native German speakers. I would like to express my deep appreciation to Almuth Payne and, most especially, to Klaus Alt, for their guidance and suggestions.

I would also like to thank many friends and colleagues who read the manuscript in its preliminary stages and gave me valuable advice and encouragement including Hubert Beckwith, Sally Freyberg, Raymond Goldbacher, Steven Alan Honley, Marion Jetton, Timothy Kendall, Thomas Kramer, Karen Lautman, Thomas MacCracken, Cecilia Op de Beke, and Marsha Scialdo.

And finally, I would like to thank Gregory Hutton, my husband and helpmate of more than thirty-five years, who has loved and supported me through all of life's ups and downs and through the many projects I have undertaken along the way.

Vera Kochanowsky
Falls Church, Virginia
August 2022

Introduction

Anna was charming and extremely beautiful in her youth, qualities that undoubtedly attracted my father. However, he had met other young, charming, and attractive women before. Why did he choose Anna?

After escaping Soviet Russia in 1922, my father made his way to Germany to attend the world-famous Freiberg School of Mines. He hoped to emigrate to the U.S. upon graduation in 1929, but this plan had to be put on hold because in that year the Great Depression brought immigration to a standstill worldwide. Despite a few initial setbacks, he was able to establish a successful career in Germany as a mining engineer, even doing special projects for the Minister of Mines under Hitler from 1936 until 1938. However, his fall from grace was swift and permanent once the Gestapo denounced him as a Jew early in 1939. Six months later, right after the start of the war, with the help of friends, he managed to escape to the Netherlands. During the next four years, as he continued to move through war-torn Europe, his main objective became survival.

During the war, while living in the south of France, Boris nearly managed to get out of Europe. He had applied for a U.S. visa immediately after his arrival in Marseille, and two years later, in November 1942, he received word that his visa had been approved. He planned to take a boat from Lisbon the following month, but just a few days after he purchased his ticket, the Germans took control of Marseille and closed the borders. To Boris' great dismay, he remained trapped in Europe. To evade the clutches of the Gestapo, whose presence in Marseille had increased markedly after the takeover, he was forced to go into hiding in the French Alps for over a year. At this point, he was in no position to marry. He had nothing to offer a woman: no job, no money, and no country—as a refugee he was stateless. He lived day to day. If he survived the war, perhaps then he could finally reestablish his career, get to the United States, and look for a wife with whom he could share his dreams.

In December 1943, with the aid of the French Resistance, Boris was able to cross the Swiss border. Although still a refugee, he could now begin to lead a relatively comfortable life. He was given the opportunity to study at the Eidgenössische Technische Hochschule (ETH), a public science and technology university in Zurich,[2] and eventually he even found mining work in Switzerland. With money coming in and the prospect of employment after the war, he felt that the time was right to consider marriage. The locale, too, was advantageous in his opinion. He admired Switzerland, its history, and its long-standing commitment to peace and neutrality. His admiration and gratitude extended to the Swiss people themselves for the refuge and assistance he had received since his arrival.

My father had been an agnostic all his life, but his interest in religion increased markedly during his final year in France because of the admiration he held for the many French religious leaders who had protected him. These brave individuals were part of the backbone of the French Resistance. Their altruism and morality inspired him to begin a serious exploration of the meaning and value of Christianity. After his arrival in Switzerland, his desire to continue his study of Christianity led him to take advantage of an unexpected opportunity. One day while at the ETH, he noticed a sign advertising a Bible study course being offered at a small religious community in the village of Gwatt. The minister who was to teach the course, a Reverend Kühner, ran the establishment which included a boarding house for young women. My mother was among the residents. The two-week course was held in early September 1944. After meeting Anna and finding himself completely transfixed by

---

[2] The Swiss Federal Institute of Technology, originally called Eidgenössische Polytechnische Schule (*Polytechnikum*), was established in 1855. Albert Einstein studied there from 1896 until 1900. In 1911 the school's name was changed to Eidgenössische Technische Hochschule.

her, my father arranged to stay on as a guest of Reverend Kühner for another week. He then returned to his lodgings in Zurich, and within hours of his arrival began an intensive correspondence with Anna that would last nearly two years.

Anna had grown up in the northern Swiss city of Winterthur, the only child of Johann (Hans) and Rosa Stahel (née Bertschi). Rosa had worked as a nanny for a few years before she met and married my grandfather. Hans was a professional cabinet maker who specialized in the construction and restoration of fine furniture. He had taken over his father's business and employed a small number of workers in his shop. The couple wed in 1924, when Rosa was twenty-two and Hans twenty-five. Unfortunately, they soon discovered they were not well suited to each other. In those days divorce was rare. Hans started spending most evenings at the local tavern drinking and playing cards.[3] His routine did not change much once Anna was born in 1926. As a result, mother and daughter were often left to themselves, and Anna never developed a close relationship with her father.

Anna relied on her mother for everything—guidance, encouragement, entertainment, advice, and most importantly, love. Although she had no siblings, Anna had many relatives in the area, including numerous cousins with whom she was friendly. She also got along well with most of her classmates and played with some of the neighborhood children in Veltheim, the suburb of Winterthur where they lived. Her uncle Heinrich Ott was her teacher from the fourth through the sixth grades, and his son, her cousin Hans, was in her class. Hans confessed to me many years later that they were rivals during those early years, and he used to pull her pigtails.

It was a pleasant enough life for Anna, until tragedy struck. In August 1939 Rosa succumbed to tuberculosis. Anna was only thirteen years old at the time. In the last photo taken of them together their mutual affection is obvious, but the effects of Rosa's illness are too. Rosa had aged, looking much older than her thirty-seven

---

[3] My grandfather was said to have been addicted to *Jass*, a trick-taking card game popular in German-speaking countries.

years. As a last resort, she had gone to a distant health clinic to try a new gold-based treatment for tuberculosis, but it failed. She died at the clinic.

Anna had lost the only person in the world who loved her deeply and unconditionally. Had Rosa survived just a few more years, past Anna's formative years of adolescence, my mother might not have suffered as much as she did. Compounding her loss, Anna had to endure her mother's funeral service. The custom within the Swiss Reformed Church at the time was to bring the open casket into the funeral chapel for the service. After the service, the coffin was closed and wheeled directly into the cremation chamber from which visible flames would emanate. Anna, having seen her mother's still rosy cheeks, could not bear to watch her being burned up looking so alive. She cried out and ran from the chapel at the sight of the flames.

Custom required Anna to wear black clothing for a year following her mother's death. She was in mourning and that was the proper attire, but it also broadcast the fact that she was different and disadvantaged. She never liked being singled out as the object of attention, particularly negative attention.

The death of his wife did not significantly change the way Hans Stahel treated his daughter. Their relationship continued to be congenial, but not close. It is possible that Hans felt a tinge of guilt over the poor relationship he had had with his wife, and perhaps that made him less eager to involve himself with their only child. He may also have thought himself inadequate to fill what he considered a maternal role. In the end, he just could not offer his daughter the love she needed. However, for the first few months after his wife's death, he hired an adult female companion for Anna who also helped with the housework and cooking. When World War II broke out, even though Switzerland was neutral, Hans enlisted in the Swiss Army and was often required to go on military maneuvers on weekends, so he was rarely at home. During his first year of service in the army, he met his future second wife, Martha Gimmi.

She was twenty-eight years old and had never been married before. When Hans and Martha wed in 1941, Anna had to welcome a new stepmother into her home.

When I knew my grandfather in the 1960s, he was a kind old gentleman who doted on me. But I also knew that he was fairly set in his ways, and that he could be extremely stubborn and show a mean temper which sometimes led to nasty arguments (mostly with Martha) about the most insignificant details. But in 1939 my mother desperately needed love, and somehow that need had to be fulfilled, even if her search for it led her in the wrong direction. There were those among her friends and classmates who felt terribly sorry for her and tried to help, but there were others, particularly young men, who took advantage of her need for love.

At this time, Anna's maternal grandmother, Anna Bertschi,[4] became a major influence in her life. Deeply religious, Anna Bertschi had lost her husband quite early and had raised their four children, Elise, Albert, Emil, and the youngest, Rosa, on her own. Her farm in Uhwiesen (north of Winterthur, not far from the Rhine and the German border) produced fruits and vegetables that she took to market in nearby Schaffhausen three times a week during the growing season. Anna, who would often spend her summer vacations with her grandmother on the farm, remembered the berries, the grapes, and especially the nine cherry trees. Those summers were full of treasured memories for them both. Grandmother Bertschi also took in boarders, generally schoolteachers, and did everything she could to provide for her family. She now took a special interest in my mother and tried her best to fill the dreadful void her daughter's death had left in Anna's life. Although she lived out in the countryside, she tried to see and to communicate with her granddaughter as much as possible. Through this more regular contact, Anna came to respect and appreciate her grandmother's hard-working lifestyle,

---

4   My mother shared her Christian name with both of her grandmothers, Anna Bertschi and Anna Stahel (née Ott), as well as an aunt, Anna Stahel, her father's younger sister who had died at age nineteen, shortly before my mother's birth.

her devotion to her family, and especially her deep and abiding religious faith, along with the positive, life-affirming philosophy she applied to all of life's challenges.[5]

While Anna's mother may have been religious, Hans was not. I do not know whether or how they observed any religious practices other than the celebration of Christmas, but it was after her mother's death that Anna became more open to religion, possibly through her grandmother's influence. Everyone in the family knew Anna Bertschi loved all her grandchildren, but they also knew that she loved Anna best of all. The feeling was mutual. They developed a close and lasting bond built on love and respect.

After completing her secondary school education, my mother enrolled in a three-year vocational training program in sewing and upholstery in Thun. From the fall of 1942 until she completed her training in the spring of 1946, she lived at the Heimstätte, a "homestead" for young women owned and run by the Reformed Church in the small village of Gwatt on the northwestern shore of Lake Thun. It is here where Boris and Anna's story begins.

Anna and Boris quickly formed a strong attachment after their first meeting. My father was handsome, highly confident, well-educated, and exotic— qualities that no doubt intrigued my mother. Yet there were many obstacles they had to face: the differences in their ages, backgrounds, beliefs, and education being among the most daunting.

Although he was a penniless refugee when he met Anna, my father had been the youngest child of a large, wealthy family in Krasnoyarsk, Siberia. His father had been an entrepreneur and had established many successful businesses in the years leading up to the Russian Revolution. My father's parents and older siblings, five

---

[5] Here follows the text of Grandmother Bertschi's favorite hymn as set down by another granddaughter, Hanni Bänzinger-Witzig: "In vain do you seek the source of good far out in the wilderness. You carry heaven and hell and your own judge in your breast. What can the earth give you, for you are but a guest and stranger? You must belong to heaven, as the longing for heaven is within you. Look up to those golden stars, they call to you so warmly, as if beckoning from afar: 'We are creations just like you!'" (German title: "*Umsonst suchst du des guten Quelle*")

brothers and a sister, all of whom were university-educated, were a great inspiration to him. His family provided him with a stable homelife and the opportunity to develop himself, both physically and intellectually. Until the arrival of the Red Army in Krasnoyarsk in December 1919, his childhood could not have been more ideal. He had had the freedom and ambition to explore his world and his talents, while having financial security and the deep love of everyone in his family. Shortly after the Communists took control, his family's property, their fortune, and his father's many businesses were seized by the new government. From that point on his family faced many hardships and crises. Yet his first fourteen and a half years had given my father a solid foundation, an unshakeable self-esteem, and a deep faith in his own abilities—traits that never left him despite the many obstacles he faced over the next twenty-five years. Even late in life, he continued to possess a kind of aristocratic bearing and attitude. He went on to proudly pursue his dreams of receiving a world-class education and establishing a career for himself in his chosen field. My father also had long harbored the desire to do great things for humanity. He had particularly looked up to two of his older brothers who were physicians, admiring them as moral heroes. He dearly wished to emulate them and do good in the world, as they had. He wanted to use his talents to make enough money to support the less advantaged, as well as to improve the condition of mankind in general through his innovative efforts in the mining industry.

Anna, on the other hand, had no such grand plans. She had been an only child in a working-class family and had attended public school only until the age of sixteen. After losing her mother, she struggled with depression and low self-esteem. Like many of her peers, she decided to pursue vocational training so that she could work in a trade. Her move to Gwatt showed that she wanted some independence from her family, as well as a refuge from those she felt had looked down on her earlier. She certainly had hopes of marrying someday and having children, goals typical of many girls her age. When my father described his life ambitions to her, they overwhelmed and excited her at the same time. She wanted to help and support the people she loved, her family, her friends, her neighbors, and she hoped that she could do some good on a small scale. But in her view, taking on the betterment of the entire world would create such a strain on her that she would end up overexerting herself in pursuit of an impossible goal, shirking her familial duties, and in the end, doing nothing well. But my father managed to convince her that she could help him move mountains by being a good wife to him.

As children, my parents had been exposed to different moral standards. My father's parents and all the married couples he knew in Russia seemed to be deeply in love and completely devoted to each other; the societal expectation was that they would remain faithful to the end of their lives. As my father relates in his memoirs, infidelity was practically unheard of and considered scandalous and abominable. Every member of his family was loved and admired by the others, which made each feel emotionally and morally strong. My mother's experience was not so fortunate. Her parents had a rocky marriage from the start and lived quite separate lives. Whether either of them found romantic solace elsewhere is difficult to say, but it is quite likely. Infidelity, including the careful keeping of secrets, seemed an accepted facet of life. My mother, always quick to catch on to subtle cues, picked up the social wiles of the society in which she lived. She knew how to be sneaky when necessary.

One of the main topics my parents discussed in their early letters was religion. While my father appreciated the teachings of Jesus, he did not believe in the supernatural or in the physical resurrection of the body after death. Like everyone in his family, my father had been a "free-thinker" and had never practiced any religion. During his last year in France, when he came into close contact with many priests and ministers involved with the Resistance, his interest in religion increased and he began to study the Bible. However, he still was not a believer. But Anna did believe, at least at first. In fact, just two weeks before they met, Anna had had a religious experience in which she had seen God. Because their religious beliefs differed so greatly, it was necessary for them to find common ground before they could seriously consider a life together. As a result, religion was discussed in great depth during the first few months of their correspondence.

Another important focus in their early letters was the broadening of Anna's education. My father had obtained a rigorous education, including two academic degrees and some doctoral research, and had worked professionally as a mining engineer for nearly ten years. From his youth he had been exposed to theater, music, and literature. She, on the other hand, had had limited exposure to the cultural arts or to higher learning of any kind. My father encouraged her to increase her knowledge in these areas and she eagerly responded to his help. He sent her numerous literary works, including Leo Tolstoy's last novel, *Resurrection*. He also often sent her picture postcards of famous men and of paintings that they discussed in their letters. In the end, Anna became more enthusiastic about learning than her teacher, even admonishing him for not delving deeply enough into the subjects they were discussing.

The problem of introducing Boris to Anna's parents soon came up. Hans and Martha quickly became aware of Anna and Boris' rapidly intensifying relationship. Hans was not at all pleased with the match, as he felt my father was too old for Anna and too poor. Also, his opinion of foreigners, especially Russians, was not high. Martha could be difficult too, but she, of the two, was the more open-minded.

Another frequently discussed topic was my mother's previous mistakes—her beauty and her desperate need for love had led to several serious romantic entanglements. Her past was a concern to them both. She tries to reassure Boris in her letters, but admits it is strange that he, with his strict moral compass, had selected her as a life partner. Boris' heavy focus on God and Christianity in his early letters may be explained by his fear that Anna would stray, and his hope that a strong religious faith would inspire Anna to marital fidelity. Based on his contact with the religious leaders he had met in France prior to his arrival in Switzerland, he sincerely believed that anyone who was a true believer must also be a very moral person. So, if Anna maintained her close connection with God, she would be less likely to be unfaithful. Early in their correspondence, he makes clear how any indiscretion on her part would disrupt his peace of mind and destroy the quality of his life. Interestingly, Anna senses Boris' disappointment as she begins to turn away from her faith a few months later.

After the war in Europe ended in May 1945, the tone of their letters changes. There were pressing questions that had to be answered: How could my father re-enter his profession after such a long hiatus? Where could he find a good job? Where could they live comfortably? Which countries would accept them? At that point philosophy, art, music, literature, and religion take a back seat to more practical considerations. The decision of whether and when to marry was difficult for my father as he felt the responsibility of having a wife, and potentially a family, weighing heavily on his shoulders. It would be a far greater burden than living only for himself. Also, Anna's parents, especially her father, continued to oppose her marriage to Boris to such a degree that neither of her parents attended the couple's wedding on July 30, 1946.

Overall, the letters show how my parents got to know each other and how they worked toward a common future. They had to negotiate the huge gulf between them, as well has Anna's family's opposition. It took much effort on both sides. Over the course of twenty-two months, they eventually came to an understanding and decided to marry. Yet, as the letters reveal, the path was far from smooth.

While the discussions and exchange of ideas between the lovers are engaging, it is Anna's evolution in thinking that is most compelling. Still only a teenager with few good prospects for the future and more than her share of unfortunate past experiences, my mother clung to what she believed would give her strength: her Christian faith and God. My father's influence on her life, as an older man with far greater life experience and knowledge, should not be underestimated. He was her teacher in many ways, almost more a teacher than a lover. And because their time together was limited, much of what transpired between them is documented in their letters. My father's views remained relatively consistent throughout their courtship; however, those of my mother changed substantially. Her letters are charming, fresh, and thought-provoking, while those of my father, who was destined to become a university professor, sometimes take on the pedantic flavor of a thoroughly researched lecture. But he, more often than my mother, allows a playful sense of humor to shine through on occasion. Interestingly, their respective qualities and personalities as revealed in these letters closely parallel those of the parents I came to know in the 1960s and 1970s.

Many readers of *Lenin, Hitler, and Me* were surprised that after all his struggles, escapes, and successes, Boris lost what mattered most to him in the end—my mother. Why did Anna make the unexpected and radical decision (for the time) to divorce my father? This question is difficult to answer, as she shared few details with me. Unlike my father, my mother did not readily speak of her past or her personal feelings. Although she was much admired for her charm, compassion, and warmth, she maintained a certain reserve, a kind of invisible barrier. It was a necessary protective tool, as she was extremely sensitive, her self-esteem highly prone to injury.

Even while keeping certain aspects of her life carefully hidden, she also generously gave of herself to others, especially to me—her time, her loyalty, her understanding, her encouragement, and the visible pride she took in my accomplishments. I could not imagine a more perfect mother, following what she saw as her primary calling—being a loving mother to her only child. She bestowed on me everything she missed getting from her own mother during a crucial time in her life. I had all the love I needed to become a strong, confident person, with the ability to tell the difference between a true, generous love and a relationship based purely on dependency, avarice, need, or ambition.

After reading and translating their letters, in some ways I feel closer to my parents now than I ever did as a child. Even after I reached adulthood, while they were living, they were still "my parents," never people independent from me, with separate lives and stories. Despite the many years that have passed since their deaths, I have been given a unique and precious opportunity to admire and reflect upon their wonderfully different personalities: my father's, dramatic and sparkling like a brilliant star, with the power and determination to take on the whole world; and my mother's, subtly shimmering as the slightest crescent moon, quietly drawing you into its mystery.

I dedicate this book to my mother, the subtle moon, in gratitude for her great wisdom, her refined character, the respect and admiration she held for people of all cultures, her deep love of nature and the arts, her unquenchable thirst for knowledge, her diplomacy and sensitivity, and her unfailing ability to bring joy to all those she encountered.

Gwatt, on the shore of Lake Thun
The Heimstätte is on the far right.

The Heimstätte
Anna lived here from 1942 until 1946.

A Note to the Reader

The letters in this volume are labeled and identified by the author's first initial: Anna's letters (A), Boris' letters (B), Martha's (M) and Hans/Vati's (V), etc. The number that follows indicates the order of mailing, earliest to latest. In some cases, the writer continues his or her letter over the course of one or more days. Those composite letters are assigned a single number.

A careful reader will come to realize that some of the letters are missing. Considering how carefully those that survive were preserved and organized, I suspect that my mother may have destroyed the ones she did not want me to read. My suspicion has been somewhat confirmed by Charles Hosler, Anna's second husband, who told me that in her last years she spent many afternoons out at their camp reading and burning old letters. Of course, those she burned may have included other letters, not necessarily ones from this collection. The symbol * indicates that the letter mentioned in the text is lost.

In some cases, I have elected to omit passages I found mundane or repetitive; elsewhere I have chosen to retain some seemingly unessential material for its potential historical value, or because it provides a unique perspective on the writer's personality.

In general, titles have been anglicized (Herr/Mr., Frau/Mrs., etc.), however I have chosen to retain the German title frequently associated with Gertrud Kurz (Frau Dr.) because the respect it reflects has no parallel in the English language.

All biblical translations are taken from the Revised Standard Version of the Holy Bible.

1944

LETTER B1

ZURICH

[Monday] September 18, 1944

Dear Anneli!

It is 1:10 p.m. I am sitting in my room and have decided to write you a few quick words. Five hours have passed since I left Gwatt, but I still feel like I am walking around in a daze. Despite the long trip by train and streetcar, I am completely oblivious to my surroundings. I can only see Gwatt, its surroundings, and the people there. I think somehow Gwatt's air has stagnated around me and it will be some time before it dissipates and dissolves into the Zurich atmosphere. I am drinking a cup of strong coffee now; hopefully, it will wake me up. In a way it is pleasant to be so intoxicated, but I would rather be completely sober. I know I will find it difficult to study in this condition. Perhaps you are experiencing the same problem? At least you have the Reverend and Fritzchen[6] there with you. I, on the other hand, am all alone.

My trip went smoothly. When I got off in Zurich, I noticed I still had my ticket. It had not been punched and taken by the conductor. I wanted to keep it and use it another time, but after a brief inner struggle, I located the conductor and gave him my unused ticket. Even though this is a trifling matter, if a person is honest in small matters, then he will likely be honest when dealing with more important things too.

I was pleased with your question and especially your facial expression when I told you what I would say to the authorities if I were asked why I had not returned to Zurich on Sunday.[7] Even in as brief a conversation as this I can see how much you value truthfulness, and that pleases me a great deal. I value your honesty, naturalness, and

---

6   Fritzchen is likely Reverend Kühner's son. The Reverend's wife and their young children also resided at the Heimstätte.
7   Refugee travel within Switzerland was strictly regulated by the Swiss authorities at this time.

sincerity. And that is not all that pleases me. You have many other worthy qualities that impress me.

I forgot to give you some suggestions for staying slim, as I said I would. One should try to:

1. Avoid drinking too many fluids (soups, etc.).

2. Stop eating before you are completely full. Eating a lot or a little is a habit we cultivate.

3. Eat a lot of fruit (especially apples).

4. Take care that your blood circulation is good, otherwise fat globules will get stuck in the body. Therefore, it is a good idea to take cold baths and showers, or rub yourself down with a cold washcloth. To this add body massage and exercise, including exercises that strengthen the stomach muscles. A protruding stomach can be a result of weak muscles or habitual overeating.

5. It would be good to have a "fruit day" (eat nothing but fruit all day) once a week. Now, in fall, fruit is readily available, so it would be easy to do this.

6. Do not sleep too much.

7. Check your weight at least once a month.

Please do not be shocked by my long prescription for the care of your body. Even the scriptures say the body is the temple wherein the Holy Ghost resides. One should strive to keep this temple clean and beautiful. This is especially important for women. For men strength is more prized, but with women it is charm and beauty. You now have much beauty and charm, which is of great value and cannot be bought with money or achieved by artificial means (such as the application of makeup, nail polish, etc.). So, take care that neither your charm, nor your beauty, gets lost.

By the way, both my father and mother had large bellies. But I, as you have noticed, do not have that problem yet, although I have that tendency. Also, you should not assume you will get fatter with age. You just need to pay close attention to your habits and follow the modern rules of physical care.

Please do not think that I value your body more than your soul and spirit. I have written so much about the body that I have left some important things out. Quite on the contrary, later you will hear only about the soul and the spirit. I know that with the help of Reverend Kühner you have learned that the most important questions in life must be given serious consideration. Controlling physical temptations depends mainly on inner strength and the development of a harmonious relationship with one's fellow human beings. If successful, one can experience God's kingdom on earth. Do not read too much romanticism into it, rather approach this lofty goal very soberly. All of man's happiness depends on the solution to this very problem.

---

10 p.m.

This afternoon I filled out some forms at the police station. Then I bought you a book by Tolstoy and a picture postcard of Beethoven by Torggler.[8]

At first glance this picture of Beethoven is not very pleasing. One should not look at it under bright light, but only in very dim surroundings, or with partly closed eyes, to mimic the effect of a screen in front of a camera lens limiting the amount of light falling onto

---

[8] The portrait of Ludwig van Beethoven by Hermann Torggler (1878-1939), after a bust by Franz Klein (1779-1840), was painted for F. A. Ackermann (1837-1903) and published as a postcard, Series 160, Number 1902. F. A. Ackermann ran one of the oldest publishing houses in Germany which was known at this time for its excellent postcard reproductions of historic and contemporary art. See https://www.pinterest.com/pin/361765782544963633/ and the Dumbarton Oaks research library website: https://www.doaks.org/research/library-archives/dumbarton-oaks-archives/collections/ephemera/names/f-a-ackermann.

the photographic plate. Under these visual circumstances you should observe the picture for one to two minutes and focus exclusively on the eyes. You will then suddenly have the feeling you can see right into Beethoven's soul. While you are looking at the picture, think about Beethoven's music, perhaps the concerto you like so much. Then observe the whole face, especially the mouth, chin, and hair, and you will see how the face expresses the essence of Beethoven's soul and spirit. This is what the painter intended. Beethoven believed God created the world. When you listen to Beethoven's music, you can get a sense of this creative spirit and strength, which is so crucial for people to experience. Jesus wishes to lead people in this direction so that they can be of service to others out of love for God. That is why one can get closer to God by listening to the music of Beethoven.

Beethoven by Torggler

I would very much like to give Reverend Kühner a book by Dostoyevsky. But before I do, I would like you to find out which books he already has, then I will look for a different one in the bookstores.

I will end this letter now and go to sleep because I am very tired and still feel like I am drunk. I hope you will pardon my many mistakes and bad handwriting. I wish you a good night and send you a big hug.

Your Boris

P.S. I enclose a program that you can keep.[9]

---

9 A copy of the concert program Boris performed at the refugee camp on March 15, 1944, see *Lenin, Hitler, and Me*, p. 210.

LETTER B2

Zurich

[Tuesday] September 19, 1944

Dear Anneli,

I am sending you a copy of *Resurrection*[10] by Leo Tolstoy along with this letter. Please read it slowly and carefully. It makes no difference how many books you read, what matters is how deeply and thoroughly you understand them. Tolstoy possessed a great understanding of the human soul; he was able to describe the smallest human emotions with astounding accuracy. Tolstoy, and particularly Dostoyevsky, believed that the worst people, even prostitutes and hardened criminals, can be redeemed. Because of his deeply religious viewpoint and his prophetic explanations, Dostoyevsky has become world renowned, so much so that he is often cited by the world's most famous theologians (including those in Switzerland).

Notice with what amazing precision Tolstoy describes the seduction of Katyusha Maslova by Prince Nekhlyudov. One can see directly into the souls of these two people. Notice later how indifferently, superficially, and irresponsibly the judge condemns Katyusha. One is full of indignation over the people and the circumstances described in the courtroom. One wants to put them all into prison! But it is possible to encounter similar cases in real life. There are those who out of complacency take no part in helping mankind, even now, when the world suffers so.

Observe how senselessly the characters described live their lives, including Nekhlyudov himself, and how the value and purpose of Prince Nekhlyudov's life change when he recognizes his misdeed and

---

10 *Resurrection*, Leo Tolstoy's last published novel (1899), tells the story of a wealthy aristocrat, Prince Nekhlyudov who, in a weak moment, seduces a young maid, Katyusha. He soon comes to recognize the severity of his error, personally witnessing the injustices of the Russian legal system at her trial, and tries to redeem himself by helping Katyusha, who had fallen on hard times after their brief affair.

its result (Katyusha's unfortunate experiences). Notice the spiritual shift in both main characters. Pay attention to how Tolstoy describes each character and try to read the book as if you were standing amongst the people being depicted. This should not be difficult when reading a book by as good an author as Tolstoy.

When I was in Irkutsk,[11] I was able to witness a final examination given by a law professor at the university organized in the form of the trial of Katyusha Maslova. The professor himself played the part of the judge, and all the other roles (the accused, the jury, the prosecutor, the defense lawyer, the witnesses, the citizens of the town) were taken by the students. I recall the scene very well, even though I was only a boy at the time.[12]

When you read this book, remember that Leo Tolstoy's daughter, Alexandra Lvovna Tolstoy,[13] played a special role in my fate. It will surely interest you. This book will help you better understand the difference between good and evil, and to discover the spiritual processes people undergo. It will also broaden your view of life and literary art.

You should only read good books, books by authors who aim to improve the human condition by clearly describing what good really is, as well as the evil that lurks within mankind. Throw away all lightweight books, like romances and those that only titillate the senses without ennobling the spirit. Sensuality alone, without spiritual or emotional fulfillment, ruins people and leads them to their downfall. One should guard against that. It is especially dangerous for girls and

---

11   Boris lived in Irkutsk, about 700 miles east of his native Krasnoyarsk, for a few months in 1922 when he was seventeen years old.

12   Reforms by Tsar Alexander II (reigned 1855-1881) led to changes in legal education at Russian universities, led by the Moscow University. There they began the practice of staging mock trials as a central element in their curriculum. See Thomas Wolf, *The Nightingale's Sonata: The Musical Odyssey of Lea Luboshutz* (New York: Pegasus Books, 2019), p. 40.

13   Alexandra Lvovna Tolstoy (1884-1979) was the youngest daughter and secretary of author Leo Tolstoy. She left the Soviet Union in 1929 and by 1931 had settled in the United States. In 1939 she established the Tolstoy Foundation. The original purpose of the foundation was to help refugees from Europe and the Soviet Union. Later, it played an important role in helping displaced Soviets, dissidents, and former Soviet citizens settle in the West. The specifics of how Alexandra Tolstoy helped Boris are unknown. See www.tolstoyfoundation.org/tolstoy.html.

young women. It is better to strive toward spiritual fulfillment, then everything in life will have a higher value and you will find greater joy in the physical things as well.

This morning I was angry with you. I thought I would surely get a letter from you by now, but nothing came. I was sad and disappointed. I have already written you three letters. The first you must have already received. This one I will take to the post office now, and the third is nearly complete and will be mailed tomorrow. This proves I fulfill my promises. And what about you?

I would dearly like to see you again and see your expression when you read my letters!

When I write you a letter it is as if I am speaking with you directly, and that does me good. I eagerly await your imminent news.

I send you a big hug,

Your Boris

P.S. I must mail this letter with this evening's post so the enclosed cake will stay fresh. I wonder whether it will arrive in good condition. I hope it will not get completely crushed.

LETTER A1

Gwatt

[Wednesday] September 20, 1944

Boris,

I have so much to tell you! Everything is dancing around in my head, so I don't know where to begin. First, many thanks for your letter, the marvelous picture postcard of Ludwig van Beethoven, and the sweet little cake. I thought of you intently as I was eating it. I don't deserve to be spoiled so!

But Boris, something is worrying me. You say you feel as if you are drunk with love. Being in love like that is nonsense. On Sunday evening, you held me to sobriety, so please keep yourself that way too! Please do!

I will tell you briefly how I feel. Since you left, I can hardly think of anything but you. But my thoughts of you are not always good ones. Often, I have nagging doubts. But they inevitably are followed by thoughts that give me courage. I suddenly realized it may be God's will that we be united forever one day. This conviction hit me so hard and gave me such comfort, that sadness and confusion no longer had any power over me. I then started to wonder why I had fallen in love with you in the first place, and in doing so, I discovered the following: Your calm, strong manner drew me to you, and your kind words seemed to do me good. Later, as I began to understand you better, I came to realize what you mean to me, and that without you I would be only half of myself. I think about your life's goal. You say you want to serve humanity and "bear fruit." I want to do the same but cannot without help because I lack your determination. I try to maintain a semblance of determination because otherwise I think I would lose myself in the smallest daily ordeals. Because you make me feel so strong, I just cannot let go of the idea that perhaps God intended to bring us together.

Now about your advice regarding personal hygiene. I must tell you that I was quite shocked by your suggestions at first. But then, all at once, I had a big laugh over it. It is so typical of you to give such detailed instructions. You know, I agree that people should be well-groomed, and for you I will try my best, but I find that with true love outward appearances are not so important.

You don't know how thankful I am to you for introducing me to Beethoven and his music. It will surely take a while for me to wrap my head around him, but I think a book that includes some of his letters might help me. I really want to understand and learn about his music, because I know it will help me understand you.

You said that one should never speak about permanence. Of course, no one knows what God intends for them, and so one must never make any promises without adding, "If it is God's will."

Your experience on your trip home with the ticket brought me much joy. I see only now how valuable it is when one can have complete trust in someone. Therefore, when you awake from your reverie and everything is gray again and you discover there is an obstacle between us, please do not shame me by hiding it from me. You must tell me the truth clearly and openly.

Boris, I do not want you to feel so alone anymore. My first and last thought each day is always of you.

With greetings and a sweet kiss,

Your Anneli

P.S. Dearest, God will surely grant you clarity and sobriety.

LETTER B3

ZURICH

[Wednesday] September 20, 1944

Dear little Anneli!

I was in town all day today and thought about you continually. I still feel quite "drunk," as I am still totally oblivious to the world around me. Everything seems so different. People I used to like very much I now feel indifferent toward. Today I saw the Italian finance minister's niece, Miss Jury from Montreux, whom I got to know at the refugee camp. I was quite taken with her back then, but today she did not interest me in the least, and I was happy to take my leave of her, as all I really wanted to do was think of you. I am surprised by this change in me, but happy about it. Then some friends of mine introduced me to a female Polish student who was interested in taking some Russian lessons from me. I did not promise I would teach her. After that I went to visit four female friends who work at the Women's Service Union. They helped me a great deal when I first arrived in Zurich and they have looked after me diligently ever since. They see me as their foster child. This time I was less happy to see them than usual, in that I noticed that I could not honestly reciprocate their degree of enthusiasm upon seeing me. I really don't know what is wrong with me. On the one hand, I was glad to see them, on the other hand, I was bothered by my reaction to them.

Above all, I would like to figure out what it is I like best about you. Is it purely a physical attraction, or is it your soul, character, spirit, or bearing that attracts me? Is it the outer attributes (your voice, mouth, nose, eyes) or the inner qualities (your conversion,[14] your wish to become more spiritually worthy)? Or is it your speaking voice, your singing, your piano playing, or your way of delving into

---

14   This refers to Anna's spiritual awakening and her new embrace of Christianity. It is referred to in later letters as Anna's "rebirth" or "resurrection."

things so thoroughly where your physical and spiritual virtues are so magnificently melded together? I would prefer to consider all these qualities together, rather than just the physical ones. I am amazed especially by the great joy I feel at this very moment as I write to you. This is something I have never experienced before. I have always been a lazy correspondent. Can you imagine, I once received three telegrams from my mother at the same time, one delivered by a friend of my parents in Berlin, one from the Rector at the Freiberg School of Mines, and one from the director of a mine, a former employer. All of them asked me why I had not written home, as my parents were very worried about me.[15]

I am uncertain whether we should be happy or not. Only time will tell whether we have the spiritual strength needed to build a lasting relationship. But, in your case, the hand of God supports you, so your soul is really on the mend and the passage of time can only work in your favor. As for me, I am still in the dark because I am hopelessly in love with you. The last straw was hearing you sing and (don't be surprised) play the piano. I doubt I can hold out until Christmas without seeing you. I am continually trying to figure out ways I might be able to visit you before then.

For the moment, I am happily looking forward to hearing your voice on the telephone Friday evening. Please tell me exactly when to call so that you will be alone and can speak freely. Above all, write me what you are doing, what you are thinking, and what you are feeling. I know that I can trust you completely and I believe all you say. I would so dearly like to be able to look into your heart and see how the little tree we planted on September 12[16] is doing.

I send you a big hug and kiss,

Your Boris

---

15 Boris refers here to a period (1923-1929) when he was studying at the School of Mines in Freiberg, Germany. He continued to correspond with his family in the Soviet Union until 1933.
16 The date of their boating excursion on Lake Thun during which they made a serious commitment to each other.

[Thursday] September 21, 1944

My dear little Anneli,

This morning I was sure I was going to get a letter from you at last, but nothing came. I was very disappointed, and I don't know what to think. There must be some reason you have not written yet. Are women's hearts so deceptive? I hope not! Please write and tell me the reason for your silence. I had hoped you might help me find inner peace. But your silence is driving me crazy.

With a thousand greetings and a loving kiss,

Your Boris

LETTER A2

GWATT

[Thursday] September 21, 1944

Dearest,

This morning I received your book and letter. You have no idea how much joy they brought me. I thank you a thousand times.

This afternoon I read some of Beethoven's letters and afterwards I thought about them for a long time. I thought of his picture, his music, and about you. Every time I looked at the picture, I felt like I was getting closer to him and to you. This made me happier and more joyful inside. Boris, you give me everything I should, but do not get from my parents. You show me how to look inside myself. I would love it if you would play some Beethoven for me.[17] Until now I have never been so inspired by music. How happy I am to be reading your book under your guidance!

This evening your other letter arrived. Believe me, I can easily comprehend your confusion and I am so sorry to have been the cause of it. It makes me hate my pretty appearance even more.

Boris, I will neither set my heart on you, nor will I try to influence you. I will let you be free. You should take your time and consider how you truly feel. But when you achieve clarity, do not let me wait one moment longer than necessary and tell me exactly how things stand between us. I will try to support you in my prayers.

You must not be angry that I did not write to you right away. I was holding myself back. I did not want to write a lot of ill-considered things in my excitement. I had to carefully think about what I wanted to say, and only then could I write to you.

I would like to tell you one more thing. I only have about three

---

17 Boris had become an accomplished pianist during his teenage years in Siberia, but he ultimately gave up the idea of becoming a concert pianist to pursue a career in mining engineering, a more prudent and secure profession for a Russian refugee.

hours of free time a day. And with those three hours I must sew and mend my clothes, take care of my correspondence, practice piano, read, and see to my personal hygiene, and I would also like to spend a few minutes with the people who live in this house with me. I am often disappointed that I don't have time to do everything I want.

As far as calling me on Friday, you can easily do that at 8 p.m. I will make sure I am alone at that time so we can speak privately. Boris, you are so good to me. I thank you from the bottom of my heart for everything, and for the treats you sent. They arrived in good condition.

Now, good night. It is 12:30 a.m. and I must go to sleep. Take one very gentle kiss from me.

Your Anneli

LETTER B4

[Thursday] September 21, 1944

Dear Anneli,

Two letters arrived just now, one from you, and the other from Frau Dr. Kurz[18] telling me all about America. Don't you see what a happy coincidence it is that both of these long-awaited letters came at the same time, almost like an act of providence?

Because I had not received a letter from you this morning, I was quite angry and would have spanked you on the spot if I could have. I think I would have the right to do so at least once a week (shall we say on Saturdays?) to discourage you from tormenting people and

---

18   During the Second World War and until her death, Gertrud Kurz (1890-1972) took a leading role in assisting refugees in Switzerland. She was also an ardent and outspoken pacifist. Even today she is seen as exemplifying the humanitarian tradition in Switzerland. Kurz saw her work as the leader of the *Christlichen Friedendienst* (Christian Service for Peace) in Switzerland as a Christian calling. She strove to provide concrete help to people (particularly refugees) who were in need or suffering injustice, without regard to their nationality, or their religious or political views. She believed in a shared political responsibility between church and state for existing political policies locally and nationwide. Gertrud Kurz first came into contact with the organization (then called The Knights of the Prince of Peace) in 1930 and became a member shortly thereafter. Originally the organization sought mainly to improve relations between France and Germany. In 1937 Kurz was appointed president of the Swiss division by the founder, Etienne Bach, and in 1938 she began steering its activities in a new direction: aiding refugees. Kurz continued her work with refugees throughout the war.

In 1942, because Germany was implementing its "Final Solution," Switzerland anticipated an even greater influx of refugees. There was a movement within the government to close off the entire Swiss-French border. Kurz felt this was unjust and fought to keep it open, addressing her concerns to Eduard von Steiger (1881-1961), a member of the Swiss Federal Council. She was able to convince him to keep the border open, but only during certain regulated periods. Between 1942 and 1944 refugees were admitted only on the basis of race or religion, rather than for political reasons. During the war, over 50,000 Jews entered Switzerland, due in large part to "Mother Kurz's" intervention. This may be why Boris felt so indebted to her.

particularly animals, especially Siberian bears![19] I tried to call you earlier, but I could not reach you at home. I did not know if you would be in Thun in the afternoon. At 2 p.m. I picked up the photos I took of you. Looking at them calmed me down a bit. At 4 p.m. I came home and then the postman arrived with both letters.

As I read your words, a sense of calm came over me. It was almost magical—exactly what I needed! So please try not to distress me anymore, otherwise there will be death and destruction instead of fruit to reap. You must have a care with me since I am the "strongest man in the world." (I set off the largest chamber explosion in civil industry.)[20]

As you can tell, I am in a good mood now, thanks to your letter. I would like to write you a thoughtful letter today, but I can't quite manage it yet. I still feel like someone has hit me over the head with a huge, heavy hammer, and my senses are still impaired. I have already taken a cold shower and tried other remedies, but they aren't helping. Do you have any better ideas? You had better take my words with caution, as you cannot always believe what people say when they are in love! Yet, I believe that my statements are truthful.

In my last letter I called you "my dear little Anneli" out of despair, as I still had not received a letter from you. It might be more proper for us to avoid using the words "my" or "mine" until we truly belong to each other in our hearts. But I believe that we are rushing ahead

---

He certainly admired and respected her for the rest of his life, even keeping a framed photograph of her in his home office. Her deep commitment to helping others and the strength of her moral, Christian convictions made a deep impression on him.

Kurz said, "We have learned from the horrible occurrences in Germany where Christianity can lead if it is only experienced on a private and personal basis and when it ignores its share of responsibility in political movements." Kurz wanted to begin the post-war period "with God," blaming the inhumanity of the war on the "godlessness of men." See https://www.linkedin.com/company/gertrud-kurz-stiftung and Adelheid M. von Hauff, *Frauen gestalten Diakonie: Vom 18. bis zum 20. Jahrhundert* (Kohlhammer, 2006), pp. 512-530.

19 Boris refers to himself as a "Siberian bear." His friends often nicknamed him "Bear."
20 Boris is referring to a mining blast here. Later in this letter he compares inspiration (God's light) to the spark needed to set off an explosion.

towards this goal, so that we could, in good conscience, do it now and remain sober about it.

You are completely correct that being in love is a kind of stupidity, and I fight against it all day long. But it is harder for me, as I am not a cool-headed "German." You know what the thirty-four-year-old Tolstoy wrote in his diary when he fell in love with a young woman (his future wife) after he had been the evilest kind of a playboy for twenty years?

"I am in love. I never would have believed it was possible for love to affect me so. I am completely mad and will shoot myself dead if things continue this way. Sonja is charming in every way. Tomorrow I will either go to her and tell her everything, or I will shoot myself dead."

You need have no worries. I am quite harmless and am not the least inclined to follow Tolstoy's example. I am more practical. Instead of shooting myself dead, I would rather spank you. But don't be afraid; if I spank you it won't hurt. But seriously, I am basically against hitting, screaming, and scolding, as I associate those acts with psychological weakness.

Before I answer your letter, I want to mention that I have a bit of a sore throat, but you need not worry about my health. My grandfather lived to be nearly a hundred years old, and my father was close to ninety when he died. Neither of them was ever sick. My father, after he had lost all his property and businesses, many of his children, and above all, his wife, had no wish to continue living, as he regularly wrote me in his last years. I would want to love my future wife as he had loved my mother. When my wife dies, I would want to die too.

Your letter made a big impression on me. It revealed to me that your soul is the mirror image of mine and that made me long to kiss and hold you tenderly in my arms. It is no great feat for a man to conquer a woman physically, or vice versa. But it is truly a great feat when a man and woman conquer each other spiritually. Then there is no subjugation, but rather a reciprocal completion and inspiration. I have never felt that way with any of the girls I have known before. But with you, I can imagine it might be possible. Yet, in some ways,

I fear making that commitment, as it would so dramatically impact our lives. We have known each other for such a short time, and we are both highly sensually disposed, which makes it more difficult to distinguish the spiritual aspects of our relationship from the physical. We must force ourselves to look at each other critically, in an unemotional way, to see if we are able to complete each other, be productive, and find a kingdom of God on earth together.

To make your task a bit easier, I would like to tell you a few things about my earlier life. I came from a very wealthy family but was never spoiled. In the year 1919, the bloodiest year of the Russian Revolution, I was abruptly awoken from the sleep of childhood at the age of fourteen and forced to become unusually self-reliant. But, in fact, I had always been quite independent, even before that. Thanks to that independence and cool-headedness, I found the inner strength to travel alone across half of Siberia, to China, Japan, India, and finally to Europe, where I worked my way through college doing dangerous work as a miner. As a young engineer, even though I was a foreigner and had no connections or family to support me, I established myself professionally and enjoyed a brilliant ten-year career until it was interrupted by political upheaval and the war.

As you say, your admiration of my calmness, strength, and stability may indeed lead you to find stability within yourself. Even cool-headed, stoic Germans, including many in the mining industry, called me "the man with the calmness of steel," as I never allowed myself to become perturbed under any circumstances. I lived through the Russian Revolution, Nazi persecution, and dangerous work in the mines and with explosives, but I was never afraid. I had only one goal: to build my capabilities, talents, and knowledge so that I might be of use to mankind. If one has experienced the hard life of a miner, seen the misery and suffering brought by revolution and war, and lived the life of a refugee, this goal becomes more vital and worthwhile than if one had lived complacently under comfortable, peaceful conditions.

As a child I taught myself to be a strong swimmer. I also studied hard at school and traveled frequently to develop myself physically, mentally, and spiritually. I believed this to be the best defense against life's inevitable pitfalls and a means toward making my goal of helping mankind a reality. If I had I found a wife who understood me sooner, perhaps I could have accomplished this more easily. A man cannot live a normal life without a woman (and vice versa—a woman cannot live normally without a man). It is not in me to seek out women purely for pleasure, even though, as I said, I am very sensually inclined. Until now I have always felt incomplete, like half of a man. Surely as a whole person, with the right woman at my side, I could be more creative, productive, and fruitful.

Anneli, think about the example I gave you. A man without inspiration, that is, someone without God's light, is like an explosive without a spark. A thousand tons of explosives, enough to destroy a hundred cities, are worthless without that igniting spark. It is precisely the same with a person. He could do more, be more, take on more burdens, move mountains, and live more fruitfully if his soul had the spark to set his whole being ablaze, giving it light and strength, enlivening and enlightening his inner soul. A woman can be that inner spark for a man (and a man can be the same for a woman), that enflames and enlivens his whole being and makes him more productive and creative.

It is terribly difficult to find that "spark," and finding it lies in the hands of God alone, as he gives this light through his spirit. Without it we are nothing, just lifeless shadows that merely "exist" without true happiness, seeking out pleasure where we can from time to time.[21] True happiness can only exist when it is combined with a creative process. For example, the birth of children, fruit on the trees, the resurrection of Jesus, your resurrection (your re-birth), the birth of inspiring ideas during a Revolution, the discovery of the

---

21 This sentence may have been inspired by Jean-Jacques Rousseau (1712-1778), an author and philosopher Boris much admired, who warns of the dangers of a society guided only by materialism: "We have only honor without virtue, reason without wisdom, and pleasure without happiness." From Rousseau's *Discourse on the Origin and Basis of Inequality Among Men*. Translation by Jane Glover, *Mozart's Women* (Pan MacMillan, 2005), p. 240.

laws of nature, and so on. These give meaning to an individual and to all of humanity. Each of these creations requires prior suffering. Think of a mother giving birth to a child, of the suffering of Jesus, of the suffering of people during a Revolution, of the great risk and exertion required of an explorer or scientist. Leonardo da Vinci stole corpses from graveyards despite the danger of being burned alive if discovered at a time when the whole world, including the Church, was against such things. Galileo, who steadfastly held on to his beliefs before the harshest judges of the time, the Church and the State, declared: "The Earth rotates nevertheless!"[22] That is why we truly rejoice after a birth. Think of the joy of all Christians celebrating Christ's resurrection despite the twenty centuries that have gone by since it happened, the joy of the French on July 14 celebrating the French Revolution (All the people dance in the streets!), and the joy shared at birthdays. Maybe you, too, have experienced this kind of joy, maybe for the first time in your life, when thinking about your own rebirth, your own resurrection!

Anneli, I have just reread your last letter and I am completely charmed. It is clear, tactful, sweet, modest, and at the same time profound and courageous. Also, your excellent handwriting, speech, and style impress me very much. It is quite an accomplishment for a little child like you! I am excited at the prospect of having such a talented pupil, as you will certainly learn much faster from me than you would at any school, and, as I see it, you have already absorbed the most essential things I have taught you so far. I have no doubt that you will make excellent progress. I am so pleased that you find everything I have brought up so far interesting. Every gardener derives pleasure from seeing his plants grow and develop to eventually bear fruit. You are nothing but a wonderfully beautiful flower who must be handled with the greatest of care.

If our relationship were purely physical, we would soon tire of each other or find other partners. How much better would it be if

---

22 Galileo Galilei (1564-1642), Italian astronomer and physicist, made this statement even after he was forced to assert that the sun revolved around a stationary Earth.

we could care for each other with genuine love and grow to bear beautiful spiritual fruit for ourselves and all of mankind. That would truly be God's kingdom!

Tolstoy said, "Man is a weak, unhappy creature when God's light is not flaming inside his soul. When that light is ignited in him, man will have more than his own strength, he will have God's strength. Each person has the freedom to choose whether to live or not to live. Not to live means to indulge in one's own willfulness, to give oneself over to the habits of society. To live means to share God's gifts of the spirit freely and be willing to sacrifice for the benefit of others. And that is the realization of God's kingdom on earth."

You know that a plant can only bear fruit when it has received a grain of pollen, that is, when it has been fertilized. Just so, a person can only bear mental and spiritual fruit if he has received God's spark (the Holy Spirit). Consider butterflies, which humans view as little nothings, that perform a valuable service by transporting pollen from flower to flower, even though they [the butterflies] do not understand the significance of that service. Similarly, for humans, it is the educators, and specifically the pastors, who, much like the butterflies, are often unaware of the value and meaning of the words of Jesus, which are like seeds that nourish our souls. But, despite their ignorance, these pastors do good work nevertheless by providing us with the words of Jesus. If the word (=seed) finds good soil, the seed will grow. Read the New Testament, Mark 4:26-32 about the parable of God's kingdom.[23]

I am convinced you have received God's light, and now you must hold on to it very tightly. Like a seed deposited in good soil getting

---

[23] "The kingdom of God is as if a man should scatter seed upon the ground, and should sleep and rise night and day, and the seed should sprout and grow, he knows not how. The earth produces of itself, first the blade, then the ear, then the full grain in the ear. But when the grain is ripe, at once he puts in the sickle, because the harvest has come. With what can we compare the kingdom of God, or what parable shall we use for it? It is like a grain of mustard seed, which, when sown upon the ground, is the smallest of all the seeds on earth; yet when it is sown it grows up and becomes the greatest of all shrubs, and puts forth large branches, so that the birds of the air can make nests in its shade."

the best of care, it will grow beautifully. I only want to help you, and I ask God to see that this light and spirit will thrive in you. If you stay on this course, you can rest assured that the errors of your past will be forgiven.[24] To help strengthen these words, I will send you my favorite picture of Jesus that I carry with me always, wherever I go. I give it to you in the hope it will bring you, and us, good luck.

I am happy you think of me often. Surely, we cannot yet make declarations of love to each other, but I hope that by Christmas our situation will be much clearer. Then we should not attempt to hide anything, but be very sober and honest about our relationship. As it says in the New Testament (Matthew 5:36-37): "You should not swear by your head, for you cannot make one hair white or black. Let what you say be simply 'Yes' or 'No.' Anything more than this comes from evil."

In response to your letter, I, too, believe you will become my better half. I very much hope I can help you feel stronger by urging you to strive for greater goals and tearing you away from the mundane trifles of everyday life. I do not imagine this will be easy. I ask only for your love and kindness in return, the rest you can leave to me.

I can well imagine you laughed heartily when you read my recipe for physical fitness. It pleases me that you are willing to consider these suggestions for my benefit and look at it in a loving way. But are you not vain at all? A woman must try to be beautiful! You see, the more beautiful you are, the happier and more enthusiastic I will be about you, the more productive I will become, and the more joy I will have in helping you. That is why God made people and the world so beautiful. Beauty has deep meaning and is inspiring in and of itself.

I am so glad you liked the picture of Beethoven and that I have succeeded in leading you toward a deeper appreciation of music and of Beethoven. But be aware that all you do out of love for another can also benefit you! That is why Jesus said, "Think only of God's kingdom, the rest will come by itself." Nearly everything we can per-

---

24 Here is the first of many instances where Boris tries to equate religious faith in God with faithfulness in love.

ceive in a non-rational way, that is with our emotions, can be more easily understood through music. I would only have to play two or three chords on the piano, and you would know right away whether it represented love, joy, or sadness. Other kinds of artists (poets, painters, sculptors, etc.) can express these same emotions by other means. We can express ourselves more quickly and clearly by drawing on our mutual understanding of music. This way we will arrive at our goal faster. Now look carefully at the following analogies:

> God=Father (represented best by the music of Bach—church music)
> God=Creator (represented best by the music of Beethoven)
> God=Superman (represented best by the music of Wagner)
> God=Spirits# (represented best by the music of the Romantics—Mendelssohn, Weber, etc.)
> #Fantastic beings who are more powerful than humans.

Even though I have not yet finished this letter, I am going to send it to you, as I would like you to receive it before Sunday.

I leave you with a kiss,

Your Boris

LETTER A3

Gwatt

[Sunday] September 24, 1944

Good evening Boris,

It is already Sunday evening. I had such a busy day I had no time to write until now. In the morning, I heard Reverend Kühner preach a sermon on Luke, chapters 11-17. He spoke very forcefully about his view of the great mercy granted by God and Jesus. I would gladly tell you more about it, but my memory fails. I can only remember small portions of it, but I hope something good will come of what I do remember.

This afternoon there was a convention of women here from Bern. Reverend Helbling from Biel was invited to give a talk about the ecumenical movement which I was able to hear. I had heard about the ecumenical movement before, but I wanted to expose myself to a new point of view.

I also played piano a bit. It is very odd, either I am hearing differently, or I am playing differently. In any case, something has changed. Earlier I would just play, now I sense there is an inner light, an inner excitement when I play. At the same time, my thoughts are always of you. I know you were invited out today; hopefully you had a nice visit.

And now, to your letter. I have trouble expressing in words how I feel. I can only thank you. I am eternally grateful that I had the chance to meet you.

Listen, I cannot answer your letter now; it is just impossible. Something is wrong with me this evening; it is awful. The dreadful feeling is like an alpine mountain sitting on top of my heart; it is like a cramp, a spasm, a horrible feeling of fear, a wincing pain that envelopes everything in a gray, sweet light. I believe it is a test. The pain is so strong I feel it physically. It is like a mist hanging over everything behind which something evil lurks. I pray and pray again that I will not fail. The best thing would be for me to go to sleep now. Tomorrow God will grant me his mercy again.

Please do not be too impatient with me about this lame letter. As soon as I am free from this devilish stress, you will hear from me again. Good night my dear. I love you very much.

Your Anneli

P.S. Boris, many thanks for the pictures, but I can't spend all day looking at myself. Please send me a picture of yourself!

LETTER A4

GWATT

[Monday] September 25, 1944

Dear,

At long last the moment has arrived, and I have been overjoyed about it all day. I believe my crisis is over now and I can write to you again.

I am so happy that your American possibilities look promising. It is just wonderful how much Frau Dr. Kurz is doing for you. I am constantly amazed, Boris. You are simply marvelous!

I am learning more and more about you. Your humor is golden. I will not torment Siberian bears all the time, because I love them too much. Furthermore, I am very curious to know how such bears thrash people without causing any pain. Very interesting!

Now seriously...

The question you raise over "my" and "mine" is very characteristic of you. It shows how deeply you think about things and how honest you are. In this respect, I am somewhat superficial, yet through this discussion I have learned a lot. I have never felt so close to another human being as to you, and I am overjoyed about it every time I think of it. I would like us to continue to grow together. Because you give me strength, I believe I can be what you need me to be (your inner peace). I would like to be everything to you. That, in a few words, is everything! That defines our reciprocal commitment.

How funny, you take the words right out of my mouth! I wanted to tell you that I understand well why you fear an immediate commitment. The course of two lives (maybe more than two, if we have children) depends on a lot of things, in your case, your work. If you think about what a horror an unhappy marriage is, then you automatically become more careful. But I can tell you I am sure you are the right man for me. You are amazed I could say something like that, aren't you? I am too, but I am convinced of it.

You captivate me. I could follow you anywhere. You are mature and understanding. You have a good, warm heart; you are calm and patient. That last quality, patience, is very important because you must realize this about me: I will be a very difficult pupil and will make many mistakes. So, you *must* be patient!

I have asked myself repeatedly if it would not be better for you marry a woman who was already accomplished, who could help you right from the start? It will be very tiresome and troublesome for you to have to struggle with me alongside your career. Boris, I sometimes am quite afraid I won't be able to make you happy.

Now back to your fear of commitment. I agree completely, we simply do not know each other well enough. I will do everything I can to remedy that. No doubt about it, we must wait until you are less emotional. It is not easy to deal with an intoxicated man, one whom I would so gladly believe, but mustn't! I would like to punch you in the jaw, so your head will straighten up again. Despite all that, I think you should be a bit more careful about what you write in your letters.

Hem! I am shocked that you dare call me "a little child." Now that you have pretty much won me over and have given me a feeling of security, you call me a little child. You may as well have said, "Hey you, dumb girl!" Take care, my self-esteem stands on very shaky feet!

Boris, your letter is just wonderful. Never has another human being spoken to me in this way. I want to read your words over and over.

I will end my letter here. I am very tired. Everything in my head is suddenly starting to dance around and I cannot think clearly anymore. Please excuse me if I have written disorganized rubbish.

Again, thank you for all the wonderful things you sent me, especially the picture of Christ. It is very, very impressive. I hope too that God and Christ are with us.

I am with you in spirit and kiss you completely from my heart,

Your Anneli

P.S. Here is a bit of honey chocolate for my Siberian bear!

LETTER B5

Zurich

[Wednesday] October 4, 1944

Anneli,

Today I received a letter from Geneva. It is from the organization that pays for my tuition. I understand the money comes from America. For that reason, they are eager to see me go to America rather than remain in Europe. I am hopeful I might be able to immigrate to America in the coming months. I would be indescribably happy to be able to realize this plan, a plan that I first hatched back in 1922. I had planned to get my education and some career experience in Germany first, then go to America for advanced schooling and to find a permanent teaching position.[25] I would have liked to realize that plan five years ago, before I became a refugee on the run. A life without work, without struggle, is not for me. I must grow, develop, and evolve. Only then will I be satisfied.

I had a nice time in Oberhelfenschwil,[26] but for me things there were a bit too peaceful. I am too young for that kind of peace. I don't want peace, I seek activity. But I am in search of another kind of peace. I am plagued with strong, turbulent inner tensions, even though one cannot sense it from my outward demeanor. These tensions constantly disrupt my mental focus. My head is often full of stupid thoughts. I always try to rid myself of them, but I am not always successful. I have high hopes that you will help me achieve the inner peace I need to reach my potential in every way. Maybe you understand this already, as you are very clever and mature, despite your youth. To make it even clearer, I would like to refer again to Tolstoy and Beethoven. Tolstoy

---

25 As a young boy Boris had dreamed of going to the United States, even hanging pictures of the American West on his bedroom wall. When Boris left Russia at age seventeen in 1922, he could easily have gone directly to the United States, but a family friend convinced him that Germany would provide him with a better education in the field of mining.

26 Located in the canton of St. Gallen

was able to find peace and to mature intellectually and spiritually after he married a clever woman who understood him. With Beethoven that was not the case. The following passage was written about Beethoven:

"He struggled so bitterly with the conflict between his natural instincts and ethical ideals as no other man ever had. The difficulty he sometimes had in reconciling his passion with his reverence for women is revealed in his diary entry of 1817: 'Only love—yes, that alone can procure for you a happier life. O God! let me at last find her who will strengthen my virtue; allow her to be mine.'"[27]

Beethoven, unlike Tolstoy, was unable to fulfill his yearning. That is why the mental and spiritual dispositions of these two men were so different.

Anneli, I know I cannot compare myself with these two men, but what is inside me cannot be explained in any better way. This same conflict resides within me as well. I have strong natural drives, as well as high ethical ideals and a deep respect for women. At the same time, I long for a love that will strengthen my virtues, support my ideals, and fulfill my natural desires. I have great hope that you will be able to give me all these things, and that it will bring you happiness to know and feel that you have succeeded in doing so. You must understand how important it is for me to know that you share my ideals and will be faithful, otherwise I would lose everything: my ideals, my dreams, and everything that lifts me above the average person and makes me courageous and strong. If one day I should have to give up these high ideals because of you, I could not be what I want to be, and my fighting strength, my inner idealism, and my respect for you and for myself would sink powerfully and dramatically. Therefore, you must understand what a big responsibility you are taking on if you wish to be my wife.

It pleases me greatly to know you would like to be a moral and refined woman and that it would make you happy to give me all that is in you. These words of yours brought me much joy: "If two people depend on God and really strive to live by God's word, then truth

---

27 Anton Schinder's quote in J. S. Shedlock (trans.), *Beethoven's Letters* (New York: Dover Publications, 1972), p. 244.

and love will surely follow." Later you said, "Boris, be completely at peace. What can happen to me if I have God and I have you?"[28]

My dear Anneli! All of this sounds like a dream come true to me. Have I finally found the woman whom I have sought all my life? I sometimes think that everything that has happened between us until now is just a dream. But when I read through your letters, I awaken again. I am always charmed by them, as they are filled with so much purity, openness, and love. I pray that God will bring us together forever and that I can fulfill all your dreams for the future. I hope that the longer we are together, the more your words, "I have God and you, Boris," will have value and meaning.

I just received your little card.* You write so little. Your silence upsets me. I wait with longing for your detailed letter. But I will not let myself be overwhelmed by anxiety because I have great hope and trust in you.

I look forward to seeing you at the end of this week. Your visit will bring more clarity to our situation, and we can discuss our plans in more detail.

I kiss you as lovingly as I can,

Your Boris

8:30 p.m.

I called you tonight for two reasons:

1. I sense that you have become increasingly uneasy since the last time we were together. Your long silence is really upsetting me. I will probably call you again tomorrow evening at 8 p.m.

---

28 These quotations are not found in any of Anna's surviving letters. Some letters have clearly been lost (*) and that may be the case here, or Boris may be quoting from a spoken conversation.

2. As I shared with you at the beginning of this letter, I received a letter today (which I am enclosing) and a questionnaire from Geneva which I must fill out and return. On this questionnaire there is a line where I can register you, should you wish to accompany me to America. This got me thinking that perhaps you really could travel with me. Although I am a bit skeptical about it, we should consider it as a possibility. Therefore, I think it imperative that you come to Zurich by the end of the week. I will need your personal information (birthplace, birthdate, the name of your parents, etc.). Also, I would like to hear from your own lips that you are convinced I am the right man for you.

If my plans to travel to America move forward, which seems likely, we must think about whether it might be better for you to end your training in Thun and move to Zurich. That way we would have more opportunity to get to know one other, and you could begin studying typing, stenography, and English.

As you see, things are getting serious. We cannot make these decisions by writing letters. So please come. If possible, send me your answer today.

I kiss you,

Your Boris

LETTER A5

Gwatt

[Thursday] October 5, 1944

Boris, dearest!

I am so sad that you are sad! I want to make you happy. Now listen carefully, I want to tell you everything that has happened. I hope you will understand. As you know, I am enrolled in a training program in Thun. I was thinking about visiting you next Saturday afternoon. To do this I must ask my head teacher[29] for a vacation pass, because normally I work on Saturdays. This lady really likes me, and because I do not live with my parents, she feels obliged to mother me to some extent. Naturally I did not want to tell her why I wanted to go to Zurich. But then she asked me whether my parents knew about it, and what was going on with me, and why I had changed so much, and so on. What else could I do but tell her the truth?

I told her briefly that I met a man last month whom I would like to get to know better. I told her that you were Russian and that you have lived in Europe for the past twenty years. Of course, she had nothing but objections. In her opinion we would have no future. "Slavs have a different kind of blood than we," she said. I didn't argue with her because I didn't want to give her more information about our relationship. Finally, she asked me to leave Sunday morning instead of Saturday. She certainly has no reason to think badly of you, but I think she believes my late mother and I are both to blame for my interest in you. I don't really know why, but it was impossible for me to tell her that I would go on Saturday evening anyway! I can fool this woman very easily. She certainly would not notice if I visited you on Saturday, but I will not do it because I see God's hand in this. Boris, believe me, it hurts me just as much as it hurts you to know we will be together for a few hours less, but I don't think our love will suffer because of it.

---

29   Mrs. Tschan

Now listen to this! Probably to make up for upsetting me, this woman invited me to the opera. Verdi's *Simon Boccanegra* was performed. I was really surprised how calm and strong I was inside. Before I met you, I was head over heels in love with this woman's son, and yesterday I could sit across from him very calmly, without having any ulterior motive. Thereupon I joyfully realized that I can only be happy with you, convinced that you and I were perfect for one another. Despite that, I sensed the effect of yesterday evening only today. Suddenly I became confused, and began to feel that the world of theater can make it more difficult for a person to establish a connection with God. As we both know, something good will come of all this only if God is truly on our side. Also, I hope that we will have a challenging beginning, so that God and the two of us will develop an unshakeable bond. That is why I decided today I will fight alongside you and face the worst with you right from the start. I won't be at your side only when everything is going well, but also when you need help.

How joyous I was this evening when I read in your letter that I might be able travel with you to America immediately!

---

11 p.m.

Now on to something completely different!

Reverend Kühner, who has been on vacation in Basel for the past several days, just telephoned. What a pretty mess I discovered! My head teacher, because of her concern for me, had nothing better to do than call my father and tell him of my plans to visit you in Zurich next Sunday! My father is quite furious about it and wrote a letter to Reverend Kühner in which he asked him to try to prevent me from making the trip. But because Reverend Kühner is on our side, he told me he would say a word in our defense. (My father doesn't believe a thing I say. He doesn't understand me and thinks everything I do is ill-considered.) But before he does, he wants to speak with me. Because he will only be back in Gwatt next week, he asked me to postpone my visit to you by one week. You see, the difficulties are beginning. I will have many, many more with my parents! Will you stand by me? Don't be too disappointed. My deep desire to be with you and to talk everything over with you is as great as yours. But we must be brave now and allow ourselves to be led by God.

This is a letter full of mere practicalities. I hope you are not too unhappy with it. You know it really hurts me when I disappoint you. I would like to devote all my energy, my whole being, to your happiness. The willpower is there, but it is also accompanied by doubt in my abilities. Boris, you can help me by believing in my good qualities, because I only see my defects.

Now then, good night, Boris. I am thinking of you and thank you for everything, everything you do for me. Please forgive me if I have hurt you.

I kiss you tenderly,

Your Anneli

LETTER B6

[Friday] October 13, 1944

My dearest,

It is hard for me to find the right words to describe my feelings for you. Every day I have been watching for the postman anxiously. He finally gave me your little card* today. What joy it brought me! The next time we meet you will see how much more tenderly we will cling to each other.

Dearest Anneli, we have never been closer than we are now. I believe our love is really beginning to grow. We have overcome many obstacles already and have made a good start. I am really beginning to fear (I fear the happiness I feel) that should our love prove strong, all our dreams will come true, and no power on earth will stand in our way. The greater our love becomes, the easier it will be for me to forget your past. You are now newly reborn through God, as you wrote in your letter* of the day before yesterday, and I will become reborn through you, as you will soon see.

I don't know why my eyes are full of tears, but I have a wonderful feeling inside me. Dearest Anneli, if you can really be everything to me, I would need nothing but you. As for God, you should consider the following passage by Pascal:[30] "Whoever seeks God, has found him already." If we seek God, God will be with us. If we become a single droplet, then it will be his doing, and he will make that droplet of water crystal clear, as pure as only God can make it. Once we have achieved that, only death can part us. If we are with God, we will be free from all human opposition.

How much I would like to have you near me, to caress and pet you, to look into your eyes, and to kiss your sweet mouth. I can hardly wait

---

30 Here Boris refers to Proverbs 8:17: "And those who diligently seek me will find me." Blaise Pascal (1623-1662), a French mathematician, physicist, and Catholic theologian, cites this passage in *Pensées,* a posthumous collection of his thoughts on religion.

until you are in my arms again. You will see that next Sunday when we are together again, we will be a thousand times more in love than before, and we will feel nobler, purer, and more valuable to each other.

My dearest, I thank you from the bottom of my heart because you have given me the "wherefore" I have always dreamed about. I can hardly allow myself to believe it has really happened. If it is true, I would no longer regret the five years I lost as a refugee and instead thank God for leading me on this difficult path.

I hug and kiss you, dearest, so tightly and sincerely as never before, and I wish you a lovely Sunday. Please be as peaceful as I am now. You know the source of this peace.

Your Boris

P.S. Please write to me every day, even if your letter only says, "My Boris, Your Anneli." That is enough for me, as there is much behind those words.

P.P.S. You should think that every little thing I send you (pictures, books, chocolate) is like a little kiss from me, my dearest Anneli.

P.P.P.S. You see, I no longer ask you if you will stay true to me, even in thought, anymore. We have come so far that this question is no longer necessary. If in twelve months, when we are living together as a single droplet, I ask you this question again, you will plant a big, strong slap on my face.

LETTER A6
GWATT

[Sunday] October 15, 1944

My dear ones,[31]

I am glad you were able to get in a bit of vacation, as you both really had need of some respite. Many thanks for your letter, the card, and the grapes. They brought me much happiness.

Now I would like to discuss a serious subject with you. I know you still regard me as a silly, troubled thing who cannot be trusted and will never amount to much. I understand why you think of me in that way. It is because you don't really understand me. Since my mother died, Vati and I have never been able to connect. When Martha arrived, the situation improved outwardly, but under the surface, things remained just about as they were before. This is because each of us is full of prejudice and we do not fully understand each other, you, just as little as I. Also, there is a lack of trust between us. Each of us believes the other wants the opposite of what would be in their best interest.

But now I would like to put an end to all of that. I want to tear down the walls between us and try to build a good relationship with you. I am full of good will and will try my best. But to be free to do this, I need to know whether you have forgiven me for all my earlier mistakes and transgressions. If you have not yet done so, I ask that you do it now. And let me share that I do not always want to take from you, but I would like to give something in return as well. I would like you to tell me freely what you dislike about me, what I lack. But also, I would like it if you would not take offense if I criticize you. You see, I would really like it so much if you could see your way to granting me your understanding, trust, and warm-heartedness. I know well that until now I have been a disappointment to you, but I am now

---

31 Anna is writing to her father Hans Stahel ("Vati") and her stepmother Martha.

ready to make good, and I hope that you both will try to meet me halfway. Let me say again that I really do not want to upset you. Rather, it is my sincerest wish that we finally can find a way to reach an understanding. So, let us not continue to play hide-and-seek, but let us speak directly, rather than through intermediaries when we have something important to say to each other. I am older now and have become more sensible, so you can and should talk to me face to face.

I am glad that Mrs. Tschan fussed at me over this matter because it has compelled me to explain everything to you. So, here are the details. This fall a religious study group met here at the Heimstätte. The participants were from eight different countries, including one gentleman from Russia. After the two-week class was over, he stayed an additional week as Reverend Kühner's guest. During that time, by strange coincidence, we got to know each other, and our relationship became quite serious.

I would like to tell you more about this man. He is about thirty-eight years old, comes from a rich Russian family, and was born in Siberia. During the Russian Revolution his father lost everything, so he has been wandering from country to country since 1922 when he was a penniless sixteen-year-old boy. He is, therefore, a stateless citizen. He traveled to Europe by way of China, Japan, India, and the Suez Canal. When he was a student in Germany, he worked as a miner to earn money for his tuition, and later he also worked there in the mining industry. In 1939, he fled Germany via Aachen across the Siegfried Line to France, until he received permission to cross the border into Switzerland. He arrived here last December. At first, he lived in a refugee camp. Later he got permission to further his studies at the ETH. That briefly covers the most important points. So that you can learn more about him, I am enclosing some papers and a photograph.

To know whether our relationship should continue, we must get to know one other more thoroughly. I know you will feel this relationship has a great many disadvantages. But, if you don't have any objections, I would like to visit Boris Kochanowsky in Zurich next weekend.

When I come home we can speak about all this in more depth. I think it is important that you meet Mr. Kochanowsky personally. He has been very busy lately and won't be able to get permission to travel for another three weeks, but he would like to speak with you too.

I ask that you please reply as soon as possible and try to take this seriously. By the way, I have spoken with Mrs. Tschan several times and explained everything to her. She had objections, of course, but she showed me much understanding and was kind to me.

With heartfelt greetings, I wish you a good night.

Your Anneli

LETTER V1

WINTERTHUR

[Wednesday] October 18, 1944

Dear Anneli,

I read your last letter. In it you speak lightly about new things and changes in attitude, such that one becomes quite distraught. You also ask that we send you word as soon as possible whether you can come home, so I will answer you right away. About this relationship with Mr. Kochanowsky, I am not able to make a snap decision about him right now. We need to sit down and talk about it more. We will expect you next weekend.

With my greetings,

Vati

LETTER B7[32]

ZURICH

[Monday] October 23, 1944

My dear, dear Anneli,

I await your next letter with great anticipation.

If I compare how I feel today with the way I felt fourteen days ago, I am shocked that I am so full of both joy and fear. Joy, because my heart and soul are completely bound to you even though we have decided to remain "free" on the outside. Fear, because the more connected to you I become, the more I fear your love will not grow as fast as mine. I experienced fear yesterday, but I attribute it more to your conversation with your parents, which without doubt had a dampening effect on you. But you should only think of one thing: that we two might be united someday. It really depends on us. In the worst case, we would have to wait until you are twenty years old.[33] It may take me a few months to find a good job. We will just have to hold out until then. The most important thing is for our love to grow. If it does, then nothing can stop us. I will do everything I can to see you as much as possible in Gwatt, although it may be difficult for me to get permission. We should also consider whether it would be a good idea for me to meet your parents.

As you can tell, Anneli, I am very serious about you. I am convinced that we belong together, and that God will aid us. I know you will be able to heal, grow, and develop in my hands.

I would like to tell you what has given my love such a strong forward push. First, it is your sincere regret about your past, and secondly your strong dedication to keeping our relationship as pure as possible.

---

32 Since Boris' last letter ten days have passed. Some intervening correspondence probably has been lost. Anna has been to Winterthur to meet with her parents. She has also seen Boris in person in Zurich.
33 The reason Boris suggests they wait until Anna is twenty years old (about fifteen more months) to marry is to circumvent any legal pressure her parents might exert.

Our love is still too young and tender to tolerate coarse sensuality. That would only destroy it, even if we were honorable about it. So, we will still have that beautiful moment ahead of us, and the longer we wait, the more beautiful and deeper the experience will be. That will be the moment we become one drop, one body, and one soul.

I just received your little card* and I am so thankful to you for it. Yes, I do have a very tender soul, even though I could easily pick you up with one hand. A gentle, sensitive soul is not a weakling, but a strong person. I was successful in my profession because I could be both hard and soft at the same time. I confronted my employees with my iron will, yet I handled them with kid gloves. They did their best for me, and everyone benefited thereby. If I were weak-willed, I would not have succeeded. That is why I do not fear our future, and neither should you. You will become the caretaker of my tender soul, a responsibility I hope you will take on without fear. You might find a younger, more handsome man, but I doubt you could find a better one.

You say if you could always be with me, all your doubts would disappear. The wonderful thing about our love is that it is constantly growing. You say that you love me more than anyone else, and yet you are still dissatisfied because you feel your love could and should be even greater. As for me, I would like to love you as much as God loves you, but that is impossible for a human being. But it is possible to wish to and to strive towards it. Despite our current despondency, we should be completely satisfied with our love. Ours is not "love at first sight," which is often of short duration. In contrast, our love grows very organically, like a seed, upward toward God. What could be better? Have patience, my dear, one day our love will be so great that only death will be able to separate us. Now we must take good care of our young, tender, beautiful love, and protect it from harm. Even though it is so young, it has already withstood much, otherwise it would have ended by now. The practical, sober discussions you had with your parents interrupted our love. But your longing for me will soon bring everything back in order. You say yourself that one should look to God. He wants what is best for us. If we do no evil, he will surely help us.

I agree that if we could be together more, our doubts would surely disappear. So my dearest, when you are depressed or in doubt, ask God for help. As I know you are an infinitely dear and loving girl, my belief in you is strong enough for me to put my soul and my fate calmly into your hands. Hold and guard them well. I know and feel that you love me. Because of your past, your soul still has scars that need to be healed. But they will heal! Love can never reach perfection (an impossible goal), but it must grow unceasingly. You could not share anything more beautiful with me than that your love for me is growing, even if there are some setbacks from time to time.

And now, I kiss you with my whole soul, deeply and tenderly, and await your next letter with longing. Your letters are my only comfort. I live in hope of seeing you again in twelve days.

Your Boris

P.S. Did you forget something at my place? I won't tell you what it was, so guess! But if you can't guess, I will be sad. Try to figure out what you might have lost.

P.P.S. The love for which we are striving is very, very rare. Yet, if one can achieve it, it surely is the best there is. So, let us wish each other much courage.

LETTER A7

GWATT

[Sunday] October 29, 1944

My dear, dear Boris,

Whew! I am quite feverish! It is 10:30 a.m., and I have been sitting and talking with Frau Dr. Kurz, Miss Bessler, a custodian from St. Gall, and Dr. Fränkel all morning. Frau Dr. Kurz told us many things, including that all refugees who were in Belgium until 1940 are now permitted to return.[34] See Boris, a little door may be opening for you! Miss Bessler told me that the U.S. will be adopting many strict regulations regarding the immigration of Jews.[35] You say this is true of other countries as well. Can you imagine how stressful it has been for me to be suddenly confronted with decisions concerning our future? Boris, try not to get depressed over this, but put your trust in the Lord. Have faith that God will set you on a straight path and lead you to where you will be most needed. Maybe the people of Europe will need you more than those in the United States? I know you don't want to work just to get rich and famous, but to help all of humanity. Therefore, be comforted and lay everything in God's hands. He will make everything right.

Boris, I would like us to consider taking on something besides your work. I would like to become a Crusader[36] and would like you to

---

34 Anna mentions this opportunity because Boris had been a refugee in Belgium for six months before fleeing to France in May of 1940.

35 This is the only passage that refers to Jews. My father wrote in his memoirs that he had "only a few drops" of Jewish blood, but that was not accurate. Both of my father's parents were of 100% Jewish extraction, though they were non-practicing. My father grew up with no affinity for Jewish religion or culture, but by blood he was Jewish. My parents did not want me to know this, and both died without telling me. I learned it later from a Russian cousin. It is possible that my mother deliberately destroyed the letters in which my father's Jewish heritage was mentioned.

36 Anna uses the word *Kreuzritter* (Crusader, literally, Knight of the Cross) here to refer to the peace movement *Les Chevaliers servants du prince de la Paix* (The Knights of the Prince of Peace), led in Switzerland by Frau

become one too. I would like to fight for good causes. I am convinced we could do much good wherever God decides to send us.

Boris, I must thank you again for the patience and love you have shown me. This has also been a trial by fire for you, and it has convinced me that your love for me is true. The fight is not over; you must believe that I will continue to fight for our love with all my strength. I believe unfailingly that God is testing me, but the time will come when God will remove this awful, unfounded fear, which still strongly afflicts me.

Boris, you should not worry that your outward appearance makes a bad impression on me. As far as I am concerned you can wear rags! You see, love explains and takes care of everything. When I see you coming toward me with a smile, when I see your profile, when you make such a serious scolding face at me, as you did in the photo, it makes me feel so happy. I love the way you walk! It distinguishes you from every other person. I don't want to love money, beauty, or any other outward quality, only your soul. You know, I am not really attracted to drop-dead gorgeous men. I value simple, discreet, but tasteful clothes. Listen to me carefully now, what do you mean by calling me a worldly lady? I do not want to be a worldly lady! I want to remain a very simple woman. But understand this correctly, I don't mean I want to be a primitive person, but a woman like Frau Dr. Kurz, with a clear understanding of the whole world. Boris, I know you could help me achieve that. I am convinced you could

---

Dr. Kurz at this time. It was founded in 1924 by Lt. Etienne Pierre Bach (1892-1986), a French pastor, upon his return home after completing military service in Germany during and immediately following World War I. Bach published regular newsletters and was involved in the first conferences that promoted peaceful cooperation between France and Germany. Membership increased quickly and the organization continued to promote good relations between Germany and France until 1939. With the start of World War II, the activities of the movement were sharply curtailed. Only Gertrud Kurz and the Swiss Crusaders continued their work during the war (1939-1945), albeit shifting the focus to providing aid to refugees. Around 1947, the Crusader movement would become the *Christlicher Friedensdienst* (CFD), or the Christian Peace Service, which is still active in Switzerland today. See https://de.wikipedia.org/wiki/Etienne_Bach and https://www.cfd-ch.org/de/ueber-uns-122.html.

turn me into something much more worthwhile than what I have been until now.

Thank you for sending me your lecture translated into German. I understand it much better this way than in French. I have long understood what bearing fruit means. I believe everyone should do as much as his talent allows. I see the great misery of our time, the sleeping church that ignores practical works, and I have a great desire to do something about it. However, despite that, I will repeat to you what is said about the morning watch in Galatians 3:6-14: "Our healing is in Christ; not in our works. It is a gift of mercy, and not our merit."[37] Therefore, I don't find it right when you say: "If we do nothing wrong, God will not forsake us." God will not forsake us, *even if we do wrong*. Through our faith in Jesus Christ, we will receive everything we need. As God promised to Abraham, because he believed, so it was with the Galatians, and will be with us. We live only through believing. The curse of our sins was taken away by Jesus on the cross; that is our only comfort. We must take more comfort from Jesus' act than our own works.

Boris, think about Reverend Kühner. God forgave him, so you should forgive him too, like a brother. Let the Christ in you grow and let the old duty-bound man die. As a sign of your forgiveness give him the book you bought for him. You would make me very happy if you do. But you must not always do everything just to please me, rather you should do it to please God.[38]

It is already past midnight. I want to wish you good night and to thank you again from the bottom of my heart for your dear letter. I kiss you as sweetly and tenderly as I can, and am always more

Your Anneli

---

37 This is from Ephesians 2:8-9, not Galatians: "For by grace you have been saved through faith; and this is your own doing, it is the gift of God—not because of works, lest any man should boast." See also Titus 3:5: "He saved us, not because of deeds done by us in righteousness, but in virtue of his own mercy."

38 It is unclear why Boris is angry with Reverend Kühner.

LETTER A8

Gwatt

[Tuesday] October 31, 1944

My dear Boris,

Many thanks for your letter.* I sensed your depression in each of your words, and immediately all I could do was to contemplate how I might help you. Because of this, it has become completely clear to me how much I love you. I know I cannot stand beside you physically, but please know that I hold you closely in my prayers. My dear, I understand well how the feelings of worthlessness and worry over an unclear future exert enormous pressure on you. But it should not be that way; you should not worry so. Just let everything rest in God's hands with confidence. You should be optimistic and patient; God will guide you on your path. Read these wonderful lines set to music by J. S. Bach. If you are here in Gwatt at Christmas I will sing them for you:

> In quiet faithfulness I love and serve my God,
> In trouble, need, and stress, He is my staff and rod.
> In God I am content, in patience I endure,
> In Him my house and I find refuge safe and sure.
> I therefore thank my God and love and serve Him still.
> What happens in this world must ever be God's will.
> I place in childlike trust my life into His care.
> In God I am content, whate'er my sphere or share.[39]

Boris, you refugees are not as worthless as you think. Through you we can learn firsthand about the needs and miseries of those living in foreign lands. You awaken us from sleep and drive us to action. Therefore, we should be duty-bound to you.

---

39 This English translation of the chorale "*Ich halte treulich still*" appears in *J.S. Bach Sacred Songs from Schemelli's Gesangbuch*, ed. Fritz Oberdoerffer, (St. Louis: Concordia, 1958), p.70.

I would like to send you my deepest thanks for the picture of Rafael's *Madonna* you sent. I don't understand much about art, but I think I now know from where the woman's virginal, pure, blameless expression arises. She has the mouth of a child, but not the eyes of one. The eyes are not looking at anything, they are directed inward. But I think if those eyes were to be turned toward you, they would look straight through you. When I compared it with the *Mona Lisa*, I was quite startled. To me the *Mona Lisa* looks like the devil incarnate. I think Leonardo da Vinci is trying to depict Judgment Day because of the darkness that surrounds the entire face. I have been thinking hard about the background da Vinci chose for this picture. You should look at it again too, it will tell you a lot.

Enough for today, my Boris, my everything. I hope you will continue to mean so much and more to me, and that you will stay with me forever. Good night my dearest, I am with you and kiss you.

Your Anneli

---

1 a.m.

My dearest,

Yesterday was a beautiful day. I thought to myself, Boris is right when he says that nature can help revive one's drive to action. That is why I am sending you this little flower, so you can enjoy a bit of nature too.

I am kissing you in my mind and I am terribly happy thinking about the kisses I will get from you next Saturday. Goodbye my† Boris.

†I am so proud of that word "my."

Your Anneli

LETTER B8

ZURICH

[Wednesday] November 1, 1944

My dear, dear Anneli,

I reread your letter of October 31 over and over. You have no idea what joy it brought me. I see it as a reward for my love and devotion to you. Yet we must admit we are only in the beginning stages of our love. But I already love you so much and my love just continues to grow each day.

Your words did me good. I find your attitude towards refugees excellent. One should always try to see the best in everything and everyone; one can reap the benefit of that oneself.

I am so glad you understand me, are clear about your task, and are full of excitement about it. Together we must now find a way to realize a future for ourselves. We will certainly have additional obstacles to face, but with God's help, our love will overcome them. The main problem remains my employment. Dearest, please help me stay patient. You see how many roads are possible, it is not an easy task to find the right one. You must be at my side with all your love, faith, and intelligence. This is how we will best find our common destiny. I don't want to make any decisions without you, as you already belong to me, as I do to you.

I think you understand much more about painting and art than I, and I am happy about that. You have a great appreciation and understanding of color and shape. I believe this is your strongest talent; you will be able to teach me a lot.

Today I received permission to travel to Bern. We will discuss my travel expenses later. You can reduce the cost of my trip by bringing some food from Gwatt. I will bring butter, sardines in oil, and you can bring bread, potatoes, and fruit. Please also bring a Thermos bottle with hot water for making coffee. I will bring instant coffee, sugar, and milk. So, we will have a real picnic for ourselves. Wonderful! Let me know which train you intend to take to Bern on Saturday and where I should meet you.

I am really looking forward to seeing you this weekend. I am curious how our third meeting will go. The first two really brought us closer together. I count the hours that still separate us. There are still seventy-two!

I thank you for the little flower. It is so beautiful. It breathes life, tenderness, and loveliness.

I thank you, dearest, for supporting me with your love, your calming words, and above all with your prayers.

There are still six weeks until my trip to Gwatt. I hope I might at least be able to see you in Zurich once before then, as I know I will not be able to get permission to go to Gwatt any sooner.

I am curious to hear your Christmas songs!

I continue to think about our future. I am convinced that if we love each other and build our happiness on God, we will easily overcome any future obstacles. This thought has calmed me these past two weeks and has led me to the fervent belief that God will indeed help us succeed. You see, I have adopted a religious attitude. And whom do I have to thank for that? You! You see, these are the fruits of your relationship with me. Are you happy about that? My love for you has taken strong root, as has my esteem. They grow without end. Out of love for you I can bear and forgive everything. Hopefully, your love for me will likewise allow you to offer me as much and forgive me my mistakes.

[Thursday] November 2, 1944

I just received another form for my U.S. immigration application. It looks like preparations are going smoothly.

I think it would be best if I immigrated to the United States first, and then you could follow later. I say this because one needs a guarantor. I have one, but you do not. But it is possible we may have an easier time finding a sponsor for both of us after the war. Perhaps your Swiss nationality might even make it easier for us. These are questions that still need to be cleared up.

If I cannot go to America, then I would prefer to go to England. In that case, I would need to prove a well-established professional status. I'm sure that Prof. Freudenberg could help me with that. It is most pleasant to live and work in England. In America, the importance of work is exaggerated, but it is possible to live well in either country.

I count the hours that separate us. There are still fifty-three! I think about the speed of the earth revolving (30km/sec) and that helps me pass the time more quickly. I miss you terribly. Everything in me cries out for you, especially my soul. And I am glad it is my soul that loves and misses you the most, because is it my soul that can help me win you forever.

My whole life long I have fought for myself alone, at times against formidable and terrifying forces. I would gain much strength if I knew that I wasn't alone in the world anymore. My dearest, I know that with your help, your love, and your understanding, I will be able to find the right path and get myself on my feet again.

I kiss you very tenderly.

Your Boris

LETTER M1

[Monday] November 6, 1944

Dear Anneli,

It has been fourteen days since you visited us. I am sending you a basket of pears. I hope they will arrive in good condition. You should write to your grandmother. She complained again in her last letter to us that you do not write. I will come back to this later.

I have gotten the feeling these last several weeks that you are not giving your wardrobe the care it needs. From several personal experiences, I know that one is not always in the mood to put a lot of effort into looking one's best, but one should not become completely neglectful of one's appearance. "Too little and too much spoils every game."[40]

I come back now to your visit and all the resolutions and good intentions you outlined. Most important to you was that we work on cultivating a warmer relationship, which I, for my part, happily welcome. Your recent behavior, however, will not bring about what you desire because, if you think about it, to win our trust you must also trust us. In the last few months, you have rarely written to us, and when you did write, it was only because you needed a quick answer. In between those hasty letters, you obviously didn't feel the need to write to us. We have found this somewhat depressing. I have often told you that you seem to come to visit us only when you need something, otherwise we are ignored. Furthermore, I am quite uneasy when I hear from others that you do not enjoy being at home with your family. It naturally follows that these people approach me with mixed feelings and look upon me as the "evil" stepmother.

You see, I also would have reason to voice complaints about you, but I have never done so. Quite the opposite, I have always told people who inquired about our relationship that it was a good one. I don't hold it against you, and have never done so, but you will understand that such a situation does not lead to a relationship of mutual trust.

40 A popular German saying: *Zuwenig und zuviel das verdirbt jedes Spiel.*

One cannot be commanded to have loving trust in another. It must come from within, from one's own deep conviction.

I understand well why you feel you should complain about the way things are now, but I ask you not to forget to write home every now and then.

With my sincere greetings,

From your Martha

P.S. You should not share this letter with anyone. It was written only for you.

P.P.S. The pears will be sent tomorrow. Please send the basket right back.

LETTER B9

ZURICH

[Tuesday] November 7, 1944

My most beloved and dear Anneli,

The nicest part of my day is the time I spend writing to you. It is as if I am talking to you personally, as if you were right next to me.

Anneli, I feel as if I am growing into you. A few weeks ago, when I spoke of the invisible threads that tie our hearts and souls together, I could not fully express that connection in words, perhaps because those threads didn't quite go deeply enough. But now I truly feel connected to you. Only a few spots remain open, there where we both have wounds that still need to be healed. But with each of our meetings, the distance between us is closing. If someone were to try to pull us apart now, it would cause great pain and we would bleed profusely. This "someone" might be time. We must combine our strength and attempt to overcome it. Let us try to see each other as often as possible to that end. Christmas will surely bring us together for good.

I am completely satisfied with you and would never want any other "better" woman. Of all the women I have met in my life, you are by far the best. I sometimes get angry with you because you still doubt that you are better than you think you are. If I were not completely convinced of that, our relationship would have ended long ago. One day without a letter from you results in agony, pain, and worry for me. It is 2:45 p.m. and I am already anxious with expectation. I hope to get another letter from you today! The mailman comes in an hour and a half.

I am very happy with your love, but it must continue to grow. I am happy that you understand this, want it, and believe that it is possible. Because of your upbringing, it is difficult for you to love truly. But I will help you learn how, because without true love, life is not possible. I will treat you as gently and lovingly as I can. In truth no one can be happy without loving and being loved. It is the same for me. I can give up a lot, but not true love. I have been yearning for it my whole life. Now that I have finally found it, my joy is unbounded. I could just kiss you for that, kiss you forever. You saw that yourself when we were together! I would like to carry you around in my arms and do with you I don't know myself what. I think a honeymoon of four weeks would not be long enough for me to become a normal person again. But ever since we first met, I have not been normal.

Any minute the postman will be here. I hope he will have a letter for me (from you!).

The postman said he had no letter for me. I didn't believe him and almost hit him. But he confirmed in a startled manner that he had nothing for me. Now I am awaiting the package deliveryman. It is an anxious hour! Now the package delivery man has come and gone and there was nothing from you! Can you imagine how I am feeling right now? I have so many disquieting thoughts in my head, but it is surely just craziness. Something or other has kept you from writing to me. I have so much faith in you, I should not let my anxiety get the upper hand. You said that it is clear to you now that you really love me. Therefore, I need not worry. I must be patient. If no letter comes tomorrow, I will call you for sure, assuming I don't do it today.

And so, I will end my letter here, with the hope I will soon have word from you.

I kiss you tenderly,

Your loving Boris

LETTER A9

GWATT

[Wednesday] *November 8, 1944*

My dear Boris,

I hope my letter* of yesterday did not cause you too much pain. In it I confronted you with all the potential pitfalls I see in our relationship. You see, my dear Boris, my belief in your strength, goodness, and purity is the source of my love for you. If these things were not secure, then everything would suffer.

Now I want to tell you briefly what happened. My head teacher Mrs. Tschan called home and told my parents everything. That is why my parents decided to come to Gwatt to see me. I had a difficult time with them and, as you could tell from my letter yesterday, I was in a bad state of mind. I had to listen to a long list of all my failings. Suddenly Mrs. Tschan, in a sheer rage, began vilifying Gwatt, the Reverend, and you. Of you, she said that it was just unheard of for an eighteen-year-old girl to be involved with a forty-year-old man. It was just impossible, and she would forbid such a relationship outright, if she could. She said my living arrangement in Gwatt was a bad influence, and when I spoke about God and faith conflicts, she shouted at me, "What, what? That is nothing, it's just fantasy!"

My parents' stance was between that of my head teacher and Reverend Kühner. They didn't voice their opinions, but I think that at any moment they could set their minds against us. Primarily, they agreed that I should be more conscious of my educational duties. I admit that I have been neglectful in this area, and that I should try harder not to let my love for you hinder my progress in Thun; otherwise, I will get myself into even more trouble, as I now have seen. I realized also that it is imperative that you visit my parents at home in Winterthur and try to get to know them better. Boris, you need not tell them everything about your future plans, just very simply explain what you hope to do. Tell them about the possible difficulties, just as they are. You don't need to say a lot, or to make things sound better than they are.

I am glad all the excitement is over for the moment, as it has quieted some of my mental anguish, and I feel more like a normal person again. It is already midnight; I need to go to sleep. I hope you can get a sense of what happened here. Here is a goodnight kiss for you.

Your Anneli

[Thursday] November 9, 1944 (early morning)

Good morning my Boris,

I am so concerned about you and hope you are doing well after receiving my last letter. I do not blame you. You are right when you say that it is the woman who determines how far a relationship can go. But I think we are an exception to this. Boris, if you can initiate things, I think it will not be difficult for me to help you afterwards. And above all, do not worry about my love for you, but help me in my fight for inner peace and security.

I kiss you tenderly…Your Anneli

LETTER A10

Gwatt

[Thursday] November 9, 1944

My dear Boris,

Your letter* really made me very happy, and I thank you for the calendar. I just devour all the words you write, and I thank you for them with all my heart.

I have finally gotten a bit back to normal and can look at everything in a more level-headed way. The end of your letter made me the happiest where you wrote that you finally have recaptured your former sense of reality. It is strange, but I, too, have come to the realization that we need to be more sober. We have knocked ourselves around with our emotions far too much lately. Also, I believe that my problems with depression stem from allowing myself to get too overwhelmed, such that I lose control and have little remaining energy to engage my better judgment. I really need to have more self-esteem and be more secure in myself, but I know that security comes primarily from God.

It is also clear to me that the source of my depression is not solely the result of last Sunday's experience. I deeply regret that I reproached you. Further, I now recognize that I must rejoice in my faith and love for you; until now I have been slinking around like a wounded dog. My dear Boris, you make me so rich with your love. I am totally convinced that you love me truly. I will never forget last Sunday. Your bright eyes, the loving way you cut and fed me that apple.

My love for you has matured such that I will no longer strive to love you as God would, but just as a person would, very naturally. For my part, through God's strength, a true godly love will come all on its own. I have already noticed progress in this regard.

Now good night my dearest. I will ask God to protect you from harm and danger and to give you strength and patience so that you can pass the difficult test you now face and find the right path. I pray he will protect our love and let it grow to his honor, and that he will allow us, if it is his will, to be united soon. I thank you, Boris, for your prayer. It did me so much good. It is good that you can pray now. It would make me happy if I could help you find the way to God.

[Friday] November 10, 1944

Good day dear Boris,

I would like to tell you what I think would be best. I will stay here in Gwatt and continue with my professional training. But if there arises an opportunity for us to marry before I complete my training, then you can put in a crucial word with my parents. It wouldn't be good for me to live in Winterthur now. I would be faced with endless struggles with my parents, and besides that, I would have no support for my faith. I doubt we would be able to see each other more there than we have here until now.

Now farewell my dearest, my Boris,

Your Anneli

P.S. We have snow already. It's enough to last until Christmas!

LETTER B10

ZURICH

[Saturday] November 11, 1944
10:30 p.m.

My dear Anneli,

I simply cannot go to sleep without writing to you and sending you a loving goodnight kiss. Also, I need to discuss something with you.

First, thank you for your wonderful letter and the fantastic cake. You should have bitten off much more. It was painful for me to tear a piece off the little heart I sent you, that is why I only bit a little bit off its side, so little I thought you would hardly notice.

I am just back from an evening Crusader program where they read a play aloud. I attended not as a member, but as a "friend," an official designation of the Crusaders.

Eight days ago, on November 4, when we last saw each other, marked exactly two months since we first met. And tomorrow evening, on November 12 at 9 p.m., it will be exactly two months since our holy light and love began to burn in our hearts, as we sat in a boat on Lake Thun. I thought about it a lot today, and tomorrow I will certainly think about it again. I believe that these two points in time hold great meaning for us and will always remain in our memories. I would be happy to spend Christmas or New Year with you, or if you will be at home over the holidays, perhaps I could spend at least one of them with you? But right now, I am just looking forward to your next visit in eight days.

From your letter I see that you are compelled to fight with yourself mightily, though love seems to be winning. Remember that I love you and have great faith in you. I am very happy with your love. Only my yearning for you makes me worry, and unfortunately that worry just seems to increase.

Recently I have been getting much more work. I believe I could take on a good deal more if it comes my way.

I wish you a good night and kiss you with much love,

Your Boris

[Sunday] November 12, 1944
8:30 a.m.

Good morning dearest,

I hope you received my letter by now. You should not think that you are alone anymore, but that there is someone in the world who thinks of you constantly and cares for you. I have an unending desire to inundate you with love, attention, and tenderness, but at the same time I feel like a prisoner. That is why, for now, all I can do is be patient and hope that someday I will be free of this feeling and that you will be able to experience the reality of that love. I have noticed lately that my appetite for learning is growing. We must try to prepare for the future and keep our thoughts and deeds close to reality. I am glad we both have our feet firmly planted on the ground, despite our perpetual drive toward the ideal.

4 p.m.

As this day quickly ebbs away, it brings about a huge yearning for you in me. I have never experienced such longing before. I miss you terribly, Anneli. I believe that when we are finally together, we would be able to shut out the entire world and drown ourselves in each other. I know you would add to that: "Yes, but in the name of God." I must tell you that I am in such close agreement with that, that I would say the most beautiful and purest fulfillment can only be granted by God. The value of our love will surely grow if we can build upon God.

I kiss you very tenderly now, with my whole heart and soul,

Your loving Boris

LETTER B11

Zurich

[Sunday] November 12, 1944
8 p.m.

My dear Anneli,

As I mentioned earlier today, I began the day with an especially painful yearning for you. I do not know why it hit me so hard. Perhaps it is because today is the two-month anniversary of our beginning. Two months ago, we rode in a small boat on Lake Thun, while Reverend Kühner awaited us with great concern on shore. That hour will remain in my memory forever.

The second reason may be that I did not receive a letter from you today, and yesterday's letter seemed unusually short. The only consolation I have is that you wrote that I am in your thoughts. Today I thought of you constantly. It is hard to be without you on the weekdays, but especially hard on Sunday. I will do all I can to make sure our separation is as short as possible.

The third reason for my anxiety is probably that on the eastern warfront at this very moment the last preparations for the winter offensive are beginning. On the Russian front the periodic exchange of troops is taking place. In the winter the Siberian troops come up; that is why the winter months are particularly hard for the Germans. It was the Siberian troops that recovered Stalingrad. In the last war [World War I] it was also the Siberian troops that stopped the German offensive forces. The Siberian and the Caucasian troops are thought to be the best in Russia. I put my hopes in them that they will be able to end the war this winter. Not just for our sakes, but so that the misery of the whole world might end. We must hope that the war will soon be over.

We must hang on to our patience especially tightly now when everything seems to be hanging by a thread. There have been times in my life I had to wait patiently and show no weakness. I always felt that I had to adhere stubbornly to my goal. Each time I did so, I was richly rewarded. Patience and persistence are extraordinarily important qualities, without which success cannot be attained. Along with these, there is another quality that belongs with them, and that is faith in God. My dearest, we must hold on and make it through this difficult time. If we can do so, nothing will hinder us in the future.

It is 8:45 p.m. At this moment two months ago, our love was ignited. I hope that God, who ignited that love, will protect it, and allow it to continue and grow. I would like to ask your forgiveness for many things. I want to protect your love and keep it safe.

I kiss you very softly and tenderly,

Your Boris, who loves you!

LETTER B12

ZURICH

[Wednesday] November 15, 1944
5 p.m.

My dear Anneli,

I would really like to meet your parents soon. Please tell me when and how this might best be arranged. I came to this decision because I do not want your parents to see you in a false light. You have already suffered enough in that they think of you as bad and reckless, and I don't want to be the cause of them continuing to think of you in that way. I want your parents to view you as a valuable person. We are both valuable people and will always be. One's value has nothing to do with having money; it is a measure of our inner selves.

We can decide how I should get in touch with your parents when we meet at my place in Zurich. Please tell me exactly when you will be arriving.

Lately, I have been feeling frustrated professionally. I feel like someone has put a huge iron chest on top of me that is hindering my progress. It is such a shame that there is no reputable mining school in Switzerland, and that there is no professor here who is really interested in my work. The mining field combines many areas of study, including numerous subjects taught by professors here (chemistry, physics, mechanics, statistics, and many more), yet none of these professors is knowledgeable in my specific area. Even if I could find a professor willing to devote his time to me, he might try to take advantage of me and my research. New discoveries are too valuable and important to take any unnecessary risks. I am still struggling to pass the entrance examinations. Yet studying for them seems like a waste of my time.

Despite this, there are many possible avenues open to me, yet none of them would be completely satisfactory. That is why the decision has been so difficult. Time is also a consideration. I really must come to a decision soon. I know you cannot really advise me, but I still want to share this with you, so you will understand what is making me so anxious. You should not think I am indecisive. No, my situation is extremely complicated, and it is impossible to describe all the details and possibilities in a letter.

I told you my older brother Joseph, who was a physician, was an excellent role model for me. I always tried to emulate him. The whole milieu in Siberia, including my family and our circle of friends, had a much stricter moral code than here in Europe. The colder the climate, the stricter the people are. Just compare Canadians, Swedes, Siberians, and even Eskimos with people from southern climates and you will see a huge difference.

Despite the extraordinarily harsh life I led, I was able to support myself in an enviable fashion until 1939. It is interesting that your years of error and mine (1942-1944) were the same.[41] It is also interesting that we both experienced spiritual revelations at the same time. We need to forget our past and shake off those events that are especially displeasing to us. I sense a powerful force growing in me through which I know I will derive strength. Where this force comes from, from my inherited good core or from God, I do not know, as it arises in me from deep within my subconscious. I know very well, Anneli, that if we want to be together forever, we must do away with our inferiority complexes permanently. Our weaknesses will then melt away. An indiscretion from either of us would perhaps not destroy our marriage, but it would certainly damage it powerfully and undermine our happiness.

You cannot imagine how highly I value your desire to become a morally pure, refined woman. You have proven that this desire of yours is true and rooted in your deepest soul. I firmly hope that you believe that I, too, have the very same desire. Fortunately, your good inner core, with God's help, has lifted you above all your earlier

---

41   Boris was scrupulous until he left Germany but indulged in some love affairs as a refugee during the war.

indiscretions. I treasure that in you tremendously. You must thank the Lord for it every day; we both must. We can help each other preserve that purity and strength.

When I read your wonderful letters, especially the last few, it makes me think of the following story by Gotthelf:

"Oh, the pain of love is the only lover in the souls of so many young women, and this lover is much more likely to be true to them than other lovers, even unto death. Nobody can see him, he does not appear in the woman's face, he does not slow her busy hands, he does not shine in her eyes in broad daylight and when strangers look at her. When the woman withdraws into her quiet bedchamber, and goes to bed, when the day's stresses are past, then this pain arises from its dark tomb and the heart throbs. The woman notices that the lover approaches, opens her arms in tearful ecstasy, engages with him throughout the night, and abandons him only when the daylight dawns, suffering the pains of separation, yet entering calmly and confidently into her daily routine, even while continually longing for the shadow to return that carries the faithful woman's lover with his pleasures, his ecstasy, and the quietly hidden pain of love."[42]

By the way, "Kochanek," the root of my name, means "lover." One can also derive "Koch" [German for cook] from my name. It so happens that I am a good cook. On the other hand, my first name Boris (when one says the final 's' very quietly) means "fighter." Isn't that strange! Should steel [German word for steel: *Stahl*, an alternate pronunciation of the name Stahel] be united with Boris, then the name would mean a "steel-hard fighter." Funny! But it might be the case, as you really could make me very strong.

I have just now received your express letter* in which you say you are worried about me and want to give me strength through your love and faithfulness and trust in God. This you have brilliantly succeeded in doing. Tears came to my eyes, and had you

---

42   Jeremias Gotthelf, pen name of Albert Bitzius (1797-1854), was a Swiss pastor and novelist. This passage is from his novel *Wie Anne Bäbi Jowäger Haushaltet*.

been here, I would have hugged and kissed you in thankfulness and love. You should always believe me when I say that you are a dear, good person whom one *must* love. I will never allow anyone to call you bad because I am dead sure that you will always follow the higher path. Praise to God who is leading you there. It is unbelievable how much power a little word can have when it is encased in love and therefore comes from God. I thank you again with all my heart.

I embrace and kiss you with all my strength,

Your tenderly loving and true Teddy Bear

LETTER B13

Zurich

[Thursday] November 16, 1944

My most dearly beloved Anneli,

If you could only grasp what a terribly big role you play in my life. I can think, feel, and do whatever I like, but the beginning and the end of everything I think, feel, and do is you, my dear girl.

You may be right when you say God has trusted you with something very precious and he wants to see if you are worthy of it. I am so happy and unendingly thankful to read your words: "I want to strive with all of my strength, and where my strength fails, there God will stand by me. God is faithful and true. He will strengthen us."[43]

You are a priceless treasure to me too, and I want to fight for you as well with all my strength, with God's help. Our chief obstacle is time, and secondly, insecurity and uncertainty. Our weapons are our love, our belief in God, and our hope in the future. We only need to overcome time, everything else will take care of itself. But now, when we are so far apart, it is doubly hard. Every day without you seems like a loss to me.

You write: "It is really strange that I, who have never been able to stay faithful to anyone, should win a man like you!" Yes, my dear Anneli, it is very strange! Even so, I am certain you will stay true to me, just as I will stay true to you. Being faithful to another is the best proof of true love, especially for someone who makes God the basis of her existence. You will love me even more when we are finally united forever. Your earlier mistakes were not the result of a depraved nature; they came about because of a faulty orientation toward life's values and poor examples during your upbringing. Now you strive for a complete, worthy, and solid happiness, rather

---

43 This sentence does not appear in any of Anna's surviving letters.

than just pleasure, which demeans the character and soul, the most precious things a person has. No, our two sick souls stand face to face wanting to tenderly care for each other's wounds and make the other whole again. When the soul is healthy again, the person will be too. If we can only hold out, the reward will not fail to come. We must help each other through this difficult time by offering each other faith, help, and love. I am glad I have such a courageous battle companion as you.

I kiss you with the tenderest gentleness, my dear Anneli,

Your Boris

LETTER A11

GWATT

[Friday] November 17, 1944

My dear Boris,

It is I who am almost tearful now. Your last two letters have made me incredibly happy, as I can sense how your soul speaks directly to mine. I am ashamed I had so many bad thoughts about you. How could I feel that way as I read those words which come so directly from your loving soul? Boris, I thank you from deep in my heart for the strong faith you have in me. You give me renewed peace. Each time I have an evil thought, it hurts me, because I know it would hurt you too. You know, sometimes I just can't understand how I can mean so much to you. But I really want to trust you completely and believe in you.

Boris, we are now tightly bound, and we will go this way into a new life, into the fight to keep ourselves clean and pure in every way. But we should not just speak beautiful words about it, but actually do what we say we will do. And there is one important thing we must not forget! When we struggle and fail, there is someone who will help us get back on our feet and give us the chance to begin anew: Jesus Christ.

Now my dearest "Kochanek," don't let your peace falter. May God grant you patience. Wait it out, Boris, my everything. I kiss you very gently and tenderly and wish you a good Sunday.

Your Anneli, who always loves you more.

P.S. Don't be sad! Look into the future with confidence. God is with us.

LETTER A12

GWATT

[Tuesday] November 21, 1944

My dear Boris,

I can see from your letter* that you are much more than just sad. I understand you well, as I too had a very long, sad Sunday. But we should not let ourselves wallow in our misfortune and hang our heads; we should be strong-minded and stoic. Maybe I am a bit better off than you because my day was full of activity, while you don't really know what you should be working on. But gather up your courage, God is with us. I pray every day that he will bless our love and not forsake us. Just think about all the people who were in love and now, because of this horrible war, have been ripped apart, neither one knowing whether the other is still alive. We should be grateful that I know you are in Zurich, and you know that I am in Gwatt, and we are both alive awaiting the moment when God will unite us. Also, we know we are not alone in this world and that there are people we should not forget and have some consideration for. In my case, it is my parents I am thinking of. We will only hurt ourselves if we are not careful.

Let us look forward to next weekend now. I still have no answer from home, but I am hoping for a favorable reply. I would be so excited to have the opportunity to bring you home with me. I believe you will get along well with my father. You know, my parents have really changed since my last visit home. The last time they were here in Gwatt they were very nice to me.

Right, my little bear, you should also stop stamping your feet, as that won't help at all. Have a little patience, and you will get your chocolate.

My dear, I, too, would like to rest very quietly in your arms knowing that we belong to each other and love each other very much. I am overjoyed that I will soon have my arms around you.

I wish you a good night and kiss you tenderly innumerable times,

Your Anneli

Good day my dearest,

I would like to thank you for your lecture about the purpose of life.[44] I understand it much better in this German translation, as I am not so comfortable with French. And now I kiss you once more and say goodbye.

Your Anneli

---

44 A translation of the lecture Boris presented at the Swiss refugee camp before he met Anna

LETTER A13[45]

GWATT

[Tuesday] November 21, 1944

My dear ones,

Thank you so much for the beautiful basket of pears. It brought me much joy; I can't wait to start eating them!

I hope you won't mind if I bring Boris home with me this weekend. I really would like you to see what a good relationship we have. It should be a cordial and cheerful occasion, rather than one of strife, in which everyone can feel comfortable and gain some benefit. Vati can even work on his stamp collection and Martha can knit or do something else. We should let Boris play piano for us a bit. Let's try to keep things informal and relaxed. It does not make much sense to discuss our future right now. It is possible to make some guesses, but what will happen lies in God's hands. The main thing is that you see what kind of person Boris is, because when you get to know him, you will better understand how I feel. Does it matter to you if I bring Boris on Saturday instead of Sunday? You really should not trouble yourselves about this at all. I will bring a cake. Boris can sleep in my room, and I can go over to Dorli's[46] to sleep. I can make the bed for him myself, so you won't have to trouble yourself.

I am sending along some things for Martha to mend. I am so ashamed that I am not able to keep my things in order; I would therefore be doubly thankful if you can help me. If am being too presumptuous, you can send them back.

Now farewell, I hope that everything is going well and that you are healthy.

With my warm greetings,

Your Anneli

---

45   This letter from Anna to her father and Martha was written before she received the subsequent letter from her father (V2).
46   A next-door neighbor and friend

LETTER V2

WINTERTHUR

[Monday] November 20, 1944

Dear Anneli,

We received your letter of November 17,* and Martha and I thank you for it. We did not have a very good Sunday, as it was entirely consumed with this business concerning this immigrant. Think about the huge age difference! The whole affair, for you and for us, is so inscrutable and hopeless that I don't care to waste any more words on it. We have explained to you in person the explicit reasons for our position.

Since our last visit barely two weeks have gone by, and now you wish to see this person in Zurich again! Why? Is this how you obediently follow our request to concentrate on your professional training? I tell you this for the last time: To really concentrate seriously on something you must not foolishly waste your time and energy on other, non-essential things. This would be completely clear to any thinking, rational person, who would certainly warn you against such foolishness. All this traveling about with this man will now stop! Do you understand me? I think you can find a better way to spend your money. How could you think that we would entertain this man in Winterthur? Our whole neighborhood would be able to gawk at your newest conquest! I could not even share details about this man publicly without people thinking that I was the dumbest person in the world. But as far as a relationship with Mr. Kochanowsky goes, compared with Swiss relationships with which we and you are involved, this one is just impossible. So, let us close the subject, and you will stay in Gwatt next Sunday.

I can tell you this whole business has kept me so preoccupied and distracted that I can hardly focus on my work. I hope in the future you will show me more consideration. Such things take so much of my time and concentration and require the strongest nerves. So, please follow my advice. It is given in your best interest.

Greetings,

Vati

LETTER M2

[Tuesday] November 21, 1944

Dear Anneli,

Our trip from Bern to Zurich was quite stormy. The snow just would not stop. I was uneasy about it, as everything looked so very dark.

In response to your letter,* it pains me above all that I cannot be the mother you would like me to be. You complain that I was not what I should have been. But ask yourself if you were what you should have been. Have you ever asked yourself what discomfort I might have endured these last three years? The heart cannot profit from these sorts of thoughts.

I had a difficult time, and I was often sad that you were unwilling to accept that things could not always go your way. You write that you would like to become a completely different kind of person, which is right and good, and which will make me happy if you can accomplish what you have in mind. But realize that one cannot become a new person overnight. Only a person who works on himself can achieve a satisfactory result, and that requires work above all, as well as the fulfilment of one's duty toward one's elders. How many children today would be thankful to have a little place in a good heart, and here we have done so much for you, and you are not at all grateful.

Above all I am sorry for Vati. He is so sad and worries about you so much. We really need to have a little peace now.

Now, head high, show that through your faith in God you have risen above these things, and renounce what makes your heart heavy. With true faith you will have the power to look at things clearly. I hope everything will come out well so that the coming Christmas can be a true celebration of love.

I embrace you,

Your Martha

LETTER A14

GWATT

[Friday] November 24, 1944

My dear, dear Boris,

I am quite worried about you and wonder how you withstood this awful setback. Yes, things have become quite serious now that my parents have declared their opposition toward us. Some other things have occurred to me as well. You must understand that after the emotional upheaval of last night I am having a hard time putting a smile on my face today. My head teacher in Thun telephoned here and Winterthur to ask what was wrong with me and reprimanded me, saying that my relationship with you was a stupid, frivolous thing, and worse. Then she started to make threats and told me that if I didn't put an end to it, they would come after you at the foreign office and you would lose your stipend and have to return to the refugee camp. Oh dearest, all this must pain you terribly. But don't give up hope. Hold on to your courage. Isn't God's strength much greater than that of all these hard, heartless people? We must try to look at everything in a very unemotional, practical way.

My parents have forbidden me to see you. Because I want to obey God's word, I find myself forced to follow my parents' command. This could keep us apart for a long, long time. However, it is impossible for anyone to forbid a person from loving another. They could put us in separate prison cells and torture us, but no one can keep us from loving each other. Boris, I believe we are standing at a decisive juncture now. We will have an infinitely difficult future ahead of us, and now we must ask ourselves very seriously whether we want to go on or not. If we are going to overcome these problems, we must have complete faith in each other. Because if we cannot see each other at all, then doubt will become our greatest enemy.

This is a lot to ask, especially since our love is still so new. But in these past two and a half months we have been getting closer and closer, despite our age and cultural differences. Now, by force, other people want to put an end to this loving relationship. There is only one thing for us to do. We must obey them while believing and trusting in God, rather than in our own strength. Nothing happens or exists without God's will, including all these difficulties that are facing us now. We should not become embittered, but stand firm in our faith and hold and protect each other in our hearts. My dearest, we must leave everything in God's hands, and not tire ourselves out pleading with him for mercy and strength. He alone has the strength to change everything. We must trust him to do what is best for us. I know this is not easy for you. Your faith is still so young and tender, and you are all alone and must deal with many difficulties. On top of that your hands are tied. But I want to help you get through this difficult time with all my heart and strength.

God's strength has illuminated this for me; let it solidify your confidence as well: "If God is for us, who could be against us?" If it is God's will that we be together, then he will find the way and means to unite us despite everything. I will take you very firmly in my arms so that you can cry your eyes out; I will do the same in yours. But afterwards we will turn into iron-clad fighters![47] An extremely sad Sunday stands before us. Bind up all your energy. We cannot, at any price, allow ourselves to hang our heads.

I kiss you and hold you very tightly so you can sense you are not alone.

Farewell my Boris,

Your Anneli

---

47   She may be referring to Boris' earlier observation about their names: Stahel=steel and Boris=fighter.

LETTER B14

[Saturday] November 25, 1944
8 p.m.

My dear, dear Anneli,

You must not be sad. People can wear themselves out with sorrow and easily lose their way. On the contrary, we should be happy God has sent us this difficult test. We should take up our fate with courage. A courageous, tough, fighting spirit steels a person and makes him unconquerable. We must instill courage and confidence in one another.

You must not worry about me having to return to the refugee camp. Earlier it was hard for me to endure the camp because it seemed like a pointless existence. But now I know the "why" behind it and would happily take on that burden too. We should consider the big events happening in the world right now, as the war is coming to an end. I will soon be free again and regain my rights.

We should show great consideration toward all people, above all to your parents. They certainly are very worried and concerned about our relationship. But it is not our fault, as one cannot forbid another to love, and one cannot be faulted for it either. So, we must give in to your father, not out of fear, but out of love for God and to protect our love. In addition, you should do it out of respect for your parents, and I, out of respect for the hospitality that Switzerland has shown me. This confrontation will bring us closer together. Now it will be easier to keep our love pure, which is something we both want.

Despite all the pain, I am very happy and proud you are showing such bravery and that this shock has not extinguished your love, but has made it stronger instead. Are you not my golden girl?!

We are already bound to each other, but now we are forced to be apart. Should our love withstand this test and stay true despite the long separation, what else could possibly threaten it? What a fantastic foundation it will be for the rest of our lives!

I am very proud of you, my sweet, courageous girl! How splendid your letter is, how strong you are! And you say that you are weak! No, no, you are no longer weak. God's strength has shown its presence in your life.

Certainly, I am sad and my heart bleeds. Today my waitress told me she had never seen me look so sad. For you it is probably not much better, my poor Anneli. But as we both feel we are in the right and have not harmed anyone, we should have the strength and courage to fight for our love. If these shortsighted people only knew how valuable having and experiencing true love is, they would explode with envy. They say they want to save you. From what? If one loves truly, then one is not afraid of anything, even death. Do they think they should threaten us with jail, refugee camp, or prison? They do not understand that every external attack they make will only strengthen our love. Imagine, if I am forced back into the refugee camp, you would surely still want to be with me, even if I were a very poor devil!

Also, I am amazed by the strength of God within you, and it all arose in just three months' time. You love in a very godly way now. One day I will be able to prove to you that I am worthy of it.

Reverend Kühner has asked the following of me:

1. I should convince you to finish your studies in Thun.

2. To ask you to keep your love for me private, and not show it in front of others.

3. That I cease writing to you daily because it excites you and keeps you up at night.

About the first: We will leave whether you finish your studies in God's hands. But I would ask you to dedicate yourself more to your studies, as it will make the time go faster and appease your head teacher at the same time. (She upsets my stomach!) You should ask the same of me. On Wednesday I will get a response from the ETH and then I will really have to exert myself to stay focused and concentrate.

We want to remain resilient and sensible. We must work hard, as we are really working for ourselves and our future. But I know that one day, dearest, you will create a home for us using your good taste and make it a heavenly nest. Every storm must end, even this one. The bigger the storm, the more beautiful the sun's rays will seem afterwards.

About his second point: I don't quite understand it, as it is clear to me that the holiest thing a person has is hidden deep within him. The deeper it is hidden, the holier it is. I never let anyone peek into my treasure house. If I did, people would either be indifferent, or envious, or would laugh at me and say they don't understand it.

On his third point: I want to give you the greatest consideration, my dearest. If they really pressure you about it, maybe we should only write every other day. We could still write a few sentences every night and in the morning too, so that we can "talk" to each other daily before we go to sleep and when we rise in the morning. The night, although we are apart, belongs to us, as we are alone with our longing for each other. It has really become painful, but out of this pain, beautiful fruit will grow. You can be sure of that.

I would like to thank you for your letter. I am trying to maintain a positive attitude, despite our hardships. Even if I had to go back to the camp now, I would still try to stay positive. But that is only thanks to you, as I know you stand behind me and will strengthen my soul with your loving words. Without that I would be lost. Then the suffering would have no meaning. I am amazed at how an eighteen-year-old girl can have such a powerful effect on me and bring me so much strength.

I see from Reverend Kühner's letter* that I was right in my suspicion that your father is most concerned about your security and future. Therefore, it is my good professional standing that is of the utmost importance. Reverend Kühner writes: "If God decides that Anna is to be your wife, then that is what will be, regardless of wars or even if you end up in Honolulu. We have no reason to dispute that Anneli and you belong together, and we would be very happy if you two are united in the future. I am sure even Mr. Stahel will be happy when Mining Director Kochanowsky takes his daughter Anna as his wife someday. What he is trying to ward off is his daughter Anna's negligence toward her studies because of her love for Boris, or because of love's trials."

I, too, believe that this is the root of the whole problem. So, if you stand beside me, I will be even more inspired to find a position as fast as possible, so that we may be married sooner. But now you must pull yourself together and grit your teeth. We will find a way through this. Let us try to support one another and help each other pass this test. We must be thankful that this problem did not arise two months ago. We are far enough along in our relationship that we can withstand much.

Let us not lose our courage. I kiss you very passionately and tenderly.

My dear Anneli,

Boris

LETTER A15
GWATT

[Saturday] December 2, 1944

My dear Boris,

The first thing I would like to say is that I miss you terribly. Come soon, my dearest. I pray you will be able to get permission to travel to Gwatt!

Yesterday evening Dr. Strupp told us about the beginning of the world, the Ice Age, and that man evolved from apes, and what all else, I don't know. Then suddenly, a little light bulb went on in my head. He is the kind of person who always thinks he knows more than God does and wants to know more than God tells us. The way to God is blocked off for these people because they do not have a childlike faith in him. People should return to that kind of simplicity. How does it help us to know that humans descended from apes? God tells us he created us. Whether he created us from apes or not really isn't so important. The main thing is he created us. I believe God's power is so great that he could have chosen to create us in other ways as well.

My judgment of this is based on my own feelings and instincts. I believe that when man strives to know too much, he botches up God's handiwork. You must understand me correctly. I do not want to throw all of man's academic accomplishments into the trash can, but if people would pay more attention to the Bible, they would be able to manage everything with greater moderation and reason. Just today I had the thought that maybe that is why so many people, intelligent people, have lost their minds lately.

I would be so happy if you could come to Gwatt, as I have an unbelievably strong desire to speak with you. Even if we cannot quite agree on everything, perhaps we can come to a clearer understanding. I rack my brains all day long over this damned godly principle of yours and your relationship to God and to Christ. It is probably better not to write too much about it in this letter. We should discuss it in person. But then please be forthright in your language and explain exactly what is hindering your faith in God. You should not be afraid it will destroy our love, because I have great hope that you, too, will find God's mercy. Faith is the gift of mercy. Read First Peter 3:1 and what follows.[48] This goes for me as well.

My dear Boris, my precious one, I will say goodnight now. When I go to sleep, I will dream of you. I kiss you heartily and fervently.

My dearest,

Your faithful Anneli

P.S. I now suddenly see that being faithful is the truest sign of love.

[Sunday] December 3, 1944

Good day dear Boris!

You know, I really did dream of you, but it was such a horrible dream that when I awoke, I was still violently upset about it. It was as if a huge stone had been lifted off me when I realized that it was only a dream.

Now I would like to thank you for your sweet letter and for the most loving kisses you sent with it. It would be better if you didn't spoil me so much. You do enough already. You should not forget that you are also my teacher, and as such you should know that you should not spoil or idolize a child. Otherwise, God will take her away.

---

[48] 1 Peter 3:1-4: "Likewise, you wives, be submissive to your husbands, so that some, though they do not obey the word, may be won by the behavior of their wives, when they see your reverent and chaste behavior. Let not yours be the outward adorning, with braiding of hair, decoration of gold, and wearing of robes, but let it be the hidden person of the heart with the imperishable jewel of a gentle and quiet spirit, which in God's sight is very precious."

Now we must faithfully stick together. You know I wait with you, and I know you wait with me. That will make it easier for us.

I wish you a wonderful Sunday. Don't be too sad, my dearest. One day, God will hear our prayer. Now I kiss you very, very lovingly.

My Boris,

Your Anneli

LETTER A16

GWATT

[Sunday] December 3, 1944

My dear Boris,

Forgive me, I want to begin by going back to our earlier discussion.[49] It interests me so much I just cannot push it aside. I would like you to explain very simply and clearly what you mean, so I can really understand your thinking, especially about the idea that I should write your biography. That really surprised me and sent me into ecstasy. It would be so wonderful, and it would bring me much joy, but there are some temporary impediments. Also, I think I should be older and more mature before I take on something like that.

First, I will restate what I think you said. Perhaps I have misunderstood you. Then I want to explain what I believe as simply as possible. Afterwards, please respond as clearly and plainly as you can to what I have said.

You say your belief in the godly principle is rock-solid. From your own experience and from history, you believe that life and true love, as the root of life, will always triumph over any negative pressures. I do not dispute this law. I can easily imagine from the examples you gave me that it exists. But I do not see faith in God in it. Faith in God is not the same as faith in life or in man's life force. It becomes faith in God only when one acknowledges that all life comes from God. God gives us the promise that his power and light will overcome everything that is evil. Christ has already given us proof of this through his resurrection, as death is the highest triumph of evil. If one can accept this, then one can believe in all miracles.

Here is a line from my morning prayer book. I hope you will recognize the wisdom in this saying: "Misery and strife will always

---

49   A discussion of this subject is not found in any previous surviving letter.

exist in this world. This is God's judgment against us because of our sins. He who opposes the God of Life will find the ruin of sin. But God will prevail."

I will conclude by telling you what I think about the much-discussed recent case, namely whether lying to save a life is a sin. I freely admit that my judgment is based on my own instincts and viewpoint. I think in this case one is duty-bound to try to save a life. One should not simply put one's hands in one's pockets and await God's help. One should handle the situation in a responsible way, so that one can answer to God for one's actions. I believe in a case like this, when there is no other way out, lying is not a sin. But one should endeavor not to harm anyone in doing so. You write: "I believe, if I were confronted with a life-or-death situation, I would always decide in favor of life, and take the sin upon myself."

But you see, it is enough if you acknowledge your sins before God. You need not take those sins on, rather you may lay them into the hands of Jesus Christ. That is why he is called our Savior. God's law is "Thou shalt not kill." There are man-made laws that go against God's law, like those of the Gestapo that turn people into animals. Therefore, I do not find it an irresponsible act if one saves a life by lying. In addition, I think you are completely right when you say you are against the Christianity that killed so many people in the name of Christ. Christ tells us not to kill heathens or non-believers. God will deal with them at the Last Judgment.

Regarding your example concerning the soldier who slapped the priest, I say the following: The priest did not handle it right! Because he offered the soldier his left cheek afterwards, which effectively challenged the soldier, the priest, in effect, became responsible for the soldier's life. One would have to know more about the exact circumstances. You wrote me once yourself that God gave us the spirit of reason, and we should turn to it in these sorts of cases. Read this passage in Matthew 5:38-39: "You have heard that it was said, 'An eye for an eye and a tooth for a tooth.' But I say to you, do not resist one who is evil. But if anyone strikes you on the right cheek, turn to him the other." I think Jesus' meaning is quite clear here. One can see the same problem with those who pedantically fulfill God's commandments to the Jews. I believe these people lack wisdom and the spirit of reason. I understand what Jesus is saying here, as the Old Testament is sometimes overly strict.

Now on to the last question of whether Jesus can be considered God's son. You answered me, "Naturally!" But then right afterwards you spoke of him as only a man. You say we are all children of God, but no one has achieved what Jesus achieved. Jesus is God's most favorite son and that is why he has a special place beside God. I have another viewpoint! It is not because Jesus was sinless that he has this special place beside God and is his favorite son, it is the other way around. Jesus is God's son and therefore he is sinless. John 3:16: "For God so loved the world that he gave his only Son, that whoever believes in him should not perish, but have eternal life." And John 10:30: "I and the Father are one." The following words are also very telling: John 14:6-7: "I am the way, and the truth, and the life; no one comes to the Father, but by me. If you had known me, you would have known my Father also."

My dear Boris, I am so happy that I finally had the time and peace to think about all this and write you my thoughts. Maybe I am mistaken about some things, but we must try to achieve clarity because we want to be mindful of the one way to God, and that is through Jesus Christ. And if you do not want to come with me, then I will do what you told me you would let me do: I will put a nose ring and chain on you and pull you along with me.[50]

Boris, I thank you from the bottom of my heart for your letter of last Sunday and the huge kiss. I hope you were not too bored, as you were all alone. I so regretted that you could not be here today. We celebrated the first Sunday of Advent. I know you would have liked it.

I do so hope you will be able to visit me on December 16. That is only two weeks away. Boris, I would really like to see you, speak

---

50 The nose ring and chain may have been for the Siberian bear (Boris) or for a bull. Boris was born on May 4, under the zodiac sign of Taurus, the bull.

with you, and kiss you. But I do not want to be a weakling. I want to be strong and wait faithfully until you can return.

Now I must complain about something! Naturally, I cannot abide your receiving other love letters[51] besides mine. I would advise you to at least reduce this other relationship from a flirtation to a friendship. I think I have the right to demand that because I am convinced you would not be able to stand it if I, too, had other love interests.

Now, good night my love, I kiss and hug you tightly and tenderly in my mind.

My dear Boris,

Your Anneli

---

51   The author of these other love letters Boris is receiving is unknown.

LETTER B15

Zurich

[Tuesday] December 5, 1944
11 p.m.

My dear heart,

Before I go to sleep, just a quick kiss and a wish goodnight. I have just returned from a concert. About twice a month I receive a free ticket from a city official I met in Gwatt. He directs the women's military service program there. He and his wife are musicians and know of my interest in music. That is why I have this opportunity.

Tonight, I heard Mozart, Haydn, Ravel, and Hindemith, including piano concertos with orchestra by Haydn and Ravel. The piano soloist was Dinu Lipatti,[52] a twenty-seven-year-old Romanian living in Geneva. He played very well. But the Ravel and Hindemith sounded like jazz to me, a lot of noise, dissonance, and sensuality. I love Beethoven.

I thank you for your letter. I am a bit on edge because I am unsure when I will get an answer from the United States. It's just crazy that they are dragging out my application so long. But there's nothing to do but wait. Maybe it's best just to leave it to fate. You are right, screaming and stamping one's feet doesn't help. Thank you for helping me through this difficult time.

I would really like to be with you at Christmas. It would be wonderful to have the opportunity to really rest and heal. I want to put my head in your lap and have you gently kiss and caress me. And I would like to be infinitely tender to you too. You are like a little kitten who needs tenderness as much as it needs fresh air.

---

52 Dinu Lipatti (1917-1950) was a brilliant Romanian classical pianist and composer whose life was tragically cut short by Hodgkin's disease. During World War II he fled Romania and, with the aid of Swiss pianist and conductor Edwin Fischer, emigrated to Switzerland, where he accepted a position as professor of piano at the Geneva Conservatory.

I hope we will finally be able to see each other again in a few days. I hope by then to have received an answer.

And now I wish you a very good night. I kiss your nose, eyebrows, and your sweet little mouth.

You are mine,
I am yours,

Boris

[Wednesday] December 6
8 a.m.

Good morning my dear Anneli, my little soul!

I just got a letter from the ETH. They have asked me to describe my doctoral work (purpose, principles, experiments, etc.). Cross your fingers for me that all this will work out. I kiss you passionately and strongly. I have such great longing for you, my little sweetheart. You are mine, understand? You belong to me and only me. (I am such an egoist).

LETTER A17

Gwatt

[Saturday] December 9, 1944

My dear Boris,

First, I want to thank you for your letter. It brought me such unending joy I cannot express it in words.

But I must tell you about something that is oppressing me today. I received a letter from my grandmother.[53] She, too, has heard about my new love affair, as she calls it, and asks me to give her a special gift for Christmas by breaking up with you. She and the rest of my family do not know the truth, and if I were to try to explain it to them, they would not understand. In any case, I know that at Christmas, when I am at home, I will be getting a lot of grief from my whole family. I am not afraid I will become weak and will leave you as a result, but I am afraid that I won't know how to answer their questions. Boris, please give me some advice, because it does matter to me whether you stand completely or just partially behind me.

If my father asks me if I have broken up with you, what should I say? Should I stand up for our love despite the risk of sending you back to the refugee camp? Or should I lie? I am at a loss as to what to do, what would be right. Help me and advise me, Boris! I know we must stay hopeful and not lose faith in God's word: "What is impossible for man is possible with God."[54]

I doubt we will be able to meet in Winterthur again. That is probably why I feel so gloomy now. But don't worry, this will pass, as I know where I can ask for strength and where I will get it, so that I can face the future with courage. But it would be awful if you were forced to go back to the refugee camp just when you are finally able to begin your work.

---
53   Anna Bertschi of Uhwiesen, Anna's maternal grandmother
54   Matthew 19:26

The first real test that was laid before us is ending. Did we pass it? I think we can surely say that we have. We must recognize that while we have passed this test, we have not yet passed the test that God is laying before us. That test is not yet at an end; it has only just begun.

Now I want to wish you a good night. How much I would like to caress and kiss you now! But even more, I would like to be there with you so that you would not have to be alone tomorrow. Another week has passed, seven days closer to the day we will finally know if we will be united or not.

I wish you a good Sunday. I am with you always in my thoughts, always! I kiss you very tenderly and long, so that my kiss will last until my next letter.

My Boris,

Your Anneli

LETTER A18

GWATT

[Monday] December 11, 1944

My dear Boris,

From your letter* I see that you are very depressed. I understand completely, I feel the same way. But we must try to cheer each other up. So, gather up all your strength (you have a lot of it in you) and wait patiently for the decision that will come. I will add a few words here:

> Father, advise us!
> Steer and guide us!
> Lord, everything,
> Beginning and end,
> Is laid in your hands.[55]

I wait with you. Your fate is my fate now. But my patience is also almost at an end at times. I just want to stamp my feet and scream, but I know that it won't help one bit. Therefore, we should begin with patience, rather than threats. I believe the most important thing for us right now is to see each other as often as possible so we can continue to strengthen our love and have meaningful conversations. I want you to tell me about all your worries and have the chance to relax here in Gwatt. I would be terribly unhappy if you end up being all alone in Zurich at Christmas.

Now I will say goodnight and kiss you as lovingly as I can. Truly, what happiness lies in the words: mine and yours!

My Boris,

Your Anneli

---

55   From the second stanza of "For the New Year" ("*Zum neuen Jahr*"), a poem by Eduard Friedrich Mörike (1804-1875). These lines appear again in Anna's letter of December 29, 1944 (A22) where the complete stanza may be found.

[Tuesday, December 12, 1944]

Good day, my dear Boris!

Another new day is here and gone and I am happy about it. We are another twenty-four hours closer to our goal. Now I would like to thank you from the bottom of my heart for your letter and for your sweet kisses, because I know they come directly from your heart.

I would like to kiss you, kiss you endlessly. Good-bye my dearest. Have renewed courage and patience, and lay everything in God's hands.

My Boris,

Your Anneli

LETTER B16[56]

ZURICH

[Monday] December 11, 1944

Dear Frau Dr. Kurz,

Please forgive this overly long, mistake-filled, somewhat disorganized typewritten letter. I hope it will be easier for you to read in this format so you can give my situation the serious consideration it needs now.

I would like to ask for your help and advice so that I, a refugee who has been enjoying the advantages and privileges of being a guest in Switzerland, can avoid being forced back into a refugee camp because of an "incorrect" relationship. I would like to avoid this, not because I am afraid of the camp, but because I do not wish to embarrass those who have been trying so hard to help me, including you, the Reverend Freudenberg, and the Reverend de Purry.

Last September, while I was taking a Bible course in Gwatt, I met Miss Anneli Stahel of Winterthur. She lives there in Gwatt and is studying in Thun. During my two-week stay, a serious relationship developed between us. Because Gwatt is in a restricted zone, I can only get permission to visit during holidays. So, we have been compelled to meet in Bern (twice) and in Zurich (once). So that our meetings do not put Anneli in a bad light, we thought it would be wise for me to meet with Mr. Stahel personally, either in Winterthur or in Gwatt, to formally ask his permission to continue our visits. When Mr. Stahel learned that our relationship was getting serious and that I was a refugee, he asked his daughter to break up with me. The reasons he gave were (1) our age difference (she will be nineteen next month, so she is half my age), (2) my status as a refugee with an insecure future, (3) he feels that the time his daughter spends with me is an unnecessary pastime, and (4) because I am a foreigner, he

---

56   The following letter is from Boris to Gertrud Kurz, previously mentioned as the leader of the *Christlichen Friedendienst* (Christian Service for Peace) in Switzerland. A carbon copy of this typewritten letter was preserved.

feels that a serious relationship with his daughter, a Swiss native, is completely inappropriate and out of the question.

Since we received his response, we have suspended our meetings, yet we still correspond by mail. Soon Anneli will return home to visit her parents for the Christmas holidays and at that time it is likely that her father will give her an ultimatum: Either she breaks up with me, or he will see to it that I return to the refugee camp. He probably has the necessary connections with the authorities to accomplish this. Anneli has asked me what response she should give.

Two weeks before I arrived in Gwatt for the Bible study course, Anneli had a revelatory experience in which she felt a close connection with God. Since then, she has made a strong effort to live according to God's word, and I, for my part, have tried to support her in this as much as possible. Her desire now is to obey her parents faithfully and honor their wishes, which since the time of her mother's death she has not done very well, probably because she was not given adequate love and understanding at home. Now that we have been thrown into this new conflict, I feel it is important for her to follow where God leads her (to obey God). It is, however, quite natural and no sin against God if she eventually leaves her parents and follows a man whom she truly loves, while still honoring her parents. She is legally permitted to do this in one year's time when she reaches the age of majority. But, for the moment, her parents have the right to make decisions for her.

Several questions have occurred to me, including:

Can her father force her to break off our relationship if she feels she can answer to God for her love?

Is a promise made under duress valid ("If you don't do it, then we'll put him away!")?

Can Mr. Stahel really get someone (his connections) to force me back into a refugee camp if she does not break up with me?

I also want to try to prove to you that our relationship is not quite as hopeless as it seems. As you know, I had a very successful career in Germany until 1939. As an assistant to the director, I managed miners in the biggest open-pit mining operation in Germany (the third largest in Europe) and at the same time became an expert in the field of blasting. I was also well-known in my profession because I had authored or co-authored several highly respected textbooks that have been translated into several languages and are held by the libraries of most technical schools throughout the world. With my previous experience, my textbooks, and the recommendations of my Swiss professors, I believe I will find a position quickly, as much rebuilding will be necessary after the war. To rebuild, one must first secure raw materials, and mining engineers will be needed for that. If all else fails, I could go back to Russia and there get proof of citizenship valid in Switzerland. Then I would no longer be "stateless." In Russia, as an experienced and well-educated professional, I could have wonderful prospects. Russia has always sought out talented, experienced people, and now, with the recent great loss of its population, Russia will be seeking people for its industry and research. Science and technology are prized much more than God in Russia now. If I went back to Russia of my own free will, I doubt very much I would be placing myself in danger, as I never declared any political affiliation and left Russia as a minor. As a Russian citizen I could, in any case, marry Anneli in a year or so and get a secure post. But I still hope, with your or Reverend Freudenberg's help, I might be able to go to the United States or England instead.

I dispute the idea that as a foreigner I am not entitled to have a relationship with a Swiss national. I come from a good, respectable family. My education is world-class, I have traveled widely, and have excellent professional experience behind me.

As far as our large age difference goes, at first glance, this really does seem like a valid reservation. But if you recognize that I am a Siberian, the danger is lessened. It is well known that the colder and harsher the environment in which one lives, the more the body's defenses against it are heightened. My family has lived in Siberia for at least three generations.[57] Anneli's mother and maternal grand-

---

57 This is an interesting observation since Boris offers little information about his family's history in his memoirs, *Lenin, Hitler, and Me*.

father were only about forty or forty-five when they died, while my grandparents were over ninety and my parents, because of the hardships they suffered during the Revolution, were about seventy (mother) and ninety (father). I have rarely been sick, and I am in good shape physically. Last year, with only one day of training, I was able to swim across Lake Annecy (2-3 km wide). With more practice, I could certainly swim much further. Should I end up as a worker, builder, or minor employee, which I would find an uninteresting livelihood, then the age difference could prove more dangerous. But as I have more creative professional ambitions, I anticipate fewer difficulties.

But this is the most important thing: Anneli is a splendid person. She has many talents and the intelligence to access all knowledge. But all of this is deeply buried, because during her childhood no one nurtured it. At home, as a young girl, she lacked the most important thing: love. None of her friends or her family knew how to wake up her soul. Thanks to God's strength, which since August has been increasing within her, I am convinced I could help her develop all that is good within her. And through this growth and development, and her new spiritual inspiration, I see the possibility for both of us to be very happy.

I could add a lot more, but I will stop here, because I know you, too, feel that Anneli would be in good hands with me.

I would like to mention one more thing. Many ministers, even famous ones, have tried to awaken my faith in God. In pre-Revolutionary Russia, I rejected the Russian Orthodox Church. I was too young then. Afterwards I was influenced by communistic atheism, and later in Germany I was of a similar mind. It is not easy to get rid of those bad influences. Through Anneli I believe I will be able to find God because I will have a living example in front of me.

It is unlikely that I could achieve anything constructive with a single visit to Mr. Stahel. If I were to try to explain the situation, he might interpret it as a challenge. I must face the possibility of returning to a refugee camp. However, that might prove a disadvantage later in that it may be harder for me to find a position after the war than if I had stayed at the Technical University. I have recently, through the kindness of one of my professors, found a job in Switzerland. If I cannot get on top of my situation within the next year, I will probably seek citizenship from Russia. By then, either Switzerland will have a Russian ambassador, or I would be able to write to the Russian consulate in Paris.

As any demand on Anneli made by Mr. Stahel or by me would only bring disadvantages for everyone, I feel a peaceful solution would be best. Our goal is to get better acquainted. It has not been possible for us to accomplish this in the sixteen short days we have spent together since we first met. Perhaps in doing so, we will discover on our own that we are not suited to each other. It is possible we only noticed each other's good qualities and were blinded to any faults because we were wrapped up in the excitement of our new love. But because we are now under pressure, it is understandable why we feel we must try to defend ourselves. As we strive to do this, we will be drawn closer and closer together, and Mr. Stahel could easily lose his daughter forever. At the same time, Anneli and I will be thrust into a much more precarious situation because I will be rushed into accepting any position I can find as soon as possible, rather than in a calmer and more considered way. Because Mr. Stahel is preventing us from pursuing our relationship, he is at least partly to blame for making his daughter's future even more uncertain. I find this struggle harmful and nerve-wracking for everyone involved.

As Anneli and I are convinced that ours is a true love, it is hard for us to give each other up. Is it right for us to let someone else destroy our love without defending ourselves? Our love, which is basically healthy and viable, is still so new that it may not be able to withstand a separation of a year or more. I am not afraid to go back to the refugee camp, but I fear that something precious may be destroyed or hindered. We have a common goal before us now, and Anneli, with her living God, could bring us much strength.

I would be very grateful if you would advise me on the best course of action. Could you send me a short reply by Wednesday, as on Thursday I am expecting Reverend Kühner? Might I speak with you on Saturday, December 16 perhaps? Then I would be able to speak briefly with Anneli on Sunday.

In conclusion, I must apologize that this letter has gotten so long. I am very anxious to receive your reply and thank you in advance for your advice.

With warm greetings,

Yours sincerely,

Boris Kochanowsky

LETTER B17

ZURICH

[Monday] December 11, 1944
9 p.m.

My dear Anneli,

I hope I can give you a clearer overview of our situation when I call you on Thursday evening. Until then I will take some time to think things over, as I would really like to find the best path for us.

What makes me most anxious is that you must suffer so because of me. I thank you for your courage and your support. I could fight anyone but you. If you were to oppose me, I would certainly be a beaten man. But as you are standing beside me, I, too, have the strength to fight.

I am amazed by the strength you find in God. I can well understand that despite our current situation your main hope is in Jesus' word: "What is not possible with man, is possible with God." In addition to this hope, I am comforted in the belief that in one year, when you are twenty, I will be able to marry you, if you still want me, and no one will be able to oppose us. In the worst case, I will have to give up on America and become a Russian citizen so that you will not be lost to me. I propose Russia as a backup plan if we can't get to America, if you do not object.[58] Do not be afraid, Anneli, we will be able to survive, even in Russia. If I apply for citizenship there, I hope I would not be at risk, as I never professed allegiance to any political group and left Russia when I was a minor. Otherwise, Belgium and France would also stand open to us. However, I doubt I could get citizenship there as quickly. But at least we would still be able to marry.

In any case, I do not want to lose you, my dearest. If your father threatens you, then any promises you make him under duress would not have any validity. I would continue to write to you, even if it

---

58 Read Anna's view on Russia in letter A49.

had to be in secret. I would find a way to remain in touch. I am not afraid of the refugee camp, but if I had to return there, it could make immigration and securing employment much more difficult and time consuming.

Your father is making a big mistake by denying us the opportunity to get to know each other better. Surely, we have followed through on his demands up until now. We have only spent sixteen days together. Because of your father, we will be compelled to take many more risks.

As I am generally a good judge of people, I feel very certain I can rely on you. You can also be sure of me.

Now I wish you a very good night and kiss you many times.

My everything,

Your Boris

LETTER A19

GWATT

[Wednesday] December 13, 1944

My dear Boris,

I am so nervous and anxious I can hardly write. I am tense because everything will be decided tomorrow. It is doubtful Reverend Kühner will permit you come to Gwatt during the holidays. But if you can find another solution, perhaps through Frau Dr. Kurz, it might work. But be careful, very careful!

My head teacher asked me today if I was going home for Christmas, to which I responded in the affirmative. Then she told me I could stay until New Year. But I really do not want to stay home more than three days. After that I want to return to Gwatt. Is it possible for you to come to Gwatt then too? It would be wonderful if you could be here while I am still on vacation. But we must be careful not to arouse suspicion. It would be better if you could arrive a few days after I do, because my parents will probably check up on me if I don't stay with them for the whole holiday. If they force me to stay home, it would of course be better if you came after the New Year. Boris, I will let you do what you think best. You are my leader. I will follow you and I know that you will fight for us with all your strength. I stand behind you and will not desert you.

Your letter gave me much courage. Certainly, one day we will find a way through of all this. But now, we must be very careful, and find a middle way. We must restrict ourselves to a minimum amount of contact to keep my parents happy and try to keep from upsetting them any further.

What did Frau Dr. Kurz say? Did she give you any advice? I can hardly sit still for curiosity. Please my dear, send me the news right away. In case you want to call, don't call before 9:30 p.m. I probably will have to work in Thun until 9 p.m. And now I thank you again for your dear letter and for the dearest of all little kisses.

My Boris, I am with you tomorrow all day in my thoughts! I kiss you with my whole heart very tenderly.

Your Anneli

LETTER K1[59]

BERN

[Wednesday] December 13, 1944

Dear Mr. Kochanowsky,

Many thanks for your clear and open letter. I am thankful that you wrote me. I would have liked to have sent your letter directly to Mr. Hans Stahel!

Please forgive me that I cannot give you a more detailed response, but in fifteen minutes I will be leaving for a day, so I can only tell you briefly what I think of your situation. You write that you would like to have my response today if possible.

All the difficulties seem to have started because Miss Anneli's head teacher was not satisfied with her student's progress. Because of this, Mrs. Kühner chimed in with a few words of her own.

I feel it would be possible to put things right again. If Miss Anneli does not finish her practicum in good standing, it will make her head teacher look bad, and therefore her outrage is understandable to some extent (although not her inappropriate language of course). Why has Anneli slacked off on her studies? Her thoughts are with you. Her evenings are devoted to writing long letters late into the night. Therefore, you must, out of love for Miss Anneli and out of friendship to her hosts in Gwatt, become reasonable and less demanding.

I know that you would like to spend your Christmas holidays in Gwatt (how well I can understand that!). But what would the consequences be? The head teacher will hear of it, and she will bring it to the Reverend's wife's attention, and she, in turn, will renew her threats to contact the foreign authorities about you. She will also likely inform Anneli's parents, increasing their resistance and bad will toward you.

This is what I recommend: Hold back for now as much as you can (certainly do not break off the relationship entirely) and stand

---

59   Gertrud Kurz responds to letter B16.

behind her with your strong love. Do what is best for her, out of love for this young girl. The year will soon be over. With time Mr. Stahel may alter his opinion. Maybe an opportunity to speak with him might present itself in the future? Your discretion will impress him (I hope so!). In any case, this is the only possible way to handle these things right now. Anything else may prove disastrous for both of you. But if her love is strong and unswerving, it will become even stronger and more beautiful through this trial, as you will live much more "one for the other," in the deepest sense.

I write you in the greatest hurry and hope you will understand me. You are both in my heart and I know God will bless every obedient follower. Surely you will experience this, and later find increasing happiness.

In deep thankfulness for your openness, through which you have brought me into your confidence.

My most heartfelt greeting,

Your Gertrud Kurz

LETTER B18[60]

Zurich

[Monday] December 18, 1944

My Anneli,

For several reasons I enjoyed being with you more this last time than the time before. As I see you so rarely, I notice the inner and outer changes you are undergoing much more clearly than if I were with you every day. I am more than satisfied. I am overjoyed to see how my little tree (you) is growing.

It is good that you are now less pessimistic than you were before. If I had been pessimistic as I went into the world alone at the age of sixteen, I would never have been able to achieve anything. A Christian without hope is a complete paradox. Jesus says that faith can move mountains, or what with man is impossible, is possible with God. Although I am only a refugee now, I have the right to hope my future will not be as unpromising as some Swiss people might think.

Our future depends on whether we are weak, broken people or the opposite. You must believe that our future depends only on us and our spiritual strength. That strength comes from our belief in God and in our love, which will grow unabated despite the storm.

I returned from my trip exhausted, but spiritually I feel like a newborn thanks to you, my dear Anneli. It seems strange, but when I walk down the street, I feel like I am carrying a huge treasure within my heart that is so deeply buried no one can see it. It is a real treasure, not a fantasy or an ideal. You may feel the same way. One cannot imagine all that is buried within a person's heart. One would need to have very special eyes to see it.

I hope I can earn enough money in the future so that we both can continue to educate ourselves throughout our lives. That is what

---

60   From this letter we learn that Boris and Anna did meet again in person the previous weekend, as they had planned (see A16), despite Anna's father's disapproval.

will be so special about our relationship, this co-development and co-fertilization, not only a little here and there, but always and continually. It will bring us much happiness, a happiness that is deep and wide and infinitely large. We have had a little taste of this joy now, so we have an inkling of what it will become in the future. But our current joy is diminished because of our long separation, and we cannot see beyond it to what our future holds. But when we are through it all, and I am really yours and you are really mine, nothing will stand in our way again. I cannot even imagine now how great the joy will be when that day finally arrives.

But we should stay focused on the present. I would like to thank you for the lines you wrote me. You see, I am right when I say you are loving. And above all, I thank you for yesterday. It remains unforgettable in my memory, just as all the other days I have spent with you have been.

Concern yourself only with nurturing your love for me; everything else will take care of itself. All your depression will vanish when your love is great.

Our letters may cross each other during the Christmas holidays.[61] We will write each other again afterwards. But you should not let your letter writing get in the way of getting your sleep. Write just a little, just enough to let me know how you are feeling, all right?

My Anneli,

Your Boris

---

61 Anna is about to leave Gwatt to spend the holidays with her parents in Winterthur, so there may be a break in their communication.

LETTER A20

[WINTERTHUR]

[Wednesday] December 20, 1944

My dear Boris,

Without letters from you my days are so gloomy. As you might think, there is much opposition against us from all sides. This afternoon I was terribly upset and angry, but now I have been able to calm down. Most of what they hold against us is not due to Reverend Kühner himself, but his wife. Her method relies primarily on force. It is not the first time she has acted this way. I have only one thing to say about her: She is loveless. If one is in the habit of writing to someone every day, one cannot suddenly cut back to just once a week. Imagine, only four times in one month! I can't imagine it.

She says it is because once a day is too much for me. She thinks she is doing a good deed, but basically, she is just afraid of my parents and my head teacher. You and I stand all alone in this battle. I have become so mistrustful in the last few days I cannot even bring myself to count on Frau Dr. Kurz.

My dearest, we will need to try to reduce our contact as much as possible, but one letter per week is too little. You can write to me on Saturdays. On the other days, I will have to see what can be done. It won't be easy because there isn't a single person I can really trust.

But we must fight. At least we know we can rely on each other. We must be patient and trust in God. He will help us find a way through this.

Try not to be sad. I want to fight for you and for our love with all my strength, but we must also take care not to hurt the other people in our lives. You understand, don't you my dearest? I would like to be with you now and kiss you for a long time.

My Boris,

Your Anneli

LETTER B19

ZURICH

[Thursday] December 21, 1944
10 p.m.

My dear, dear Anneli,

I do not want to write very much today, as you have received so many of my letters at once and therefore have a lot to read. I thank you for your fighting courage. Have no fear, my dearest, victory is there where true love exists. We should have no fear of other people. We must just take care that our love is real, true, and pure. Everything else is trivial. Where there is true love, there too is God.[62]

If it is too risky for us to meet on your way to Winterthur, then we should try to meet on your return trip. If you like, I could meet your train and ride with you to the next stop. Then we could skip a train or two while we talk in the station. We really need to talk.

I kiss you,

Your Boris

P.S. Write me exactly where and when I should meet you, and which train I should board.

[Saturday] December 23
9 a.m.

My most sincerely beloved Anneli, my little heart,

Today I feel like a criminal because I didn't write you at all yesterday evening. I want to tell you everything point by point.

---

62 Perhaps a reference to the Latin hymn which begins: "Where charity and love are, there is God." (*Ubi caritas et amor, Deus ibi est.*)

Yesterday evening I went to a holiday church service for refugees at the Grossmünster,[63] and then afterwards I attended a party for refugees. I sat next to the Reverend Lehmann. He spoke to me about our situation and said he spoke with Reverend Kühner last Friday. I told him I had the feeling that Reverend Kühner would like to pull us apart gently. He said that was not the case at all, that Reverend Kühner is quite happy about our relationship. So now, my dearest, we should believe him because we do not want to think badly of other people. Nevertheless, we do not want to put up with too much interference from others; nor should we, in any case, let our love be taken away. It could be that Reverend Kühner, Frau Dr. Kurz, and maybe your father, too, just want to see if our love is true, rather than simply an infatuation that might eventually burn itself out. All right, we will undergo this test for a time, maybe another three months. Any longer might cause us to become embittered. If we cannot establish an understanding with Reverend Kühner, Frau Dr. Kurz, and especially your father, it could certainly lead to unfortunate consequences. Your parents could lose you for a long time and I might be compelled to find a position in a hurry. It would be better to do the job hunting calmly. We should explain this to your parents at some point.

If our relationship comes up in conversation while you are at home during the holidays, please ask your father to allow me to come to Gwatt. Tell him that you want to obey him, but you are very serious about this relationship, and that any pressure from him will only bring us closer together. If he gives us more opportunity to get to know each other, we may learn sooner, rather than later, that we are not well-suited, and secondly, we would be able to make our decision more rationally, since our knowledge of each other would be so much better.

If you think it would serve a positive purpose and if it comes up in conversation, tell your father I would be happy to meet with him in Gwatt or in Winterthur, perhaps at a restaurant, so our meeting won't seem too official in nature.

So, my dearest, I lay our fate in your hands. Do all you can.

---

63   One of the four main churches in Zurich

LETTER B20

ZURICH

[Wednesday] December 27, 1944

Dearest Anneli,

Your parents will soon receive the following letter from me:

> Dear highly honored[64] Mr. and Mrs. Stahel:
>
> I would be very grateful if you would grant me the opportunity to meet with you. I hope our visit will bring complete clarification and reduce the tension of the current situation. I know you have had many worries on my account, and that has weighed heavily on my heart. I thank you for your future confidence in me.
>
> With great respect I send you my greetings,

I am not writing much to you today, as I hope to see you soon.

I hug you very tightly,

Your Boris

---

64 The German salutation *Sehr geehrte* is customarily used in formal letter writing.

LETTER A21[65]

WINTERTHUR

[Wednesday] December 27, 1944

My dear Boris,

It is 9 a.m. on Wednesday and I am still in bed as I write. You know I was very sad yesterday. I want to tell you exactly why. Mainly it is because our contact has been curtailed, and yet we both feel we need to learn so much more about the other. When I thought back to last Sunday, it seemed to me you were a little less sure of yourself. This would not surprise me, as you are really taking on a big burden, and I am still almost a child. But please tell me if you think something is amiss. Also, there is this Miss Olga who gives me a stomachache. You know, I want to learn not to be jealous of you; it really has no place with true love. It is an all-consuming fire that makes people unhappy. But I think each of us has a duty to avoid giving the other cause to be jealous. What would you say if I were to sit around until midnight with a man who I knew was interested in me? You are likely uncertain how you will react to Olga's attractive pull. She invites you to Geneva, but out of consideration for me you tell me you don't want to go. But two days later you suddenly must go see Reverend Freudenberg in Geneva. Then when I ask you if you went to see Miss Olga too, you respond angrily, "No." But that "No" sounded much like a "Yes." Someone in Gwatt already told me about it. Now you can see what a mean person I am. Watch out, Boris, maybe you are mistaken about me.

I must say I feel bad about writing these things, but I cannot suppress it, it bothers me so much. I am such a bad girlfriend to you. I concern myself so little with you, and then I grumble when you go visit other women who are probably much nicer to you! No, seriously, I am not a good woman for you; I have no idea how you feel inside.

65   This letter refers to earlier communications regarding a Miss Olga and some bad news Boris received from the ETH. Those communications are lost.

I don't know what you will do now that you have received such an unsatisfactory answer from the ETH, and there is nothing at all I can do to help you. What I really want to do is just sit and cry. I'm sure you had a very sad Christmas, dearest, and I am only thirty kilometers away, but I am imprisoned. Yes, this is really something to cry about!

Boris, please forgive me this jealous outburst. I admit it is a sign of insecurity, probably spurred by the fact that we still do not know each other well. There is probably some egoism mixed in it too because true love only wishes to give, not take.

Boris, you are still true to me, right? Completely? Otherwise, there is no point or value in continuing our relationship. You should be an example to me!

I kiss you very fervently. I will not give you up to another, you belong to me. You said it yourself, so it must be true, otherwise I will become furious!

Boris, I am yours completely too! I kiss you again.

My Boris,

Your Anneli

LETTER A22

[Type-written letter]

Winterthur

[Friday] December 29, 1944

Good evening, Boris,

I want to send you a quick New Year's greeting and will do so using the typewriter. I suddenly got the idea today and thought I might learn something new in this way. My mother is letting me use her brand-new typewriter. She even gave me a letter to type for her. Now I am on my third letter, and I am enjoying it, partly because I know it will please you if I learn to type.

I am quite sad today because I would have liked to start the year with you, being near you, and with your kiss. The coming year will be one of great decisions for many people, and for us too.

So, let me wish you all of God's future blessings. Boris, let us begin the year with a prayer:

Lord God, let this horror on earth end, and allow us to find and help all people who live in misery. Help us open our eyes and know that you are the Lord of Lords. May he bless our love and make it fruitful, in his name. May he give us strength and faith and allow us to be united soon. Amen.

Farewell now, be of good cheer, and read this short poem by Mörike once more:

> May the New Year begin with him,
> Who moves suns and moons
> Across the blue tapestry of heaven.
> Father, advise us!
> Steer and guide us!
> Lord, everything,
> Beginning and end,
> Is laid in your hands.[66]

---

66 See also letter A18.

I should long ago have sent you a greeting from Dr. Strupp. He said he takes you for a very hard-working man. That is all for now. It is midnight, soon my eyes will close.

I kiss you very gently and tenderly,

My Boris,

Your Anneli

LETTER A23

WINTERTHUR

[Sunday] December 31, 1944
11 p.m.

My dear Boris,

I miss you very much, but since I cannot be with you, I will at least write to you. My dearest, I thank you from the bottom of my heart for your New Year's letter* and your good wishes. Your wishes are my prayer too: That all the realizations God has granted me will be preserved and will bear fruit, especially for you, so I can really bring you good luck.

Yesterday I read "Faith and Science" by Brunner.[67] Naturally, I could not understand everything, but I found some passages very worthwhile. For example, I recognized his depiction of the one-sided Christian faith of medieval times. His opinion that science can go hand in hand with faith really pleased me. I was unsure about this issue before, simply because I recognized how disastrous it would be if science replaced faith. One talks a lot nowadays about modern science admitting its limitations. In my opinion, science and research only show their true value if they are built on the rock-solid ground of faith.

It is now 1945.

As far back as I can remember, I have cried on New Year's Eve, maybe out of pity for myself, or simply because of sentimentality. But today I am happy and full of hope.

How are you? You told me that you feel your strength is unbroken. That makes me believe you are and will be full of hope and will begin the year with new, joyful courage.

---

67 Heinrich Emil Brunner (1889-1966) was a Swiss Reformed theologian and Professor of Systematic and Practical Theology at the University of Zurich from 1924 to 1953. See "Glaube und Forschung: Festrede des Rektors Prof. Dr. Emil Brunner, gehalten an der 110. Stiftungsfeier der Universität Zürich, am 29. April 1943," *Universität Zürich: Jahresbericht 1942/43* (Zürich: Orel Fussli, 1943), pp. 3–20.

Boris, we both know there will be many difficulties ahead of us, and I am actually happy about that, because, as you say, it is much better if everything doesn't fall easily into our laps. But we want to ask God to make some good come out the pain we are now experiencing, and through it make us stronger, purer people.

Goodbye for today. I kiss you for the first time in this new year from my heart. Boris, you are my everything.

My dearest,

Your Anneli

Wedding party at the marriage of Hans and Rosa Stahel (1924). Back row, far right to left: Anna Bertschi (mother of the bride), Anna Stahel, née Ott (mother of the groom), Anna Stahel (younger sister of the groom). Far left: Jakob Stahel (father of the groom).

Bachtelstrasse 12
Anna's home in Winterthur

Rosa with Anna (1927)

Rosa Stahel (1938)

Hans Stahel (1939)

Anna and Rosa (1939)
Last photo of Rosa before her death

"Rebhof"
Anna Bertschi's home in Uhwiesen

Anna Bertschi (c. 1952)
Last photo before her death

Hans and Martha on their wedding day (1941)

Anna and Martha (1941)

Anna in Gwatt (Fall 1944)

Boris (1945)

1945

LETTER A24

Gwatt

[Thursday] January 4, 1945

My dear Boris,

You can hardly imagine how happy I was to receive your letter.* One day here in Gwatt without a letter from you seems interminable. Today you are in Winterthur meeting with my mother. I had some trouble falling asleep last night because I was a bit restless, wondering how your meeting would go. I hope the two of you were able to come to an understanding. Boris, my dear, I am so thankful for your help. You will now have a clearer understanding of my situation. I tend to be too emotional and that can be a problem.

Yesterday Frau Dr. Kurz was here to give a lecture. Afterwards she led a discussion about post-war problems. It was extremely interesting, and I was sorry you could not be here.

I was overjoyed to receive your very thick New Year's letter.* I believe I have been searching too far afield in my attempts to understand you. I will now try to base my understanding of you on what I already know from our own close interactions. If my mind weren't so muddled, I would have understood everything by now. That is why I am doubly glad that you are a bear and have so much patience.

I have really taken your letter to heart, particularly where you explain that to succeed one must have a clear conscience and maintain an inner calm to the very end. I must thank you for these words; they are immensely valuable for me in that I tend to get upset so easily. I so hope some of your peace will rub off on me, not just for my sake, but so that I can be a better, truer partner to you.

Now I kiss you firmly and sincerely in the hope that everything went well for you today.

My Boris,

Your Anneli

LETTER M3

[Friday] January 5, 1945

Dear Anneli,

As you probably know, I had a conversation with Mr. Kochanowsky yesterday.

This man, who certainly is well educated and probably also has much knowledge in his field, did not give me a bad impression. But this does not mean all our objections have been laid to rest. How things develop further is up to you, and it will depend on whether you complete your professional training, which I certainly hope you will do. Above all you must learn to accept that things cannot always go your way. As far as your relationship goes, I think Mr. Kochanowsky is much more sensible than you are, and I would like to recommend that you follow his example.

I will now briefly tell you the real reason I am writing. On Tuesday evening Vati telephoned me. Among other things, he told me he wanted to go to Gwatt next Sunday. But in my conversation with Mr. Kochanowsky, I learned that he, too, was hoping to go to Gwatt the same day. Because of your father's planned trip to Gwatt, I advised Mr. Kochanowsky not to go, because at that point Vati was unaware of his intention. It is something I did not wish to explain or discuss with Vati over the phone. That is why I want to tell you that all this was not intended to thwart your visit with Mr. Kochanowsky.

Now I have something else important to tell you. Lately I have had the feeling that you are not taking care of yourself properly. I assume that this is at least partly due to your relationship with Mr. Kochanowsky in that I sense this man is not so concerned with outward appearances. During his visit yesterday, this gentleman appeared well-groomed in general, but I can hardly believe that despite his financial circumstances he need go around in such tattered shoes. Or, if he were made aware of it, that he could not arrange to find some better ones. Being well-groomed and neatly dressed has nothing to do with vanity. I believe these problems are more due to carelessness and a lack of attention to those details I have often mentioned to you. All right, enough of this.

I hope you have a good visit with Vati on Sunday. I send you my warm greetings.

Yours,

Martha

LETTER A25

Gwatt

[Friday] January 5, 1945

My dear Boris,

I was upset because I learned that Reverend Freudenberg was here today. You might have spared yourself a trip to Geneva if you could have arranged to meet with him here. All this fuss on my account! I am to blame that our relationship has become so complicated and that you are not allowed to visit Gwatt. Please forgive me, Boris!

So now I would like to write you a "Sunday"[68] letter. Sundays are really the worst days for us. It is the day we miss each other the most. Therefore, I want to give myself some time and some peace and quiet to write you a good letter.

Boris, I want to ask you something. When I was with you last week,[69] you asked me why I love you. At that moment I could not find the right answer. Afterwards I tried to explain it to you in a letter, but I was still not happy with the result. I am still thinking about it and am surprised how thoroughly I must contemplate the question each time I try to answer it. In the first place, I must admit I have an inner timidity, almost a fear, of the word "love," or better said, of the incorrect conception of the word. I have only just started to recognize what true love is. My relationship toward everyone in the world is new, or better said, it is only just beginning. Because of this, new questions and problems continuously arise in my mind that I must somehow find a way to address myself. But this is difficult for me to do because I am not good at expressing the exact nature of these problems and questions, because most of them are of a very

---

68 Anna is writing this letter on a Friday, but she is calling it a "Sunday" letter because either she wishes to write in more depth than she would normally on a weekday, or she hopes Boris will receive it and read it on Sunday.

69 All communication related to the planning and execution of this meeting has been lost.

intimate nature, and because I have so little time at my disposal to really study them.

I am terribly grateful for the book you gave me by Dr. Bovet.[70] It will help me enormously. I learned that the right path, the one that leads to spiritual health, can be found by holding fast to the laws of God. We should not be troubled about ourselves; we will be forgiven through Christ and freed from our sins. But why is this possible only because of Christ's death and resurrection? That I cannot say. Just as you said, I want to be a Christian, but I have not yet recognized Christ.

Boris, I have another question. Would you agree to become like a pastor to me? Perhaps you might even be eager to do it? But think what enormous selflessness it would require, because most of the problems I now have revolve around you. On second thought, I think it might not be a good idea because I might cause you pain or maybe even frighten you at times. But I would like to ask you from the outset, if I have doubts, please do not be sad, but take it as a sign that I am fighting an internal battle. Pray that God's strength in me will be victorious and help me right myself as well as you can. Do you agree that my asking you to pray for me sounds a bit strange? But I ask you to do so, not just for my sake, but for yours as well. Boris, you are the only person I trust; that is why I turn to you.

Anneli

---

70 Swiss neurologist Theodor Bovet (1900-1976) was also a Christian marriage counselor. Detailed typewritten notes from his lecture "*Not und Hilfe in der Ehe*" (Need and Help in Marriage), his books *Risse in der Ehe* (Cracks in Marriage) and *Vom Stand des Christen in der Welt* (The Status of Christians in the World) were found with the second set of letters (see Postscript).

LETTER A26

GWATT

[Sunday] January 7, 1945

My dear Boris,

First, I want to thank you for going to Winterthur. Now you can see more clearly how things really stand, as I am always in a state of confusion. I am sure you approached the situation skillfully and I hope we will succeed. I, for my part, will do my utmost, and will work as hard as I can.

I met my father today in Thun and we had a good conversation about style, design, paintings, and architects. Our relationship did not come up, which is probably good. I wanted to keep our discussion about it to a minimum.

My dearest, I am so glad, so happy, so elated over your letter. Your letters give me much strength, and so much more. What would I be without you, my everything?

I am having terrible doubts about my faith right now. I am even wondering whether God exists. That is why I still fear old people so terribly. Boris, please tell me again what the difference is between a dead person and one who is living. You see, at such moments, I would be ever so happy to be with you, physically near you, so I could calmly rest my head on your shoulder and tell you everything that is on my mind. I have so many questions, but these are questions that I simply cannot write down in a letter, and when I am with you, I forget them all! Basically, my questions have to do with the two poles you told me about, the godly and the worldly, and how to find a middle way between them. As I am terribly afraid of the worldly, I find this difficult.

But through all the struggles and troubles that plague the soul, there is a saying that always comforts me, and it should comfort you as well: "If you are now faced with more and more temptations,

temptations that you were not even aware of earlier, take it as a good sign that you encounter them now, much like a sentry encountering the enemy ahead of the battle line."[71]

Dear, I fight for you too, and with myself, because I really want to belong to you and love you truly, but I can only do so with God's strength and spirit. I want to make you very, very happy.

I really wonder if my pastor would think I love you truly, or whether it is only egoism. But I don't really think it is. Boris, I really would like to see you soon, very soon! I hope the days will go quickly so you can be a free person again and use your God-given strengths, and so I can help you.

I miss you so terribly, I miss your eyes, your dear laugh. I kiss you now, my dear, dear Boris. You are my precious treasure.

Your Anneli

---

71   From Heinrich Vogel's (1902-1989) 1936 publication *Die eiserne Ration eines Christenmenschen* [The Iron Rationalism of a Christian Person]. See https://www.stmichael-online.de/kampf.htm and https://en.wikipedia.org/wiki/Heinrich_Vogel.

LETTER A27

GWATT

[Monday] January 8, 1945

My dear Boris,

Even though it is already quite late, I need to tell you something urgently that I just learned tonight because it is important for our future. A class is being held here for refugees who will be leaving Switzerland after the war. Maybe you already know about this Swiss refugee program run by Mr. Olgiati, who is a supporter of the Quakers. It was he who gave the lecture tonight. He is just back from a trip to France, Spain, Portugal, England, and the United States that was sponsored by an American Quaker organization. He spoke about the preparations being made in the United States and England to help refugees, of the possibilities, and about his impressions.

Concerning the United States: America is wary of rising unemployment which may come after the war. It is unlikely that they will take many refugees, primarily only those who are citizens of other countries and secondly, only those who already have visas. But these people will have to undergo strict scrutiny. And thirdly, they will accept a small number of others under certain circumstances for special reasons.

This only confirms what you already told me. In general, he said that each immigrant who wishes to go to the United States must understand clearly that he should lower his expectations. Furthermore, women will be accepted as citizens more quickly and more readily, so that it may happen that the wife will have to support her husband, which could easily lead to marriage crises.

Mr. Olgiati claimed repeatedly that the Quakers in the United States are very eager to help foreign refugees. In England, a lot of postwar preparations are being made, but there is not much information about how they will help immigrants.

Boris, I miss you very, very much. It has been so long since I last had a letter from you. You should tell me what you are doing, so I won't have any reason to get jealous. I am ashamed of myself, as I believe jealousy is a bad thing. No, I really want to experience things with you, to enjoy things with you, and to be sad with you. How did it go in Lucerne? Did you come to some sort of understanding with Dr. Bendel?

I want to thank you for the wonderful little treats you sent me Sunday; I ate them all up at once. Then afterwards I felt sick. But they were so good! See what a baby I am!

Now good night my Boris. I kiss you until you explode with delight.

My dearest,

Your Anneli

LETTER B21[72]

ZURICH

[Friday] January 5, 1945
10 p.m.

My Anneli,

It is truly amazing what strength you give me with your few words. It has been five hours since I read your letter, but I still feel fire burning in my heart, so I must write you a short letter before I go to sleep.

Even if we only write a single sentence to each other at the end of the day, it will help keep our love alive. It is quite normal for us to think of the other just before we retire, to press the other firmly to our heart and give each other a goodnight kiss in our minds. Perhaps some people might laugh at our idealism and romanticism, but that shouldn't matter. We may feel obliged to remain sober outwardly, but we cannot allow our dreams, our healthy idealism, and our fantasy, which lift us up to the high heavens, to be lost. They are the basis of our happiness. We should continue to dream and retain a pure, childlike outlook. Many people, even your age, are no longer childlike. We should always try to remain like little children in our hearts. It is a valuable trait, one that Jesus valued highly. We need to be sober when it comes to fighting for our survival. We must have much patience and knowledge and work hard. But at home, when we are alone together, our joyful, happy, childlike souls must come out into the light, and there we will be forever in love, like we are now, but even more so. Our current separation may cool our love, but let us try to imagine a future when we will be together and strive, day by day, to make each other happy.

By the way, when I was at your house in Winterthur, I saw a portrait of a woman in the dining room, across from the piano, who

---

72 Boris' letters of Jan 5, 6, 7, 8 and 9 were sent together. In them Boris responds to Anna's letters of January 5, 7 and 8. Boris is bundling his letters together to conform to the new restrictions imposed on the frequency of their correspondence.

looked a lot like you. I was quite delighted with it. Now I can guess what you might look like when you are older, and it pleases me very much. Is it a picture of your grandmother?

Your parents spoke of your mistakes and weaknesses. Can you tell me what they are? Truthfully, even if I try very hard, I cannot imagine that you were ever really so bad. I attribute your prior mistakes to poor upbringing. Surely, we both have made mistakes in the past, but we will not focus on them anymore, agreed?

I have somehow managed to create a long letter out of what was supposed to have been a short one.

Here is a kiss for you, my golden girl, my everything,

My Anneli,

Your Boris

P.S. By the way, I sent you some stockings because I thought you might be able to use them. You are NOT to knit me a sweater in return for them! You should use the time to catch up on your sleep instead. I do not want you over-stressing yourself. You should take care, understand, my little dear heart?

[Saturday] January 6, 1945
9 p.m.

My dear Anneli,

I have just returned from Lucerne and found your wonderful letter. You can just imagine how happy I was. I will answer it right away, as you touch on many important issues.

My dear, you must not upset yourself because I could not come to Gwatt to speak with the Reverend Dr. Freudenberg "because of you." Getting angry will only make you old and ugly before your time. That is why I forbid you to do it! Also, it was not because of you that I couldn't come, it was *because of us*. I am even more to blame for "your" mistake than you are. Besides, it wasn't really a mistake at all. You always behaved correctly, and the result would have been the same regardless. This is just our lot right now.

I can tell you now that I almost came to Gwatt today. I didn't want to tell you earlier so you would not worry. When I told your mother that my trip to Gwatt on Monday, January 8 was not approved and that I would have to go to Lucerne instead (just halfway to Gwatt), she telephoned your father to find out whether he was planning to travel to Gwatt too. Because he indicated that he was, she advised me not to go because she felt it would be better for her to speak to your father about it first. I think that was very nice of her, don't you? I think it shows that your mother is well disposed towards us. I cannot be totally sure, but I think I made a good impression on her. Maybe you can ask her what she thought of me? She told me I was even better looking in person than in the photograph she had seen of me and, even more surprising, that I looked young for my age. Most importantly, I discovered that she, too, feels that love is not subject to human laws, but only nature's laws and God's laws, and when two people love each other, no future citizen's union can stop them through a plenary assembly. Only the two involved can determine the outcome of the relationship.

I see you are making good progress in your study of Russian. To reach any goal the main thing is not so much one's ability, but the enthusiasm one has for the subject. It is also important to know the purpose of the subject at hand. That is how it is for me in any case. I find learning just for learning's sake silly.

You say you wish me to become like a pastor to you. You also write that you know Jesus redeems us from our sins and makes us free, but you don't understand why this is so only because of his death and resurrection. I will explain it this way: Suffering→Creation→Joy. This is God's order, or what I call the godly principle. Jesus demonstrated this in the most absolute terms: suffering unto death followed by creation (the resurrection). Joy is found in the two thousand years it has lasted, and in the belief that it may last forever. Jesus had to die for this to be true. But when one really understands his suffering and the purpose of that suffering, then one realizes that it is only through suffering that improvement is possible. In this way our understanding of life is deepened. Think also about other forms of suffering, for example, a mother giving birth to a child. She does so gladly because her suffering is creative.

Good night my dear heart.

[Sunday] January 7, 1945

[Dear Anneli]

To get a better understanding of my beliefs, I advise you to read the brochure "The Faith and Science of Men, the Prayer of a Scholar"[73] which includes a prayer by Kepler.[74] I am completely in agreement with it.

In my last letter I wrote that I believe the significance of Jesus' resurrection lies in the salvation of mankind and the union of the godly and the worldly. Through salvation and spiritual equilibrium mankind can help his fellow man in a creative way. But if, on the other hand, people only think of themselves, then humanity is doomed. The result can only be death and destruction. Jesus leads us to be at least as concerned with others as we are with ourselves and to occupy ourselves creatively with our God-given abilities. We must be thankful for them. Think about most people. What do they do most of the time? They worry about their daily bread, their basic survival. Yet most of the things they use in their lives (even ordinary things like matches, printed books, glasses, and so on) are products of the hard,

---

73 "*Glaube und Forschung von Männer, das Gebet eines Gelehrten*"
74 Johannes Kepler (1571-1630) was a German astronomer, mathematician, and astrologer, a key figure in the seventeenth century scientific revolution, best known for his laws of planetary motion.

creative work of people whom they often not only disparage, but even curse. These are Christians who stand only on one foot (one pole) in life. They are simply short-sighted, ungrateful egoists. Instead of thanking God deeply for the gifts a creative spirit has wrought, they denounce them (including, perhaps, even the Bible they are reading!). They ignore political and social matters[75] even though they claim to strive for peace. Yet they ferociously criticize those who do concern themselves with these crucial matters, while contemplating very egotistically how they might get into heaven.

But thankfully Christianity is much celebrated and practiced nowadays. I put great hope in it. But people must understand Christ correctly and not distort his message. I know that being a Christian means to love and serve, and I find it absurd that I still do not know how to do it. Jesus clearly shows us how to live without destroying or restricting ourselves, or hindering our growth. And what does living mean exactly? To answer that it is best to think about the fruit tree. One must provide it with nourishing soil and a lot of fresh air and sunlight so that it can develop and grow. Then it will bloom and eventually bear fruit. With mankind it is just the same. Our love is like that too. We see our love as a source of strength that will nurture our growth.

We should avoid and even fear all that might destroy our future growth. Together we must fight against those influences with all our might. We are already building a love that lives, breathes, and defends itself. It is vital and worthy of life. It joyfully anticipates the development of fruit that may come. The anticipation of that joy helps make us strong. Think how it will be when we bear fruit together, then we will truly be one.

When you feel you are finally free of your past, then your next task will be to let God's spirit continue to work in your heart and mind so that you can develop a spiritual equilibrium through the harmonious unification of the heavenly and the worldly. If you can achieve that, then you will cease being so anxious and upset. You will find peace,

---

75 His view clearly echoes that of Frau Dr. Kurz.

joy, and self-confidence, and all your thoughts, feelings, and activities will be directed only toward creativity, as you will be brought to it by the creative strength of God. It will become our common goal.

Now on to your question of whether what you feel for me is true love. Your question is not an easy one and it may have been posed incorrectly. Your question was: "Can you see the foundation of true love?" Just to see it is not enough. To know whether love is true, there is only one question to ask: Are you willing to make any sacrifice to be with that person and share every burden with him, or not? Do you feel you have the necessary strength for that? Even more difficult, could you imagine risking your life for him? When I was in Lucerne recently, as I passed a half-frozen lake, I thought to myself: "If Anneli were drowning in that lake, would I jump in to rescue her?" I answered, "Yes!" Of course, my life might not have been lost in doing so, perhaps only put into jeopardy. But one can measure true love by the level of sacrifice a person is willing to make, if necessary.

Another important facet of true love you noticed yourself: You find great satisfaction in being everything to your beloved and devoting yourself to him completely. You want to immerse yourself in his life so you can share his thoughts and experiences. When he is happy, you are happy. When he is sad, you are also sad. These are the clearest signs of true love, as this is the beginning of sacrifice. However, sacrifice is not as much of a burden when it is joyfully done. That is true love. Ask yourself also whether it would be easy or difficult for you to stay faithful (in thought too) throughout our long separation. We are already making sacrifices for each other, as we must bear the pain of that separation. But we are doing it for the sake of our love. Otherwise, I might just say, "Oh well, this is just too complicated. I will seek out a different girlfriend in Zurich, and you can find yourself another boyfriend in Gwatt or Thun. Then at least we can have fun every weekend. No need to take expensive train trips or upset your parents." The sacrifice a person is willing to make of his or her own free will brings meaning to life and is the measure of true love.

Another important question: Would you like to have a child with me, or does your love not yet go that far? For this the highest trust and esteem is necessary. Because your child, in whom we both become one flesh, is part of you. The child is the fruit we would create together.

You will find many answers in Dr. Bovet's book. Too bad we cannot read it together (another sacrifice). There is much emphasis on faithfulness. I feel I am already completely at your mercy, my entire fate rests in your hands. If you were to be untrue to me, you would not only destroy me, but also our family life, our children, and all the work I would be able to do, or rather not be able to do, because of the disturbance you would bring to my life. You must understand how very tender and easily damaged my soul is, despite the inner strength I have, as it is with my soul that I would like to entrust you.

But have no fear. You must take some time to get to know me well. I, too, must see for myself whether your love is true. But as I am already planning my life around you, I am betting that it is. But whatever happens, know that you can trust me.

Dr. Bendel showed me his recently published book. In the preface he thanks his wife for her help. This made me think of you, Anneli. We must live together in all things, even in my career. One day you will become inspired too, once you come to understand my field better. Read Kepler's prayer[76] in Brunner's brochure. Even though you may find it a bit challenging, our love will give you added energy to do this and to learn languages, typewriting, stenography, and to help me with my professional correspondence. In these endeavors too, we would become completely united spiritually and mentally.

---

76   Perhaps the prayer referred to here is Johannes Kepler's "Astronomer's Prayer": "Thank you, my Creator and God, for giving me such delight in your universe, this ecstasy when I look at your handiwork. As far as my finite spirit has been able to comprehend, I have shared with others the glory of your works and your infinity. If anything I have said misrepresents you, or if at any time I have sought my own glory, graciously forgive me. Through Jesus Christ my Lord. Amen." See https://www.justprayer.gracespace.info/astronomers-prayer-johannes-kepler/.

I am excited and hopeful. I believe we will succeed, as we have laid the foundation already. Even our separation (our freely given sacrifice) ripens and improves our love. I believe it will continue to be an uphill climb, but the most difficult and most dangerous obstacles have already been surmounted.

Do you know that I long for you terribly? It is the same for you, I know. Hopefully, I can get to Geneva, and then we can meet in Bern. Your mother has given us permission to meet once in January and once in February in Bern, and at Easter in Zurich or Winterthur. Hopefully, your parents will eventually welcome the chance to get to know me a bit better. As I already have made two trips this month to try to meet with your father,[77] it is financially impossible for me to get to Bern now. It is unfortunate, as each of our meetings brings us more strength and joy. I would like it best if I could visit you on Sunday, January 21, two days before your birthday.

We will see each other soon!

I wish you a good night,

Your Boris

[Monday] January 8, 1945
9 p.m.

My dear Anneli,

I thank you for your letter.[78] I am so sorry we cannot spend a few days together so I might try to answer all your burning questions. Your soul is undergoing a real transformation; it strives toward true goals and offers to make unselfish sacrifices.

---

77 Details of these attempted meetings are not known. Presumably, Boris traveled to Winterthur twice, but was unable to meet with Hans. Perhaps his meeting with Martha occurred on one of these trips.
78 Anna's letter of January 7, 1945 (Letter A26)

You write you are having a difficult time finding a middle ground between the two poles, between the godly and the worldly, as you have a horrible fear of all that is worldly. Hopefully, you understood me correctly, but only expressed it unclearly. Because if you stand between the poles, then you will have the benefit of neither. You must stand *on both poles*; that is, you must unite the godly and the worldly within yourself (the ideal). There must be: (1) understanding, reason, science, research, and intelligence and (2) heart, feeling, faith, and intuition. Read the enclosed review of Romain Rolland.[79] It refers to his clear intellect, strong convictions, and the ironclad strength of his creative power and spirit. Remember what I told you about Tolstoy and Beethoven? It always comes back to the same thing: the significance of the two spiritual poles and using them as a basis of judging yourself, your neighbors, and even countries. Only Jesus could be God and man at the same time, yet every person must strive to unite the godly and worldly within himself.

You ask what the difference between a dead and living person is. A dead person is one without love; a living person has love. Love inflames and develops creative strength. God is the eternal creative spirit which made the whole world and continues to create forever. Love=God.

You wonder if your love is true? You wish to bring me joy, to be everything to me. Tell me why? I believe that it is through the joy and spiritual stability I receive from you that I can become more creative and bear fruit. If that could happen for me, I think you would derive great joy from it as well, as through your efforts something creative would result. If you hope to develop creatively through me, it shows that you have a healthy core.

It would only be egoism if you were only to seek superficial advantages (e.g. fun, carefree living) without making any sacrifices yourself or taking on any of my burdens.

---

79   Romain Rolland (1866-1944), French dramatist, novelist, essayist, art historian, and mystic, was awarded the Nobel Prize for Literature in 1915.

Tell me, could you find a good photographer and get a portrait of yourself made in profile? None of the photos of you I have are very good.

I wish you a very good night and send you a kiss,

My Anneli,

Your Boris

[Tuesday] January 9, 1945

It is very early morning. I was at the ETH all day yesterday. I was just on the phone with Guinard, a cellist I met first in Lucerne and then again in Gwatt. He has invited me to a concert this evening. I must hurry. That is why I will answer your letter[80] more thoroughly tomorrow, now only briefly.

My meeting with Dr. Bendel went very well. More about this later.

I am very happy you are a little baby and that you got a stomachache from eating the four *Küsschen*[81] I sent, not because you got a stomachache of course, but because it proves you are still a little baby. I would have done the same thing (but only after lunch). You should and may stay a baby until you are a hundred years old. I am especially fond of babies, with all the mistakes that go along with being a baby. I, too, make many mistakes and want to continue doing so.

Concerning my U.S. application, I presented myself exactly the way you suggested. But I must do everything I can to succeed. It will be a fight to get there, or at least to England, so that I can really learn the language.

Now I must close. I kiss you very firmly.

My baby,

Your Boris

---

80 Anna's letter of January 8, 1945 (Letter A27)
81 A *Küsschen* is a fancy chocolate confection. The name means "little kiss."

LETTER B22[82]

ZURICH

[Tuesday] January 9, 1945
11 p.m.

My little baby,

I just returned from the concert which included Mendelssohn's violin concerto and Brahms' first symphony. This Brahms symphony sounds a lot like Beethoven, powerful and aggressive, with rapid alternations of tension and relaxation. This kind of music enlivens the spirit and makes one feel strong. Too bad you could not have come with me; you would have enjoyed it.

I know you long to see me, but I still do not know when I will be able to get to Gwatt. I'm afraid it may not be possible this month at all, as I already have two other trips planned. Dr. Bendel has also invited me to visit him in two weeks. I hope I might be able to see you the first week of February, if your father does not object.

Now I wish you a very good night. I am quite tired. It is very cold in my room. In the mornings it is usually 11 degrees and in the evenings 13.5 degrees.[83]

I kiss you,

My Anneli,

Your Boris

---

82 Boris begins his next letter the evening of January 9 and mails it together with his letters dated January 10, 11, and 12.
83 11° Celsius = 52° Fahrenheit; 13.5° Celsius = 56° Fahrenheit

[Wednesday] January 10, 1945

My dear Anneli,

I will now answer your letter.

Concerning U.S. immigration, I hope to make it through as an exceptional case, as I only have distant relatives in the United States who would be hard for me to locate. I know it will be difficult for me at first. Americans are mostly inconsiderate and very businesslike. If a person doesn't pull his weight, then that is the end of him. But for me is it especially important to be in America, even if I cannot establish a big career there. It would be enough to just go there and learn the language. I don't have any illusions. Even so, I am resolved to move forward, as the implications for our life are enormous. It is a terrible shame, and a big disappointment for me, that there is no mining school in Switzerland. Yet recently I have been able to work productively, and I advise you to do the same.

Dr. Bendel told me he would be happy to be a reference for my U.S. visa application if I would first assist him with some of his work. He says that way he can honestly say that I worked for him. I am not sure about his true goal, whether he wants to test me somehow, or whether he himself is not secure in his own work. Perhaps he wants to get the scoop on my discoveries; I really don't know. He says he will call me in about two weeks to discuss it in more detail.

Lately I have been spending most of my time at the ETH attending lectures and staying warm. I have no heat in my room! I went to Geneva to fill out some immigration forms. I also wrote a letter to Mrs. Tolstoy[84] in New York and then I wrote a fourteen-page letter to a certain young lady (Miss X) who lives by Lake Thun, but that shouldn't concern you too much. And last night I attended the concert. Today I went to a

---

84 Alexandra Lvovna Tolstoy is mentioned in letter B2.

lecture (on Religion and Psychology), and tomorrow evening I will visit a family who will introduce me to Prof. Brunner. I am excited about meeting him. I know our conversation will be quite an experience.

I must leave for the university now.

I kiss you,

My Baby,

Your Bear

11:35 p.m.

I am just back from the lecture. Now back to your letter.

I see you experienced some anxiety because I only mailed your letter on Tuesday. But Anneli, we planned that you would get a letter on Wednesdays and Saturdays. Reverend Kühner thought we should only write once a week, and your mother was opposed to me writing to you more often. I think we must leave it at that, but you can choose the days (Tuesday, instead of Wednesday), if you like. We are not writing any less often than before, despite the "more rational" system we are obliged to follow now. I hope you had plenty to read with my fourteen-page letter and the two pages of enclosures I sent. You should also take time to digest the letters, otherwise there is not much point in writing so much.

Dearest, I, too, would like to see you very much, but we probably must wait until the first Sunday of next month. We just must hold out. It is a damnable shame that it is so far to Bern. It is a sacrifice, but this test will measure the greatness of our love.

Now, with a kiss, I wish you good night,

My Anneli,

Your Boris

[Thursday] January 11, 1945
midnight

My dear Anneli,

This evening I finally got to meet Professor and Mrs. Brunner. I was able to converse freely and comfortably with Professor Brunner in a home setting. It was an experience I will remember for the rest of my life. What a shame you could not have been there too! I will give you all the details tomorrow, as it is very late now and I am tired. I was at school all day today.

I kiss you many, many, many times,

My dear Anneli,

Your Boris

[Friday] January 12, 1945

My dear Anneli, my little heart!

I understand your disappointment that we cannot have more spiritual contact. I feel the same way. You are undergoing a spiritual transformation and therefore need support. I am going through a kind of transformation myself, so maybe my influence would not be so useful to you right now. But I hope you will gain more than you will lose through your contact with me. Because your faith is stronger than mine, you may be able to answer some questions more readily and correctly than I, despite my longer experience and greater knowledge of people.

I will try to recount the conversation I had yesterday with Prof. Brunner, who is a world-class personality. It will be hard to give you all the details. Personal contact is always best. That is why I sent you to Bern to see Frau Dr. Kurz, as the conversation you had with her will likely stay in your memory for many years. Maybe one day you will have the opportunity to advise a young lady yourself. By then you will have had much life experience and, as a result, will be more confident. I will try to reconstruct the conversation I had with Prof. Brunner. In two and a half hours he could only answer two of my questions. So here, in a nutshell, are some of the most important points he made:

He once said in a lecture I attended that if a person cannot have faith and be a believer, the fault lies with him. I wanted to lay before him my own philosophy, namely that if one takes the Bible literally, then one would not be allowed to lie, because a lie is a sin against God. I gave him different examples in which people had to lie. In each case love was the reason behind the lie; love was more important than the truth. I told him that when I lie, I am admitting that I committed a sin, and that I consciously take that upon myself and regret it. He said, no, it is NOT a sin to lie (e.g., lying to an evil person, or to the Gestapo to save someone's life) when the reason for the lie is love. Even killing because of love may not be a sin. Killing out of hate, however, is a sin.

As you see, it always comes back to the authenticity of love. If real love is behind it, one can do anything with a clear conscience, even killing, without committing a sin.

As he gave me such a rigorous answer, so different from what I had heard in France, I strayed from the original question a bit, and laid before him another important question: whether Christians may work to further the cause of social freedom.

In France, ninety percent of the sermons I heard maintained that man is too weak and evil to solve anything himself, and that it is futile for him to try to attain peace. Only Jesus can offer mankind salvation when he comes again.

I found this too weak a view and countered it by saying, "All right, if all people make mistakes, then I would prefer that rulers, prime ministers, and kings be good Christians, rather than atheists, so that their rule will be based on love."

I also said that in many cases I prefer the Protestant view over that of the Catholics, but in this case, I find the Catholic view stronger. He said I was completely correct, that Protestants must take up this question more actively, particularly French Protestants, some of whom escaped persecution in France by emigrating abroad and were thus presumed by many to have become degenerate and weak.

The next time I see him I will ask him the following questions:

1. How and when does one attain personal contact with God? As I wrote you, my view is that this can only happen through the practical application of love toward one's fellow man, especially as it applies to one's closest relationships (e.g., husband and wife), and through one's involvement with creative work which benefits mankind. How does a person speak to God? For me God's word is still a puzzle. I can only imagine what it might be like. Perhaps it manifests when a researcher makes a new discovery or is the first person in the world to have figured out the solution to a problem, almost as if "someone" told him the secret, even though, naturally, no one actually spoke to him, and he himself had not known it previously.

2. My thoughts on the godly principle (Suffering→Creation→Joy)

3. Creative spiritual energy and the necessity of two poles for creative productivity.

4. Whether it is right to punish someone else. Is it permissible in some cases and not in others, or should one always offer the other cheek?

I have had many debates with famous preachers and professors of theology in France on these topics. So far Prof. Brunner seems to agree with my point of view. In my opinion many Christians, and naturally non-Christians like Nietzsche too, understand Christianity incorrectly because they think it lacks strength. In my view, Jesus was the most courageous and spiritually the strongest person who ever walked the earth.

Huge fields of knowledge rely upon just a few rules, even just a few words. If one has mastered them, the rest can easily be built upon them. But if you have no foundation, you will only sway between heaven and earth, instead of building and resting balanced securely upon these two poles.

Today I will send you only three *Küsschen* instead of four, to spare your little tummy discomfort.

I will also send you (as a sample) a *real* Russian cigarette. In Russia it is called *Papizossa* (plural= *Papizassi*). But you may not smoke it! If you are tempted to smoke it, then give it to someone else, understand, my sweetheart?

I was hoping for a letter from you yesterday, and because of my impatience (even though I doubted I would really get one) I went to the post office and inquired prior to the normal delivery time. And there, instead of a letter from you, I got a tax bill! The disappointment was doubly hard to bear. Perhaps I will get a letter from you today. In another forty-five minutes the postman will be here!

The following lines come from the pamphlet by Dr. Bovet I sent you: "True love seeks to help the other under all circumstances, and suffers for the sake of the other, and wishes to take the beloved's burden onto himself, even if it is a sin. Only in this unique relationship can we get a sense of the all-encompassing mystery and life-changing attitude brought about by contact with the living God."

I have your letter* now. You ask whether I might send you more than two letters per week. I feel bound by the promise I made to Reverend Kühner and your mother. But you write that Reverend Kühner feels that there is now no reason to restrict our letters, but that does not mean I may write to you more often! If you want me to write three times a week, then you must broach the subject with your parents and Reverend Kühner, as I do not want to go back on my word.

I expect to take my exam at the beginning of next semester (in the middle of May) rather than at the end of March because I will not be finished studying by then. I had to miss many of the lectures and lost much time culling the lecture material from books.

I am so happy to learn that my letters bring you much joy and strength. That is the main reason I write. It would be better if we could see each other more often, but we should try to focus only on the positive throughout our separation.

Your letters invigorate me like oil on a fire. Each one shows your inner excitement, and I can sense new strength in you. You are really a dear girl. But you must work hard on your spiritual side. You cannot imagine how dangerous your past is for your soul. Only true love, much tenderness, tact, and patience can help you extract yourself from its bad influences. That is only possible through God.

In this hope I kiss you and embrace you tenderly and wish you a wonderful Sunday.

My baby,

Your Teddy Bear

LETTER A28

[Tuesday] *January 16, 1945*
9 p.m.

You, my dear Boris,

Even though I received your dear and eagerly awaited letter today, I still feel sad and dejected because we cannot see each other more often and spend more time together. We really must get to know each other face to face, even if we must fight for the opportunity.

I do not think I answered your question of why I love you well enough. It is not right for me to love you only because you are my sweetheart, that is, only because of your relationship with me, or just because you love me. I must love you as a whole being, as a person who has a relationship with everything and everyone else, not just me. True love exists without being returned; it is unconditional.

I need to learn more about you. I must be able to observe you and to see and hear how you interact with other people. Only then will I get a complete picture of you. Right now, I can only see you in the role of a lover. I must have the chance to evaluate you in an unemotional, critical way. I know from the outset that you will be able to pass this test, but it is still necessary and important because it will enlarge the foundation from which our love can grow. Also, Boris, it is important for you to know me better so that you will not harbor any false illusions about me. Surely, if things continue as they have in the past five months, something good will become of me. But I am not completely over the hump, as I know there will still be many temptations and trials ahead. But it is not a sin to be tempted, only to give in to temptation.

I am not at all jealous that you went to the University ball, because I am now convinced that a person who is jealous does not love truly. Our love must never become restrictive under any circumstances. I believe each of us knows how far we dare go without risking infidelity. If you enjoy it, then you should certainly go dancing. I already told you that I will not, because I know it would be dangerous for me.

The topic I selected, the difference between works of service and works of creation, seems complex at first. But I think that both concepts can be reduced to a common denominator. Both are done for God and are related to each other in this way. But they must be regarded in terms of that same denominator.

Here are my thoughts about the newspaper article you sent me: I am uncertain what position I should take, but I think it is very contrary to what I hear here in Gwatt. I believe it is precisely these "atheists" defended here who are registered at the civil registrar's office as Christians, who are not really Christians at all. But I question whether it is right for me to judge them. A Christian should and must be active! What do you think about this?

You write that sometimes you have inner tensions that almost drown you. What are these worries you have? Won't you tell me about them? I really would like to help you be happy and strong.

I have just one more question. What is a person's soul really? I have never discussed this with anyone. I think that maybe the soul is the sum of the heart and the spirit, but I am not sure.

Now good night my dear. I kiss you very tenderly and passionately.

My Boris,

Your Anneli

LETTER B23[85]

[Saturday] January 20, 1945
7 p.m.

My dear Anneli,

You asked me to tell you more about my past life. My very first memories are from the date of my birth, May 4, 1905. That year was very special because of three major events: the Russo-Japanese War, the Russian Revolution,[86] and most importantly, my birth. You yourself can attest to the fact that this was the most important event of 1905 in that it affected your fate much more than the Russian Revolution or the Russo-Japanese War did. So, the proof of this is quite clear and undisputed.

At about 5 a.m. on the morning of May 4, I came into the world. Because it was so early in the morning, I was still asleep, naturally. But the attending physician did not notice, and instead of taking my particularly deep spiritual traits, my character, and my usual habits into consideration, he started to spank me. Of course, I soon woke up and was incensed by his actions. At that time, I had only one weapon with which to defend myself: my voice. But to bring it up to full power I needed to inhale for a couple of minutes, until my Siberian chest was fully expanded with air, and then I let my rage burst forth. Even though the doctor and my mother, who had just brought her ninth child into the world, had had much experience in such cases, they were surely taken by surprise by the strength, the sound, and the beauty of my voice, even though I was not concerned with beauty at the time, but only wanted to get revenge.

---

85 Boris' letters of January 20, 21 and 22 were mailed together.
86 The Russian Revolution of 1905, a massive political and social revolt, was at least partly inspired by the events of Bloody Sunday (January 2, 1905) when soldiers fired on a crowd attempting to present a petition to the Tsar. While the revolt led to certain reforms, it also set the stage for the Revolution of 1917 which ultimately brought the Bolsheviks to power and resulted in the establishment of the Soviet Union.

I would like to tell you about two other punishments I endured, so that I can bring a close to this chapter. I was only punished a total of three times in my youth, and each time I was completely blameless.

The second instance happened when I was about three or four years old. My father and brother were working at a table, and I was crawling underneath it. Suddenly, and for no apparent reason, my father became angry and took a strap and started beating me. Even though I am older and wiser now, I still do not know why I was punished and why it came without any warning, which surely goes against the basic rights of man. I never was able to forget or forgive my father's misdeed.

The third incident occurred when I was eight years old and in kindergarten. During our long recess we played "Robbers and Pirates" in the courtyard. I was the leader of one of the bands of children. The other group, our "enemies," was led by the most beautiful girl in our class, the director's daughter, with whom I was head-over-heels in love. So, my group stormed the other group according to the rules of the game, and I caught the opposing leader, took her by the hand, and put her into our "prison." This action was spotted by the director from a distance away. Suddenly she was on top of me and punished me. As I felt completely innocent, I began to cry bitterly from rage and shame in front of my classmates. I was the leader of the Pirates after all!

As a child I was unusually calm, obedient, quiet, and reserved, so much so that my teachers always pointed me out as an example. I was also dubbed a *Wunderkind* by some because of my piano playing ability and my good grades in high school and Berlitz School (English). Luckily, I never let that praise go to my head. I was very level-headed and self-possessed. As a child I observed and studied the outside world carefully. Even then I consciously tried to develop myself in many areas to become as strong and knowledgeable as I could. I wanted to achieve much in life, benefiting myself and others, as a knight would. These were my thoughts when I was a child. I developed myself physically by teaching myself to swim. My spiritual development came through music and theater. I attended concerts, plays, and operas regularly from the age of six or seven on.

My spiritual development was also influenced by:

1. My sister, fifteen years my senior, who was extremely kind and gentle toward me.

2. The many intellectuals (doctors, lawyers, etc.) and artists (actors, singers, and painters) who were often guests in our home.

3. The surrounding landscape, especially in summer when I would lie for hours in the glorious fields amid beautiful flowers with my face to the sky and would listen to the wind in the forest and the mountains and the sound of the river. (Read Jules Verne's novel *The Courier of the Czar*[87] in which my birthplace and the Yenisei River are well described.) I was especially excited when a storm would hit, particularly in the mountains, where it could be seen and heard so wonderfully.

I thank my inherited qualities and my surroundings for my spiritual development. Meeting and observing many different people also had a big influence on me.

I will stop for now, as I need to do a bit more work.

---

87 Jules Verne, *Michael Strogoff or the Courier of the Czar* (Breinigsville, PA, 2020) vol. 2, ch. 7, p. 100: "He knew the Yenisei, its width was considerable, its currents strong. Ordinarily by means of boats specially built for the conveyance of travelers, carriages, and horses, the passage of the Yenisei takes about three hours, and then it is with extreme difficulty that the boats reach the opposite bank." "At this place, the Yenisei is not less than a mile in width and forms two arms of unequal size through which the waters flow swiftly. Between these arms lie several islands covered with alders, willows, and poplars, looking like verdant ships anchored in the river. Beyond rise the high hills of the Eastern shore, crowned with forests whose tops were then empurpled with light. The Yenisei stretched on either side as far as the eye could reach. The beautiful panorama lay before them for a distance of fifty versts." (Fifty versts equals about thirty-three miles.)

11 p.m.

My dear Anneli,

I am so tired I only want to give you a goodnight kiss and go right to sleep. I worked all day at home. I hope you sleep well too, my Anneli!

Your Boris

[Sunday] January 21, 1945
3 p.m.

My dear little soul, my Anneli,

The day after tomorrow you will be nineteen years old, and I would like to write a few words in honor of your birthday. It is still very cold in my room. I hope that the cold will not have an adverse effect on my heart, as I would like to say a few words to you from this heart of mine.

A birthday is a big occasion for everyone. But for you this day has an especially significant meaning in that you have experienced something this year that will have a great impact on your life, your new relationship with the living God. A person who has established contact with the living God becomes a completely new person; he derives his spirit and strength directly from God. This is extremely rare. In many of our letters we have tried to explain exactly what the terms "a new person" and "a living God" mean, and we have established that a new-born person is one who possesses God's spirit, strength, and the light of God's grace. It may also be called love. A life without love is like death (heartless and loveless). People who do not have love cannot distinguish between good and evil or between creation and destruction. They must make do with occasional pleasures, which they often find through ruinous means, or even sadistic, abnormal ones. They do not comprehend eternal virtue, which one can only seek, recognize, and understand in the deep recesses of the soul and mind. It brings people true joy, rather than just simple gratification. Only those who are imbued with the spirit of God (love) can access what is most fundamental, most valuable, and most necessary for creativity.

Now that you have received God's spark, you must hang on to it tenaciously and cultivate it so that it can grow. Otherwise, you may lose it. Seductive thoughts are the most dangerous. You must consciously fight against them, because if you cannot master them, then all will be lost in the end. They will always pull you down lower and lower. That is why Jesus said even a sinful thought is a sin. If it is God's will that we be united, it will be easy for us to fight temptation together, as we will both be living in the same spirit (Jesus), and through mutual support and confession, we will be able to rid ourselves of negative thoughts. But right now, things are difficult for us. I believe that your depression and feelings of low self-esteem are caused by these pressures. I advise you to read the Bible, or other good books, or to listen to good music, or if that is not possible, just get a lot of sleep so that your nerves can rest. Work and exercise can help release tension too. The best medicine is being in the care of the people who love you, that is why I can well understand your wish to be near me. It is the same for me.

I am exceedingly happy and thankful to learn that I have helped you find clarity and helped strengthen your belief in yourself. I am especially proud of your desire to become a good and capable person and that you feel my influence has been a positive one.

The more a person strives only to satisfy himself, the more powerfully he restricts himself. People who are only concerned with materialistic things are the poorest excuses for human beings. They only use their wealth to benefit themselves, pamper their bodies, buy expensive food, pursue sensuousness, and so on. Perfection, on the other hand, can only be attained through an equal awareness and use of the body and the spirit. A person's strength and capability are profoundly enhanced when he has found a balance between the head and the heart, that is, between emotion and rational thought. This balance can be best achieved with God's light. For a person to work creatively, all inner hindrances must disappear; that is, he must be "redeemed." Jesus wanted to redeem mankind and to put people to work creatively in the service of all humanity. Only through his spirit (the spirit of love, in which the worldly and the heavenly are united in perfect balance) can man be reconciled and create a heaven on earth. To work and live in this spirit is the greatest gift anyone could wish for, and I wish it for you on your birthday.

As a symbol of God's spirit being equal to nourishment, I give you the following: milk and honey for your body and secondly, a book by Dr. Bovet which will balance the healthy body with an informed mind so that you can ponder and get clarity on the important questions that interest you so much right now. So, read it slowly and thoughtfully.

I want to do all I can to nurture you. I believe that is why you love me so much. If you felt I was trying to destroy you, your love for me would waste away.

I wish you much happiness and the fulfillment of all your wishes and dreams.

---

11 p.m.

I studied all day long again. I am very tired now and will go to sleep. I hope that you are satisfied with the Russian offensive.[88]

I give you a very big kiss on your little mouth,

My Anneli,

Your Boris

P.S. I can't wait to see you again! Should I come on Saturday, or on Sunday? If I can, I would prefer to see you on Saturday. Hopefully, Reverend Kühner will not make any difficulties for you, as your mother has agreed that we may see each other twice before Easter in Bern.

---

88 Boris is probably referring to the Vistula–Oder offensive, a successful Red Army operation on the Eastern Front in January 1945. It saw the fall of Kraków, Warsaw, and Poznań.

[Tuesday] January 22, 1945
6 p.m.

My dearest,

I just came back and read your wonderful letter and now I must go to the post office quickly so you will receive your birthday presents on time. By coincidence, the lady who works in the store across from my lodging told me she saw us together when you were here during your vacation. She knows you, as she also lived at the Heimstätte not long ago.

Your mother told me that an acquaintance of yours from Winterthur saw us in Bern last week[89] and told her about it. That is how she knew that we had met there. The world is truly small!

Returning to the pole concept, you and I agree about history and the usual actions of mankind. It is difficult to define these poles and that is why there is so much confusion about this concept. In the first place, the words we use (like spirit, soul, and faith) are understood differently by different people, and secondly, they are defined clearly only in the narrowest sense. In the broadest sense they overlap with so many other concepts, and that is part of the reason for this confusion. But don't let it worry you. Just be aware that there are two poles and seek to develop them equally.

Now I must end my letter, otherwise I won't get to the post office on time.

I kiss you sooooooooo firmly,

My Anneli,

Your Boris

---

89 This meeting in Bern took place most likely the weekend of January 13-14, although there is no mention of it in the letters.

LETTER A29

[Tuesday] January 23, 1945
9:30 p.m.

My dear Boris,

My birthday is almost over, and I really don't want to write much this evening. I only want to thank you from the bottom of my heart. Boris, you really shouldn't have gone to so much trouble on my account. Yet I know every little thing I receive from you comes directly from your heart. I really can't tell you how thankful I am for the book you gave me. I think it will really help me, maybe not right away, but little by little. It always takes me a long time to absorb things.

Just yesterday I finished Tolstoy's *Resurrection*. I thank you, too, for this book. I have never encountered a book in which I could immerse myself so deeply and personally. I am so excited about it. I thought a lot about you while I was reading it, and I was able to ascertain how the spirit of the book and your spirit had much in common. After reading Tolstoy's description of the superficiality of the Russian Church, I understand your hostility toward the church much better. But I think to some extent the modern-day church recognizes its earlier failings and is trying to make up for them. Yet, they have an unimaginably difficult task before them. Therefore, we ordinary Christians must try to help the church by warning it against making new mistakes.

My dear, it appears now we will not be able to meet next Sunday. I received a ticket for a concert on Sunday from Mrs. Kühner for my birthday, and of course I must go, or she will be offended. So, we will have to postpone our meeting until the weekend of February 3.

I don't believe I even know how much you mean to me. I would only know if I were to lose you. The longer I love you, the more real my love seems. In other words, I don't love myself in you, but only you. I am terribly happy you are enthusiastic about your work, and I am not even a little bit jealous of it. I feel driven to tag along after you, to follow you in whatever you do so I can understand everything you understand. It has dawned on me and I am convinced now that it is a thousand times more important that I love you than that you love me, and that this will never lead to jealousy. True love knows no jealousy; it only gives and requires nothing in return.

I will say goodnight now, my dear. I hope that we will finally see each other again in twelve days. I kiss you very tenderly and thank you again for the wonderful package and for all the delicious, mouth-watering treats. Boris, you need not send me so much; I really get enough to eat here. You must try to gain some weight yourself. You have a long way to go to gain twenty kilograms![90]

I would be happy if the Russians do not get too far west; I don't trust them much. I don't know much about communism, but what I do know does not appeal to me. If Russia's power becomes too great, then communism will become a big force in the world. Above all, I should try not to spoil things with the Russians in case I end up becoming one!

You'll stay my Boris, won't you?

And I will keep being your Anneli.

---

90 Boris had been a muscular, athletic man in his earlier days, but had lost a lot of weight due to the privations of the war years. Twenty kilograms equals about forty-four pounds.

LETTER B24

[Wednesday] January 24, 1945

My dear Anneli,

When I learned in your letter that you were so happy with the birthday present I gave you, I was probably more joyful than you were! I hope it will always be that way with us. You know this gift comes directly from my heart. How important it is to be able to make someone happy. It is an art.

Look at some of the measures taken in Russia and Germany to cultivate happiness. There are civil organizations called "Strength Through Joy," which make it possible for the poorest people to take wonderful trips and vacations.[91]

You say you feel my spirit has much in common with Tolstoy's spirit. You are getting to know me well! I feel the closest affinity with Beethoven, Tolstoy, and Ibsen, as they epitomize feeling, sense, and reason.

I could describe my experiences from 1940 on (in Belgium, France, and now at the ETH) like Tolstoy describes the trial [in *Resurrection*]. How superficial and stupid people can be! For precisely this reason Europe is facing ruin. If Hitler had managed to get Russia on his side, he could have easily conquered the whole world. As Romain Rolland, the French Tolstoy, said: "As Europe sleeps in its drunk and stupefied state, the world dies, poisoned by its clever

---

91 Boris is referring to the Nazi "Strength through Joy" program which was established as a subsidiary of the German Labor Front in 1933. It was an attempt to organize workers' leisure time while serving the interests of the government at the same time. It was, in effect, a means to instill Nazi ideology and propaganda into the minds and lives of German working-class people. Likewise, in Soviet Russia, a worker would be treated to annual short stays at sanatoriums (health spas). Under Stalin many individuals got state-funded vouchers to visit such institutions so they could rest and reflect on socialist ideals. See https://spartacus-educational.com/GERjoy.htm and https://en.wikipedia.org/wiki/Prora and Claire Voon's review "The Utopian Leisure of Soviet Sanatoriums," *Hyperallergic*, December 8, 2017, https://hyperallergic.com/409691/holidays-in-soviet-sanatoriums-maryam-omidi/.

and shabby egoism." The world suffocates, it is true. Perhaps you remember what I said to Frau Dr. Kurz in your presence in Bern? I will repeat it, so that you can better understand Tolstoy, Rolland, and even more important, the spirit of Europe: Clever, shabby egoism has made people superficial and indifferent to the creative words of the living God which has caused all of Europe to become denigrated, spoiled, and to fall apart like a house of cards.

In this I have never been deceived. Now I can see that even since my arrival in Germany in 1922, my beliefs have been correct. As a brief example, I will tell you about one of many similar personal experiences I had. When I was a refugee in Belgium, I had all my documents and references with me (they are still buried there) as proof of my expertise. Being a top expert in blasting in Germany, I offered to advise the director of the Belgian mine under whom I was working in 1940. He told me: "Belgian engineers are the best in the world, we don't need any foreigners." Just imagine, this was during the war when every technician and professional was desperately needed. Consider also how and why the Germans forcefully took everything and everyone useful to them from the lands they occupied and sent them back to Germany. In France, too, there was much of the same spirit, and even here in Switzerland, where I honestly didn't expect to find it.

I encountered the same closed-minded egoism at a work camp where I offered to help make technical improvements for no compensation. I showed the director the book I had co-authored and assured him I was intimately familiar with all the latest mining operation methods in Europe. His answer: "My dear friend, I have been working in this field for over thirty-five years. I do not need any help. I am aware of everything that needs to be done."

And now at the ETH, even though I have proof of my experience and references from the most respected professors in Europe, I continually encounter very odd responses. The rector at the ETH told me my references were not sufficient. I told him that one of them was a world-renowned professor whom he should know. He replied that he didn't. Then I told him that Professor Niggli at the ETH knew him well and was prepared to confirm it. He told me he would check with him, but he never did. A couple of days ago I spoke with Professor Stupi, my main professor. I mentioned that I had gained admission to the ETH without taking any tests because I had written a scientific paper that had been highly praised by experts in the field. He then said to me, "But I cannot tell how much of it was written by you and how much by others." I was speechless at that. My name was at the top of the list of authors, even above the names of better-known men.

There may be several reasons why I received this treatment. It could be mistrust, lack of ability to appreciate the value of people, indifference to the value and practical usefulness of my work, or perhaps an unwillingness to give a foreigner a free hand. All of this results in terrible short-sightedness and laziness.

Now I would like to touch upon the second subject you brought up in your letter, the church. As a child and later, as a young man, I was put off by every kind of church and religion, not so much because of the nature of the church itself, but because I could see for myself the detrimental influence it had on people. When I was in Gap two years ago, I read through the New Testament and was deeply influenced by it. I became convinced that humanity can only be saved by the spirit of love, the kind that is supported by both the heart and the mind. My denial of the church was based upon its faulty conception of love which had no basis in reason. The cultivation of this senseless, blind love seemed to be its goal, along with self-preservation. (The faithful must try to secure a place in heaven as soon as possible.) This kind of thinking turns a Christian into the worst sort of egoist, concerned only for his or her own welfare.

It is also difficult for me to accept the church's requirement to believe in the supernatural. For a modern scientist this is as unnatural as believing a stone can fall up instead of down. No doubt there are many things in this world that are unexplainable but that are still natural. I can also imagine that there is an eternally creative and omnipotent power in the universe that is the beginning and end of all things which may be called God. But I do not believe this is the same God that spoke to Moses, Paul, and others in the Bible. The church says one should not rely on reason and rational understanding, but just have faith and be guided by one's feelings. Therefore, faith rests mainly on one pole, something I would have difficulty accepting. Perhaps people living 2,000 years ago, or even 300 years ago, could have that kind of faith. Today it is more difficult. That is why the church has lost so many intellectuals and humanists (highly moral people who do not believe in a personal God, like Tolstoy and others). I imagine Moses and Paul truly believed that they heard the voice of God. Their writings relate directly to the spirit and are therefore very valuable. Perhaps their experience was like that of modern people (e.g., Newton, Kepler, Copernicus, Galilei, and Leonardo da Vinci) when they became inspired and suddenly discovered a truth that no one else had known before.

I hope one day modern religion (perhaps a form of Protestantism?) will support a similar transformation in thinking. I believe even Prof. Brunner is of this mind. People understand the laws of matter and energy well, but the laws of the spirit are incomprehensible to most. The only light shed upon them is offered by Jesus. But the suffering of Jesus at the hands of man is interpreted differently by different religions. I believe in only one thing: the spirit of reasonable love. I believe that with it, human beings will be able to understand one another and surmount many of life's obstacles.

You say you have a pressing desire to know me better and to tag along after me so that you can experience what I do and understand all I do. You have no idea how happy those words made me. If you had no interest in my thoughts or inner life, our relationship would be become boring. Even sensuality would in time become boring too. If we have this sort of foundation, even the sensual, which I don't wish to undervalue, will take on a completely different meaning. It will become the most important source of our strength.

I will end here for today.

[Thursday] January 25, 1945
11 p.m.

You, you, you!

I have just returned from Professor Zimmerli's lecture about the death penalty and am very tired. But I just could not go to sleep without giving you a goodnight kiss. I guess I am just a little baby. You can tell that I am a baby too by the way I gobbled up that whole big cake you sent me (for which I thank you so very much!). Fortunately, I did not get a stomachache. That is because I have the stomach of a horse. It is probably not good for both of us to be little babies. One of us should surely be stricter and play by the rules, or we could take turns. One week you could be the baby, and the next week I would be. You should know from the outset, if you happened to have something really yummy, I would want to eat it all up first. (Of course, only after a meal!) This might give us some problems!

You said once you are bad at keeping financial records[92] and are wasteful with money. In that case, I would advise you to write me your view on the value and purpose of money.

Your Boris

---

92   Anna kept excellent, detailed financial records during both of her marriages.

LETTER A30

[Monday] January 29, 1945

My dearest, my Boris,

I want to tell you briefly how I feel about money. Earlier my goal was to become rich and beautiful! Now that has changed, along with everything else, and money is not so important to me, maybe partly because I still do not have to pay my own expenses. It plays a subordinate role. The main purpose of money should be to simplify business transactions. I am thinking particularly of trade in earlier times. Also, I think one should use money to help one's neighbor and fellow human beings. Just as you say, it should be used first for self-preservation, then to improve oneself and help others, and finally for creative efforts. Dr. Bovet says that one is answerable to God as far as how one uses money. Also, it made a very deep and positive impression on me when you said that you pay attention to how people use money. I will be able to learn a lot from you in this area, as I think about these things far too little.

Now I want to give you a huge number of goodnight kisses. Too bad you can't feel any of them.

All I can think about now is next Saturday. Boris, you are really my only, my everything.

[Tuesday] January 30, 1945

Good evening, Boris,

I need to tell you something important. I have told you this many times before, but it doesn't seem to make any difference: I love you so very much!

I received no letter from you today. Maybe you had no time to write, but I hope I will be happy tomorrow [if I get a letter from you]. If anything was decided, you would tell me at once, wouldn't you?

Boris, just to see you again at last, your dear eyes, your hands, your dear way of walking, and then also to listen to your soul a little!

Today I am in no mood to write. Rather than write a jumble of disorganized phrases, I will just say goodnight and wish you well.

I kiss you very tenderly, my Boris,

I am your Anneli

[Wednesday, January 31, 1945]

Good day dearest,

How will you look? What will you say? These questions are always on my mind. Today is Wednesday already, and soon it will be Saturday. I kiss you once more.

To my love,

Anneli

LETTER B25

ZURICH

[Tuesday] February 6, 1945
11 p.m.

My dearest, my Anneli,

How important our meetings are! They bring us ever closer together. If we had more time together, we would certainly blend into one droplet very soon.

When I think about you, your manner, your character, I have three emotions: a passionate excitement about you, deep thankfulness toward you, and a great desire to give you everything I have. However, right now I have so little, both materially and spiritually. But I think even the small amount I have would be enough to make you happy. Even though neither of us is extraordinarily great, the two of us possess multi-faceted positive traits and we will, with our modest talents, create much happiness together. It already brings me much joy just watching with what earnestness and excitement you absorb and react to everything I give you now.

I miss you terribly and dearly wish I could kiss and embrace you. As you say, I am a baby too because I need tenderness as much as I need bread and water. Without tenderness life is terribly cold and barren.

I just returned from an orchestral concert which included Saint-Saëns' violin concerto. The violin soloist was from Winterthur. They also played Mendelssohn's *Scottish Symphony*. I believe the French inherited the gracefulness and aesthetic of the Greeks, as one can hear in Saint-Saëns and others. The symphonies of Mendelssohn are also wonderful. I am not surprised that the Romantic period, which was rooted in emotion and fantasy, was so fruitful and creative. A man without fantasy cannot be creative. People who belittle fantasy do not understand its value.

It is late and I must go to sleep. I kiss and embrace you with all my strength, and at the same time most tenderly and gently, as this strength is full of love. Even if one were to be crushed to death by this kind of strength, it would seem to the beloved to be tender and gentle.

So, here is a kiss, my Anneli, my dear,

Your Boris

LETTER A31
GWATT

[Monday] February 12, 1945

My dear Boris,

I just re-read your letter* of last Saturday; it made me happy and excited. Today I had some bad, mistrusting thoughts about you, but now I am won over again by the warm, honest tone of your letter. It became clear to me today that we must not allow our doubts about whether we love each other enough to marry to grow. Our long separation plants these misgivings in our imaginations. We should root them out!

How extraordinary! When I read the Geneva committee's letter, I suddenly felt much stronger. I knew that once the moment of decision arrives, I shall know exactly what to do. From this I concluded that all this waiting has been a real detriment to us.

I am not at all afraid of being untrue to you anymore. As far as flirtation goes, it is no longer of interest to me. A serious love cannot grow without being nurtured. I will give our love all the care it needs to grow. After all, what would I rather have, what more could I wish for, than you, my Boris!

I kiss you!

[Tuesday] February 13, 1945
10 p.m.

My dear Boris,

I thank you wholeheartedly for your letter of today, for all the worries you have had on my account, and for all the love you give to me.

There is nothing else I want to tell you today other than just to thank you for this and to kiss you.

If nothing hinders me, I will go to Winterthur on February 25. I think I must confront my father again.

Now I will say goodnight, Boris. I am with you in my thoughts, and I kiss you.

My Boris,

Your Anneli

P.S. You must not be sad anymore, my dearest; my circumstances have changed for the better. I will go through your letter in greater detail tomorrow. Now I will sleep. Farewell!

[Wednesday] February 14, 1945
7 a.m.

Good day my Boris,

I want to send you a little kiss quickly. You are my big baby. I don't know if I dare call you that! How are things going with your work? Are you making progress? I would like to have a chance to watch you while you are working sometime.

LETTER B26

[Saturday] February 17, 1945

My dear Anneli,

I just got back from the movies. I saw a Swedish film entitled *Appassionata*. That is also the title of a piano sonata by Beethoven. It was a sad film, and it ended with a suicide because of a woman. I don't care for films like this because they always put me in a bad mood. But now I am particularly surprised at what you can do, all on your own, with a letter. Each one of your words affects me like oil on a flame. When we are finally together for good, our love will be enriched because of the continuing positive effect we will have on each other. Certainly, there may be some sadness, as we are only human after all. Yet successful marriages do exist; there are couples who are genuinely happy together.

I am so glad you feel you can tell me all your thoughts. I think this is one of the main reasons that you have "conquered" me. We must remain best friends and rely on each other completely.

Sometimes I feel like getting on the first train to Gwatt to be with you. One just becomes impatient sometimes! But time is going by. Once the war is over, we will be able to get a clearer idea of where we will go and what I will do professionally. Now we are completely in the dark about everything. It may be a struggle for me to gain acceptance in my new country, but the inconvenience will only be passing, as all the knowledge that has laid dormant in me these last five years is still there, at my disposal. Also, I am benefiting greatly from the work I am doing now. It has increased my experience and knowledge of current research and learning techniques. So, I will be even more valuable in my profession. With persistence one arrives at one's goal. Yet five years is a damnably long time to be inactive.

Our love can play a huge role. Each time I think of it, it fills me with the deepest gratitude. Your desire to help me brings me great joy. It is clear to me that if you always feel this way, I will always want to do the same for you. Here lies the kernel of God's spirit: not *I,* but *you. I* am only here to help others, especially those who are closest to me. I find that you already possess a wonderful spirit, despite all your inner struggles with "I." I love you for that too.

I kiss you, my Anneli,

Your Boris

LETTER A32

GWATT

[Friday] March 2, 1945
9 p.m.

Good evening my dear Boris,

I have already learned a lot from you. Most importantly, I am slowly getting a broader perspective on the world. I have been thinking a lot about what you told me, and it now stands me in good stead. In school we are studying design which interests me a great deal.

It is too bad that we cannot be together, even for just a few minutes each day. I would have innumerable questions to ask you and innumerable problems to discuss with you. I looked through some of Beethoven's letters and found some passages that agree with your views:

"The aim in the world of art, as indeed in the whole of creation, is to advance freedom."[93]

"Blessed is he who has suppressed all his passions, and then addresses all of life's affairs with pure energy, unconcerned with success. Let motivation be in the deed, not in the outcome."[94]

I too strive for this. It is becoming free of oneself and then standing straight and strong on both legs against all storms.

"I have so often cursed the Creator and my existence. If nothing else is possible, I will defy my fate."[95]

---

93 This extract is from a letter Beethoven wrote to Archduke Rudolph on July 29, 1819. See Shedlock, p. 270.
94 See Ludwig Kohl, *Neue Briefe Beethovens* (Stuttgart: Cotta, 1867), p. 101-102.
95 Beethoven wrote to Dr. Franz Wegeler (1765-1848) on June 29, 1800, referring to his growing deafness. See Shedlock, p. 20.

I think this reflects the fighting spirit in Beethoven you love so much.

"And when I contemplate myself in relation to the universe, what am I, and what is he who is called the greatest? And this again shows the godly within man."[96]

Then I found a passage in Ludwig Richter's book: "The world's realm and God's realm, the world's spirit and God's spirit, the world's child and God's child, these are the great opposites on earth that mankind does not see as valid, because he cannot recognize them. But whosoever has won a godly childlikeness, or who has taken it on, on the other hand, recognizes the difference between the world's spirit and God's very well. Flesh and spirit."[97]

Now I ask myself whether this philosophy also relies on a poly-system? What do you think? You told me that Pascal said that Christ unifies both God's spirit and the world's spirit within himself. Furthermore, even J. S. Bach wrote: "There where God and mankind are united is my most blessed salvation." If so, then the pole theory is also maintained here, because if man is to be complete, he must stand strong in his physical world while being supported by God's spirit. Gotthelf writes about this too: "The worldly and the truly spiritual are much closer than most people believe." Similarly, Dr. Bovet speaks about piercing through both worlds!

Your Anneli

---

96 From a letter to Countess Giulietta Guicciardi, dated July 6, 1801, see Shedlock, p. 32.
97 This quote is from German artist Adrian Ludwig Richter's (1803-1884) autobiography *Lebenserinnerungen eines deutschen Malers*, published in 1885 by his son Heinrich.

LETTER A33[98]

GWATT

[Tuesday] March 6, 1945

My dear Boris,

I was mistaken when I thought I had found something lighter to read when I started the novella *The Saint*.[99] This story of Thomas Becket is terribly complex, and I can't quite grasp it fully yet. I mean I can understand the story, but not this strange man, Thomas. My understanding of psychology is still too insufficient. I am enclosing a copy for you with this letter. If you have time, read it. It is beautifully written. Maybe later you can help me find my way through it.

Your book has already taken hold of my heart. It has wonderful things in it. It is like a precious treasure to me, and I guard it jealously. I look forward to looking at it with you.

I am amazed how you have stood by me all this time. This winter I was not quite normal at times; I had gone off and gotten lost in religious concerns. I think religion is not for me. I want truth, not religion. Lately, I have been going around in a daze. I am constantly amazed by the realization that everyone else is another "I." This is a very significant discovery for me. I continue to be amazed when I put ordinary things aside, and nakedly observe birth, growth, and death. It is a great awakening when one suddenly realizes that one is a living being just like animals and plants. How small and ugly everything human appears when looking at things this way, especially all the hustle and bustle. Really Boris, I am disgusted by the world, above all by war and all the wickedness there is. I am sometimes even sickened by my own hatefulness.

Taking this view, a new question arises: What is the meaning of life? The thought that we only live to die is so hopeless. We must

---

98 Anna later wrote "Realization" in the top margin of this letter.
99 *Der Heilige*, published in 1879, is a short historical novel by Conrad Ferdinand Meyer (1825-1898), a Swiss poet and novelist. This book is mentioned again in Letter A47.

be here for a reason. Invariably other questions follow: Why does an animal live? Why does a plant or a flower live? I find no other answer than just to bring joy to those who see it. What is a tree's purpose? To bear fruit. With that I arrive at the point where you led me before: We live so that we can both enjoy the world as a wondrous creation and live in the service of that creation, not just for ourselves, but *within* that creation. One must shake everything around a bit to really understand this truth. It is the source of much strength.

I am writing you this so you can know what I am thinking about. You know all this already, but for me it is a new experience.

I will say goodnight for now. I miss you a lot too, my dear Boris. Take a big kiss from me.

[Wednesday] March 7, 1945

Good day my dearest.

Here is a quick thought. You write that you long to merge into a single droplet with me. It is exactly here where reality and idealism must have equal weight, otherwise it might lead to a terrible disappointment. One should not assume that "becoming one droplet" is achieving a total mutual understanding, because there is no such thing (as Dr. Bovet says). There is always something in the soul that will remain a mystery to the other, and perhaps this is the most crucial part of the attraction between two people. I am glad that I have no such illusions about marriage anymore. I see quite clearly how terribly difficult living together as a couple can be, and that this difficulty can only be borne successfully by a truly great love. I, too, look forward joyfully to being united with you. I am also happy about our differing points of view and about our reconciliations. I think you know what I mean.

Boris, I would like to give you some advice. Give yourself a little time off from all your worries about the future tomorrow. There is nothing you can do right now anyway. Read the wonderful story of Thomas Becket; it will give you a little diversion. So, now I kiss you very tenderly.

My Boris,

Your Anneli

P.S. I would like to see you again soon!

LETTER A34[100]

GWATT

[Thursday] March 8, 1945

My dear Boris,

In your last letter* you wrote that during a concert of Romantic music you started thinking about how a true Christian should behave. You concluded that a true Christian should have complete trust in God and should obey God's words and commands without fear. He would cease to kill, lie, fight, and punish. You see these things correctly. A Christian should have complete faith in God and follow God's commands. But realize that we are talking about a Christian, not Christians. Remember even Christ on the cross suffered because believed that God had forsaken him. Matthew 27:46: "And about the ninth hour Jesus cried with a loud voice: 'My God, my God, why hast thou forsaken me?'"

Now I will explain what I think being a Christian means. A Christian is someone who believes that love is rational and sensible. He is not free of mistakes or weaknesses (there is no such person), rather he is someone who *knows* he may always come back to God, despite his sins. I believe it has more to do with thinking than feeling. This is the key premise of Christianity. Thus, the Christian stands up strong, with open eyes and ears trained upon his fellow man and knows why he lives.

Now to your point about not killing. I must say, if someone pressed a gun into my hand and commanded me to shoot these people, I am not sure what I would do. Also, concerning lying, I am not completely clear. I think if it was a matter of life and death, I would lie too. This sounds lazy, but I think one should listen to reason, which is also a gift from God, and not stubbornly adhere to the letter of the law. As an example: If you broke your leg, you would not sit back and believe God will make your leg whole again.

---

100 In later years Anna wrote "Good thoughts about religion" at the top of this letter.

Rather you would be reasonable and go to a doctor, and for that no one (except perhaps a crazy person) would suggest that your trust in God was lacking.

You are quite correct when you say everyone would prefer to stay on this side of life for as long as possible. As Gotthelf says: "Going to sleep here to an awakening in a different place, which we call death, is something horrible even for the most faithful Christian." For me death is still something foreign and terrible, but I believe that with age and maturity one learns to prepare for it; one *must* prepare for it.

Now I will address punishment. Punishment and rage are not the same thing. Rage=Hate. One can punish out of love. For example, think about educating children. Parents are required to punish their children, but they do it, not out of hate, but out of love. It should be that way throughout your life. God does the same thing.

Boris, I really treasure your realistic thinking; it is the same ability that Tolstoy and Rolland possessed. You are right, we are all bad Christians, both clergy and congregation. We chatter too much, have too little faith, and do too little to help others. But despite that, there are people who take religion seriously and make an honest effort to serve God as well as they can.

Further, you suggest that the church helps too little. Yes, that is correct, but we all help too little. Realize also that there are many people who do not want to be helped. I fully agree with you that anyone who so distorts Christianity that its errors and weaknesses are hidden is a fool. But an honest person would not do this.

I want to tell you how I first came to the church. Everything I know about goodness I learned from the church. I discovered that there are people who think of things besides themselves and their own welfare. I derive my whole philosophy from this experience. You must remember that from the very beginning Jesus acknowledged that his followers throughout time would only be a small flock.

You wrote that the Holy Spirit is the balance between two poles. I have thought about it, and I don't quite agree. The Holy Spirit is a power that comes from God. The Holy Spirit can promote the balance between two poles, but it cannot be the balance between them. This balance can also be achieved by an atheist, but when the balance comes from God and goes to God in a creative way, that is what we call peace. Complicated, isn't it?

You wrote me that a person must be silly if he cannot recognize his insignificance in comparison to God. But aren't most people just like that? Most people experience exuberant emotions about God from time to time, but they could just as easily be directed at Jove, or some other entity instead. Real faith is something unemotional, it is knowledge. You will, of course, disagree with this. But you are mistaken, Boris.

You see, I find myself at a very awkward stage right now. I have lately strayed from a sober faith, that victorious certainty which rises above everything, and am now in a fitful emotional muddle whose cause is fear. I am not getting anywhere. I always seem to be barking up the wrong tree, but I hope I will find the right path eventually.

Your lecture about music was wonderful and made me happy; I learned something from it. I am so proud of you.

Now listen Boris, if you can come on Saturday, please be so good as to call me from Bern and let me know you are coming, otherwise I will not mention it to anyone here. Or, if you would rather, call me tomorrow evening. I hope you can come; everyone here would be very pleased to see you again. Maybe you could ask for permission to travel to Thun? Aren't I an impatient thing!

Good night Boris, I kiss you tenderly,

Dear,

Your Anneli

LETTER B27

Zurich

[Thursday] March 8, 1945

My dear Anneli,

Today I was annoyed as I seldom am, and because of these annoyances I find that my longing for you has greatly increased. I need sunshine and warmth, and *that is you*!

Some laughable things are the cause of my annoyance, which now seem even more laughable. But the aggravation still cost me the three fingernails I chewed off today.

It is all on account of gas rationing. Even though my landlady receives two extra units of gas because I rent a room in her house, she doesn't want me to use them. She would rather keep them for herself. Today she asked me not to cook dinner at home in the evenings. For me this is a question of money and coupons. Also, a cup of coffee in the afternoon helps me get more work done.

Earlier this week, one of the four women at the civil service office for refugees came to see me. All four ladies there, as Christians, have felt duty-bound to help me since my arrival in Zurich. One of them came to visit me during her lunch hour (I was out at the time) and brought me some fruit and other food. When she discovered how very cold my room was and saw that I was using my coat as a blanket, she brought a blanket the next day. I was out again when she stopped by. My landlady took this very badly, believing this meant the people at the refugee office thought she was not taking care of me properly. In brief, she told me that she would be happy if I would find myself another living arrangement. She was particularly angry this time because when she let the lady into my room it was a mess. I told her she should have brought the lady into the living room instead. It was a big ado that went on much too long. It was just stupid. My landlady has shown me kindness in the past, but now my feelings of thankfulness toward her have suffered colossally because of the petty attitude, ill will, and coarseness she exhibited. You mustn't worry about my bad mood. These problems are only trivialities. But it is sad that people are so unkind, even though, in the end, it is to their own disadvantage.

Today I was running around all day looking for another room but found nothing satisfactory. All the landladies I met made bad impressions on me. They were cold and businesslike.

I have been trying to save money this month by riding my bicycle to the university on most days. I only rarely take the tram.

And now to your letter. I doubt that I will get permission from the foreign office to go to Gwatt very soon, as it depends on the military authorities. It may take a couple of weeks. But if I can get permission to go to Bern, I might risk going to Gwatt from there. Maybe it would work one time?

Your Boris

LETTER B28

ZURICH

[Wednesday] March 28, 1945

My dear Anneli,

My trip to Gwatt is still at risk. On Monday, after receiving tentative permission from the foreign police[101] in Zurich to visit to Gwatt April 2-17 (dependent on approval from Bern), I received a rejection notice from the foreign police in Bern. I then wrote a letter to Reverend Kühner asking him to intervene. Because the military authorities have approved my application, it should be easy for me to get permission to travel, especially if I can get Frau Dr. Kurz to vouch for me too. Please encourage Reverend Kühner as much as you dare to help me get this straightened out as soon as possible.

I would really like to arrange to stay with you for at least a week, and I would be very unhappy if nothing comes of all this trouble. So, please do what you can.

I kiss you,

Your Boris

---

101 The security organization in charge of monitoring the movement of foreigners in Switzerland

LETTER A35[102]

GWATT

[Thursday] April 19, 1945

Good day dear,

Quickly, here is a little good morning kiss for you. I don't understand where I am getting the energy to wake up at 6 a.m. every morning, but I think it is good, as I find it easier to work in the morning than in the evening.

Boris, I do not want to be a piously religious person, but a sensible one instead. The world interests me more than heaven does. I wonder what you will say to that? I think maybe I am changing my mind again, hardly to my credit. I am starting to think over my earlier experiences again. I crow about faith, even if I go half-crazy in doing so. Maybe it is just the survival instinct.

[Friday] April 20, 1945

Good day Boris,

It troubled me yesterday[103] that you are afraid of trusting me completely because I had spoken to Reverend Kühner about us. I understand that. I would feel the same way too. But I will try hard to inspire your trust and remain open to you from now on so that I can understand your soul better. You know, when I make a mistake, I do not do it on purpose; it is done unconsciously.

I can imagine you are full of tension awaiting an answer from Bern, even though you say you have little hope. All things being equal,

---

102 Anna later wrote "A change in thinking" at the top of this letter.
103 Evidently there was communication with Boris on April 19. No letter from Boris survives.

I think that it would be good for you to work. You would feel more productive. But of course, I am unable to see all the advantages and disadvantages.

I don't believe that my depression is just imaginary. Until now I had never thought it was an inherited trait, but now I can see that it might be. Just as there are those who are naturally funny, there are also people who naturally have a depressive nature. That is something that just is; it does not arise through random circumstance. I see that clearly now. I am not troubled by any specific problems right now, but I am still feeling depressed. It is a painful, overly sensitive emotion that manifests itself as physical and spiritual tiredness and sadness. But these feelings go away very harmlessly if one guards against them. But they can resurface again when one is faced with an abnormally difficult problem (which acts like poison). I would really like to know what a psychologist would say about this.

I would be happy to translate another letter for you. I would do it very gladly because it is for you! Thank you so very much for the umbrella, the picture, the little kiss, and the letter. I am sending you a couple of flowers so that your room won't be quite so lonely. Now I kiss you very tenderly.

My Boris,

Your Anneli

[Saturday] April 21, 1945

Good day my Boris,

I was just now suddenly hit with a terrible dread of all the problems that sit before me. One can't simply put them aside or defuse them by reading words from the Bible; one must study them and work through them.

I believe you are calmer and surer than I in these situations, don't you agree? For me this will come with maturity. So, now I kiss you very tenderly, my Boris. We will see each other again soon, right dear?

My dear Bobussja,[104]

Your Anneli

---

104 Boris had many Russian nicknames, many of them being variations of Bob.

LETTER A36

Gwatt

[Sunday] April 22, 1945

My dear Boris,

Thank you so very much for your letter;* it filled me with happiness. I loved the picture of da Vinci. It is interesting to compare it with the portrait of Michelangelo: da Vinci with his strong, sharp expression and his truth-searching, all-penetrating look, next to Michelangelo's sad, painful face and his expression of complete devotion. Yet even in Michelangelo's figure one sees the incredible strength behind it, especially if you look at his hands.

Boris, it is so difficult for me to discuss God and other related problems with you right now because I don't feel I dare believe in anything at all. Even God is a question mark for me; it is only a word. I thought I had found the one and only correct path. Others confirmed that I had, representing all else as false. But then you come along and tell me that things are different, and I see truly that it might just be as you say. How can I know which is the truth? That is why I want to avoid this whole subject for a while, until I have recovered from the fear that has oppressed me these past few months. By the way, I read an article by a psychologist who believes that all theology built on the teachings of Paul generates fear because it is dogmatic. Maybe he is a freethinker[105] too, but he is right. I now want to concern myself with life and collect new experiences, in the hope that I might become a more mature, sensible person. I agree with you that a sensible person is one who stands upright, securely balanced on top of both poles.

Concerning my depression, you might be right. Maybe it is just a matter of weakness of will, as I never before have had the fears that have arisen in me over the past few months. I hope they will com-

---

105 A freethinker is someone who rejects religious dogma. Boris often described the members of his family in Russia as freethinkers.

pletely disappear in time. In the future I will want to be more careful when I say, "I believe."

You can still write to me about all your thoughts and beliefs despite this. I get much pleasure from seeing what interests you and how you search. As far as confiding in each other, only when one trusts completely can one love completely. But I am still very young and sometimes still quite immature, so I understand very well why you may be a little afraid of trusting me. Do not worry, I will earn your trust in time. My trust is not quite perfect either, otherwise I would not be jealous of you.

I am so sorry you ran into such problems with your landlady. Let me give you a piece of advice: Try to be nicer and kinder to her than you have been in the past. Maybe that will help.

I thank you also for *Der Freischütz*![106]

So, now I kiss you sweetly, my Boris. The time goes by, doesn't it? And yet it still goes too slowly.

My Boris,

Your Anneli

---

106 The libretto of Weber's opera by Friedrich Kind

LETTER A37

[Tuesday] April 24, 1945
9:30 p.m.

Good evening my Boris,

Today I finished reading *Der Freischütz*. I will now explain how I interpreted it. Overall, I think the story shows the victory of good over evil. Max, the main character, represents the common man. Agathe and Ännchen are the embodiment of love. In Caspar and Samiel lie the power of evil. I also find it well depicted how the world, in the person of Prince Ottokar, does not forgive, but love (Agathe) and God (the hermit) discover a new path. I think I finally understand what romanticism is now (I only had an inkling of it before), especially in nature. But I see it in *Der Freischütz* too. But here the most beautiful and deepest truth is somewhat veiled by its romanticism. The action is so exciting, and I wonder how Weber came up with the music to go with it. When I get the chance, I will go and see the opera.

Boris, I can sense from your letter* that you are unhappy that I am turning away from my faith. But you need not worry; it came about very naturally through my soul searching. I must let the whole matter rest and let it evolve on its own. As my soul matures, it will arise all by itself into the light. I have only one thing before my eyes now: perfection and love for my fellow man. By perfection, I mean purity of the heart, which is becoming free of oneself. I thank you for your explanation about psychology. I had thought about it in a similar way. As soon as I have some time, I will consider it even more carefully.

I can well imagine you have many conflicting thoughts these days, as the decision of where we will go after the war is drawing closer. I, too, have thought over the advantages and disadvantages of your taking a position in Bern if it is offered to you.

Advantages: You would have far more freedom to travel. You would be able to help Switzerland a great deal during the war and in the initial period right after it. If Switzerland really is interested in mining in the Ruhr district,[107] then I think you would have a good chance. You could work productively, and that would do your soul and disposition good, and you could count on good recommendations from those you know in Switzerland. Your contacts in Swiss industry might help your chances of emigrating to the United States. You would also have a financial advantage and have a full year to prepare for your next step in peace and would not fall into the "strudel" of emigration right now. If in the future you wanted to become a Swiss citizen, this position would also be an advantage for you. Further, if you were interested in doing so, you could help Switzerland build up its strength. I would also have the advantage of having you with me for another year.

Disadvantages: You would be obliged to serve for one full year. It could be that in one year the United States might be in an economic crisis and you would have a harder time getting there. You would lose your [refugee] stipend. You may well experience some irritations at this job, and you would have to stop working on your doctoral research. I would not continue it now anyway because of your current circumstances. You can probably find a better way to pursue it later.

So now I will give you a goodnight kiss, my Bobussja. I kiss you very gently and thank you also for your sweet little kiss of today.

---

107 Boris had worked in the Ruhr district in western Germany for many years before the war.

[Wednesday] April 25, 1945
6:15 a.m.

Good day my dear,

Of course, it would be dangerous if our interests were to diverge, but I am not afraid of that because I know we will always seek out a peaceful resolution. In addition, we also have a very great goal in front of us: to help the world where and however we can. But we will only be able to do that when we are united.

Now, I want to kiss you very tenderly because you are certainly also hungry for tenderness. I thank you so much, and I am looking ahead with joy to our next meeting. Another little kiss, and now I must go.

My Boris,

Your Anneli

LETTER A38

[Saturday] April 28, 1945
6:25 a.m.

Good morning Boris,

Last night I conversed with Dr. Strupp for a while, and through this discussion I learned the meaning of the word conservative. He is very much in favor of peace and believes that all innovations come about all by themselves. He, too, believes that one should endeavor to develop oneself fully to better help all of humanity. Further, one should not throw away the old before one has created the new. I told him I saw a bit of passivity in his view, to which he responded that all young people are radical, and all old people are conservative. He may be right about that. He said that Social Democrats are "neither fish nor fowl." I was quite taken aback at this, as I had envisioned it as the ideal party. But Dr. Strupp said the political middle way is always the weakest. What do you think about this, Boris?

Last night I had a horrible dream. I dreamt I was in Berlin. Everything was completely strange to me, and I lost my way running through the streets during an attack, in constant fear I would be knocked over at any moment by the hordes of soldiers storming by. You know, the war has been much in my thoughts lately, and the question you raised earlier (What will happen to the German people after the war?)[108] becomes ever more pressing.

In reference to your conversation with Mr. Beyen, I think few theologians would directly answer the question: "What is your conception of God?" They would evade it by saying one should not even try to imagine God. As far as the renewal of the church goes, I would like to hear what you have to say about it. I know your ideas, but I am not sure how you would implement them practically.

---

108 Where and when Boris raised this question is unknown.

I hope you have a nice Sunday tomorrow and won't feel too lonely. I kiss you very tenderly, so it will ease the strain of your trip tomorrow.

My Bobussja,

Your Anneli

---

1 p.m.

Dear Boris,

When I opened your letter and found *Egmont*,[109] I let out a cry of joy. I am so happy and excited about it. I thank you from the bottom of my heart. You know Boris, I am so happy to be free of the whole faith business because it was not the right way. I am sure I misunderstood much of it. But I blame the church because it directs its teaching at simple folk. The church should help people see clearly, but it only allows people to see what and as far as it finds appropriate.

Here is one more very long and strong kiss,

Your Anneli

---

109 *Egmont* is a play by Johann Wolfgang von Goethe (1749-1832). The title character, Count Egmont, a Dutch general and stateman, lived from 1522 to 1568. His execution led to a national uprising which eventually resulted in the Netherlands' independence from Spain.

LETTER B29

Zurich

[Saturday] April 28, 1945

My dear Anneli,

Today, for the first time, I received no "Sunday" letter from you on Saturday.[110] I thought you said you were going to send one. I hope you did not run into any difficulties. The lack of a letter from you and the political events (Himmler, capitulation!) taking place now are making me nervous. I had to escape to the movies to distract myself. It looks like important world events will be taking place on my fortieth birthday. If you read the eyewitness accounts of concentration camp survivors, one must thank God that the world will finally be rescued from this insane, sadistic person, better said, this devil.[111]

From the start, even before 1933,[112] I could see how Nazi fever was being artificially instilled in the populace by propaganda speeches, pushing the German people bit by bit toward total belief in the "Nazi Ideal," in the Führer, and in the future of a great German Reich that would last 1,000 years. It was only because of complacency and indifference that Hitler was able to destroy all his opponents one by one, right in front of everyone's noses. Really, a hideous time lies behind us. Coming generations will perhaps not even be able to believe that the Germany that produced such great people as Bach, Goethe, and Kant could have sunk so low. It will certainly prove to be the lowest point of all German history. But others are not completely innocent either, as there were plenty of Nazi supporters up until 1939.[113]

---

110 Anna did write him a letter but likely finished it too late to reach him in time via regular mail. She sends it express and it arrives the next day (on Sunday).
111 Hitler
112 The year Hitler came to power
113 It was only after *Kristallnacht* (November 9-10, 1938) that world opinion turned decidedly against the Nazi regime due to critical news reports published around the world. Having learned a lesson from this, the Nazi government made sure all subsequent persecutions of the Jews and other non-Aryan groups were shrouded in complete secrecy. See Martin Gilbert,

I am extremely thankful I was able to get through this maelstrom in one piece. I am curious to know what will happen in the coming years.

In yesterday's newspaper I read a sort of horoscope, a list of predictions and suggestions organized by birthdate. For May 4 (my birthday) this is what was written: "A great event in love is going to occur. Make a decision about a job after weighing the pros and cons." Even though I rarely put a lot of stock in these sorts of things, it seems, at least for me, these particular statements ring true.

I hope you are well and that I will soon have some news from you. I kiss you very tenderly and gently.

Sunday, April 29

My dear heart!

Your express letter calmed me down a lot and brought me much joy. I thank you for sending it and the many kisses you included. My joy is substantiated in the first place by your cry of joy when you received *Egmont*. It is colossally important that we both have and pursue the same interests and that you learn about important historical personalities because they usually represent a unique spiritual philosophy. One cannot achieve a valid historical perspective just by knowing one's neighbors, which is what most people do, even if one moves frequently!

My Anneli,

Your Boris

Kristallnacht: Prelude to Destruction (New York: Harper Collins, 2006), p. 268.

LETTER A39[114]

GWATT

[Tuesday] May 8, 1945

My dear Boris,

Last Sunday, just like the Sunday we spent together earlier in Bern, was a day of pure joy. Really Boris, these hours with you are so enriching. I thank you for all the patience and love you give as you teach and explain things to me. What a special joy it was for me when I found out you had prepared something about psychology for me. That was very sweet of you.

I am in the middle of *Egmont* right now, and I am so excited about it. I hear Beethoven's overture all the while, storming around in my head. It is amazing how he set it to music and how one can picture Egmont exactly, his boldness and daring as he goes riding gallantly about. I don't identify as much with Egmont's character as with Faust's, yet I still like him very much. I am increasingly amazed by Goethe. He must have possessed an unmatched understanding of humanity.

Boris, I think I am much closer to you than before, and I am happy about it. It is said that complete love is achieved when I am you and you are me. That makes sense to a certain degree, but it is also true that it is by loving that one discovers the real self (the true "I") for the first time, but in terms of the other.

I am sending you a few flowers with my letter; you should throw away all the old ones. I now will give you a little kiss and stroke your hair. You are a dear person Boris, the dearest I have known until now.

My Boris,

Your Anneli

---

114 Boris and Anna met in person on Sunday, May 6. This letter was written on May 8, 1945, V-E Day, which would have been marked by major celebrations throughout Europe.

LETTER A40

GWATT

[Thursday] May 10, 1945

My dear Boris,

I just received your letter.* It was a big surprise and it made me very happy. It was so sweet of you to send it express. I am sitting in a chaise longue right next to the lake. It is a beautiful day, and I am enjoying the sun. I hope you are enjoying it too. This morning I practiced piano and made better progress than usual (I had warm hands!) and that gave me renewed courage. Yesterday evening I went to typing class for the first time. I have an excellent teacher. He has humor, but he demands complete concentration from us, which is very important.

After I finished reading *Egmont*, I read a critical review of it. The reviewer said *Egmont* was a youthful work of Goethe's, and more of a self-portrait than a historical representation of Egmont. I, too, felt the author took a lot of liberties. (Goethe himself says it was a difficult work for him to write.) But for me, the most important thing is to really understand the character of a man like Goethe's Egmont, and from that understanding find a new orientation towards life: to have pleasure, but not allow that pleasure to govern you; to be free of yourself, but to be led by the goodness of your own heart.

Even though *Egmont* is a youthful work, Goethe clearly reveals the spirit of Christ in it. His words show this and prove that he already had a deeply developed understanding of people: "He has my safety and happiness at heart but considers not that he who lives but to save his own life is already dead."[115]

Little Claire[116] is also beautifully represented. Personally, I am against such worshipful, gushing depictions of love. I believe that true love can only exist between equal partners. (Bovet says the same

---

115 Quote from Act II, scene 2 of *Egmont* (1788)
116 The heroine, who is in love with Egmont

thing.) This refers not only to the person's social class, but to the totality of the person.

With us, I know that you are superior to me, yet I still feel I am on the same plane with you. If I felt that I was below you, my love and enthusiasm for you would dwindle to nothing.

Little Claire's love must not have arisen out of mere impulsiveness, otherwise she would never have had the strength to sacrifice herself for Egmont. There is a lot more to this work, but I can only digest it a little at a time. The Dutch people have faced a similar situation, as have all Europeans, in the last few years. I now have a little better perspective on that time.

---

10 p.m.

By chance I heard a lecture this afternoon about the situation in Holland currently and before the war. The speaker said that successful rebuilding can only take place on the plane of Christian faith. After the lecture I had a conversation with Dr. Strupp. He told me he didn't understand the lecture at all, and then we began to talk about Christianity. Some of what he said was similar to what you say, but he is more removed from the situation than you because he cannot yet see the strength that lies in Christ. He asked, for example, what help would it be to someone in material need to tell them to build on the rock of God? He feels that it is time a reformer came along because the church no longer has any power. In 1914, when World War I began, the church did nothing. Between the wars it did nothing. And when World War II began in 1939, it also did nothing. An earlier discussion was reopened: How difficult communication becomes when every religious person feels his or her own religion is the only correct one. I want to leave this topic now. I find it to be total chaos, a complete stupidity in the spiritual and physical world. But despite that, life is so beautiful! But it is hard to find the right way.

I am enclosing your photo. I think you should have some copies made because it is an excellent picture.

Concerning the Pentecost holiday, I have no answer from home yet. I can rent myself a bicycle.[117]

Dear, I will say goodnight now. I am quite upset over all these silly spiritual questions. I simply can't find my way through them. But I will stop thinking about all this now. I think everything will become clearer with time.

Now a little goodnight kiss from me, my Boris,

Anneli

---

[117] Pentecost was on May 20 in 1945. Boris and Anna are planning to take a bicycle trip during the holiday, but Anna needs her parents' permission.

LETTER A41

GWATT

[Saturday] May 12, 1945

My dear Boris,

First, I want to share the news that I did not get a refusal from Winterthur for our bicycle trip. Now you can apply for police permission. Hopefully, we will have some luck with this. Listen, I forbid you to buy anything for this trip, understand? Otherwise, I will be very angry! I will purchase some food I know you like, as much as my financial circumstances allow, and will take on the major portion of the expense. In any case, I do not want our trip to have a negative impact on your efforts for the future. Now you must promise to obey me, Bobussja, without grumbling!

I thank you very much for your letter* of last Saturday. It made me happy because I could sense the liveliness and excitement growing in you. I was particularly pleased with the passage in which you described your new approach. You write you want to be a realist who unites the heavenly and worldly. You see, that is exactly what I mean when I say I want to be a sensible person. By sensible I do not mean a cold and calculating person, but one who very clearly and soberly understands why he lives and organizes his life accordingly.

Frau Dr. Kurz asked me to send you her greetings. She was here today to attend a Crusader meeting.

I attended a very interesting lecture on the Free German movement and the German Protestants given by Miss von Kirschbaum. She is Prof. Barth's secretary in Basel. The question centers on whether the [Swiss] Protestants should join the Free German movement which has claimed its objectives are inspired by Moscow. Several have already joined up, others hesitate, others are distrustful. There was an extended discussion in which the theological implications were dissected. Some felt the church should not join it. Others, including

Frau Dr. Kurz, say that the church should not shrink from getting involved with politics. The church made a mistake before by hiding behind its own walls. Prof. Lehmann, who was also here, said very rightly that we cannot make decisions now for the distant future, or even for tomorrow, but only for today. One can understand why the church, after the experiences it had with the Nazis, hesitates to fall in with the Communists, and yet it may have to if it doesn't want to hide behind its walls again. I don't see why Christ couldn't work with a Communist in an hour of need, or with a Democrat or a Socialist. Frau Dr. Kurz said very characteristically: "If you are so very sure in your Christianity, why are you afraid of communism?"

In addition, I heard many sad things from a German who lives at a work camp in Valais near Montana.[118] He spoke of the horrible circumstances in the refugee camps. There is a kind of political insanity there; they do beatings and the like. The camp is divided into three different sections based on the beliefs of the inmates: Communists, Christians, and egocentrics. He said that the Communists swore to him that if they were released, he would be the first person they would take a knife to. A former Spanish fighter taking a nice spring walk with him suddenly said, "Oh, this is so boring, I want to see blood!" He also spoke of three Italians who had to leave their comrades at the camp because they were not Communists and were instead labeled Fascists. The three got permission to go home, but then they were immediately denounced by their former Communist comrades and were taken to prison instead. When one hears things like this, one becomes anxious and fearful for the new Europe. These people will bring Europe to the brink of a new Nazi generation.

I will say goodnight now, my dear. I kiss you very tenderly. I look forward to the next time we can be together.

My Bobussja,

Your Anneli

---

118 A remote area in the alpine canton of Valais in southern Switzerland

LETTER A42

[Wednesday] May 16, 1945

My dear Boris,

I am so very enthusiastic about Schiller's *Don Carlos*![119] I can't tell you how thankful I am for your help in furthering my education. I also thank you for the picture of Bizet,[120] with whom I am not at all familiar. Yesterday I read about Martin Luther briefly, and now I want to see if I can find more literature on this period.

I believe I now comprehend the myth that was based on a completely faulty understanding of Christianity. It instilled and supported people's fear of God's wrath and the superstition that arose as a result. It also disgracefully misinterpreted Paul's words implying that God's authority can be meted out by popes, emperors, and monarchs. I believe I understand it now because I went through such a period of fear myself. But it is wonderful to see how out of the darkness of that time people suddenly awoke one by one and eclipsed the Christians who had come before.

I am sending back your recommendation for the refugee camp with this letter. This is exactly what I like to see! You don't just talk, you act. What really appealed to me in your last letter* was that you believe you will succeed in the future.

So, I must say farewell now. I hope you have recovered from our bicycle escapade. I wish you a good Sunday and kiss you very, very tenderly.

My Bobussja,

Your Anneli

---

119 A tragic play in five acts by German author and philosopher Friedrich Schiller (1759-1805)
120 Georges Bizet (1838-1875), a French composer, most famous for his opera *Carmen*

LETTER B31

ZURICH

[Saturday] May 26, 1945

My dear little heart!

I should really be working now, but your last two letters were so sweet, I just had to take a few minutes to answer them. But I have so much to say and am so full of love for you, I just can't find the right way to express my thoughts.

I feel our last trip helped bring our mutual understanding to a higher level because it allowed us to experience common, everyday things together. In general, a person behaves the same way when it comes to monumental events as he does with small, ordinary things. That is why day-to-day experiences can also be instructive.

The comforting words in your letter* did me good. I believe you are correct in what you said. But I am not going to apologize, as I know I still have much energy within me, even now. When we are together for good, I know we will be able encourage each other and spur each other on, as we are both realistic and industrious. The only apology I will make is I will admit to a six-year period of inactivity.[121] One should not minimize its influence, but I don't want to let it get me down. You will help me fight against that, won't you? You are right when you say I am in chains. So, please help me find the patience and persistence to remove these chains of refugeehood.

I agree completely with what you say about sensuality. Sensuality can dry up true love and can make people ordinary. Whereas virtue leads people on a nobler path.

I am happy to hear about your interesting reading projects and your joy in learning. I am also pleased by your clear thoughts on different personalities and characters. I regret that we can't discuss these things more fully. It is hard and tedious trying to do that in a letter.

---

121 Boris is referring to the war years, during which he could not pursue his profession.

If your mother asks you about our bicycle trip, tell her the truth. But I would also be clever and mention that we slept in separate rooms. I think you know what would be best to share to stay on good terms with your mother.

I read in the newspaper that masses of people are traveling around Europe now. One and a half million Russians will be leaving western Germany and going back to Russia, and one million troops will be brought to the west. Also, many refugees are leaving Switzerland daily. Hopefully, the U.S. will not impose a general immigration blockade against foreigners; that would be the end of my dreams.

I am very much looking forward to our next meeting. I would like to open myself up to you more. For this to happen we must both be in a suitable mood.

I kiss you and stroke you very tenderly,

My Anneli,

Your Boris

LETTER A43

[Wednesday] May 30, 1945

My dear Boris,

I thank you for your letter and the new little picture. I was longing to hear from you. As I can see from your words and your handwriting, your inner tension continues to grow, and I think it will be harder and harder for you to be patient. I, too, can hardly allow myself to think about it, as I would like to give time a vigorous push.

Boris, lately I have been reading a book about the twelfth century, *Zwischen Kaiser und Papst*,[122] a very lovely book, but I haven't quite finished it yet. It deals with the topic of divesting the pope of all secular governing power. It also discusses one of the earliest anti-papists, a monk by the name of Arnold of Brescia, another bit of church history. I must say, the hair on the back of my neck stood up on end when I read about all the mischief the church has done in past centuries. How very long it has taken (nearly 2,000 years) for the essence of Christianity to be partially understood! I understand it to a degree, particularly the fear of straying from the spirit of the Bible. But the words of St. Augustine: "Love [God], then do as you will," should have enlightened them.

I am also horrified by all the trickery and deception people used to attack one another. It still happens today, but people are better at covering it up. It struck me the same way in *Prince Serebrenni*.[123] To help me better understand this novel, if you have time, please be so good as to send me a description of the typical

---

122 Full title: *Zwischen Kaiser Und Papst: Ein Roman um Arnold von Brescia* [Between Emperor and Pope] by Emanuel Stickelberger, (Stuttgart: F. R. Steintopf, 1934). It was published again in 1948 under different title: *Der Magdalenenritter* [The Magdalen Knight].
123 This novel by Aleksey Konstantinovich Tolstoy (1817-1875), second cousin to the more famous novelist Leo Tolstoy, takes place during the reign of Ivan the Terrible (1533-1584).

Russian and his character. That is all I want to write; I still have so much work to do today. But one day I will find the way to Christ, and then I hope things will go better for me. Then I will be free of myself.

I kiss you very tenderly and joyfully look forward to your letter of tomorrow. Boris, I wait with you full of impatience for what will come.

My Bobussja,

Your Anneli

LETTER B32

[Wednesday] June 6, 1945

My dear Anneli, my little heart,

From your letters I sense that you are bit out of sorts and at odds with yourself. But I believe you are missing only one thing, love. But I mean love in the complete sense. You are so young yet, and spiritually delicate, and it is spring now, and the sun shines and nature laughs, but you are alone, without loving words, without gentleness, with only your monotonous work in Thun. You see the same people every day and they do not offer anything new or inspiring. There are also so many unresolved issues about your future. I understand this very well, dearest, but from 150 kilometers away I am, like you, chained up right now, and can do very little to help you. It makes me sad, and yet, I am happy today. Today Mr. Freudenberg called me. He is expecting me at the beginning of next week, which means the two of us can be together the next two weekends! Isn't that wonderful?

Anneli, you must not brood anymore; you should focus on looking ahead to next Saturday with joy. Can you register me for two nights? I will meet you in Thun at the train station. Write me when I should arrive.

Could you practice the symphonies of Mozart a bit so we can play them together? I have not yet sent you my photograph, as the copy did not turn out well and I am too stingy to have another photographer redo it. You will get it later for sure.

I will end my letter now because I need to go into town soon.

I kiss you tenderly,

My Anneli,

Your Boris

LETTER A44

[Thursday] June 7, 1945

Dear Boris,

Everything is ruined. Yesterday evening I checked with Mrs. Kühner (Reverend Kühner is away). She said the Heimstätte is filled up and there is no more room. I proposed that I would give you my room and I sleep in one of the common rooms. It would have worked out fine that way. She responded that it was not at all necessary for us to see each other so often and she would not allow it because of her responsibility to my parents. I knew she was set against us, so I said nothing more and left.

About an hour later she came to my room and asked me what I was planning to do now. I told her right out that I would be going to Bern Saturday and Sunday. To that she said she would not give me permission to do that, as she could not answer to my parents for it if I went, and if I were not sensible enough to hold back, then others would have to step in. At the same time, she complained that I have been isolating myself too much, staying away from everyone. She also said she had tried recently to get closer to me. I replied that I had not noticed her attempts to do so, and that the only times she spoke to me were to complain or argue about something. She then said that in the future I must ask for permission to see you. I told her I would not be able to do that. Everything in me was raging against her.

Could you leave Zurich early on Sunday morning and get to Thun in the afternoon? Maybe I could slip away for a few hours without being noticed in the middle of the afternoon. Write me your answer in Russian in case someone else opens and reads your letter before I can get it.

I am still in crisis mode right now. I don't know what these people want from me. I would have liked to have the chance to discuss all of this with you in person and learned more about your trip to Geneva.

Despite my best intentions, my dissatisfaction with Mrs. Kühner is growing. But try not to get upset about it, that would be pointless. We will find a way to meet somehow. We must not allow external things to cause a rift between us.

You can imagine how I angry I was. Yet, I don't really find it so terrible that we must give up on our visits once in a while, as it is not a make-or-break situation for our love.

I kiss you very tenderly and await your answer,

My Bobussja,

Your Anneli

LETTER A45[124]

[Tuesday] June 12, 1945

Dear Boris,

I thank you for your letter.* I am just as overjoyed about our relationship as you are. On Sunday I readily noticed how you clung to me and how your love has grown. Believe me, it is becoming more difficult for me to speak to you in a cool, unemotional way. But I did it because I am convinced that this is the best way to serve our love, rather than just by stroking your head.

I am incredibly happy to see that your drive toward truth and absolute honesty is so strong, and I thank you also for the trust you have in me. I will make every effort to be worthy of it.

I must tell you again how much your conversation with Mrs. Kühner made me marvel. It revealed your great spiritual strength which allows you to see the big picture and then arrive at your goal with calmness and wisdom. Just witnessing this exchange strengthened my faith in your future success. Today I will be with you in my thoughts with both hope and worry.

I doubt I will have time to write again this week, but it will soon be Saturday and we will see each other then. I will await word from you about your arrival time. I hope you had a good trip and found lodging. In a rush, I now offer you my sweetest kisses.

My Bobussja,

Your Anneli

P.S. Please pardon my bad handwriting; I am writing on the train.

---

124 Boris was able to visit Anna in Gwatt on Sunday, June 10, as Anna mentions in this letter.

LETTER B33

[Tuesday] June 19, 1945

5 p.m.

My dear Anneli,

I thank you for your dear letter.* Things are going for me exactly as they are for you. I am so sleep deprived I had to take a two-hour nap this afternoon.

I feel psychologically worn down too, mainly because I am continually wrestling with the problem of our livelihood but have no patience for it. Yesterday I and four other engineers in my situation attended a meeting of a refugee engineer organization, part of the Geneva international committee for placement. This is the organization that is supporting me. I found it disheartening that three out of the five in my group already knew where they were going. It has been established that technical specialists will only be considered for immigration once military forces grant the civilian government the freedom to rebuild. Provisionally, everything depends on the military. Until now I have only been in communication with the military authorities in Bern, not with the civilian government, which has temporarily lost its power.

I agree that I am spending too much time on external things. I thank you for so many things, Anneli. You have become my little heart and soul, and I am happy you value the internal so much. If we are modest in our future desires and put our main value on internal things, we will make out fine.

I have become completely distraught over all the last-minute changes, frantic letter writing, and the extra traveling I have had to do. Perhaps my agitation has caused your work in Thun to suffer since you have not been able to work in peace. Despite this, we should not close ourselves off from each other completely. We must fight for our future very doggedly; our cause is a worthy one. You cannot imagine how much it hurts me to see you struggle emotionally. I feel as if I am responsible for it, yet I am not to blame. But I know full well that once we are free to be together your worries will be allayed, as my first and last goal will always be to make you happy, not with riches or material things, but by bringing you inner joy. Thinking about our love makes me happy and gives me the strength to fight. If you believe what I say, you, too, should find the strength to fight.

We must be as balanced and productive as possible. The most important thing is to get plenty of sleep. Sleep steadies the nerves. Tell me if my letters and enclosures divert you too much from your work. Please make any suggestions you believe we should consider, so we can both be productive and avoid emotional suffering. Maybe we should write less? We can write more succinctly if we are very tired or have too little time. If I come to see you in two weeks, would that be too great a distraction for you? I doubt I can postpone the trip, and our joy in seeing each other will be so great, it would be hard for me to give up this opportunity! So, I await your suggestions. So that you can relax a bit, I will wait and send this letter tomorrow.

I just finished reading an article about Russia by Hewlett. He writes: "Life is perpetual forward movement. Inactivity is a form of death." I believe this may be the precise cause of our current difficulties. But we should guard against our own impatience and illusions. Our inertia is only temporary. As we are both actively improving ourselves, we are not really experiencing inertia at all. Let us try to avoid subjecting ourselves to constant emotional turmoil; it could prove harmful. We must rely on our sense of reason to keep us out of that blind alley.

Boris

LETTER A46

GWATT

[Thursday] June 21, 1945

My dear Boris,

I thank you so much for your letter. It really cheered me up, especially because you agreed with me that we have been concerning ourselves too much with trivial things lately. Think of Jesus, who said: "Why do you ask, 'What shall we eat, what shall we wear?'"[125] On the other side of this stands the prayer: "Give us this day our daily bread."[126] Give them equal weight. It is true that your situation is difficult, but I think you are a little too cautious and maybe a little too particular.

Maybe you should restrain your desires a bit and ask yourself what part of the world could best use your talents. Where is the greatest need? Where can I be of the greatest use? When I think of it that way, I always think of Germany first. Wouldn't it be there that your knowledge and abilities would be most valued, rather than a country that already has plenty of resources? If the Americans see your good work in Germany, you might have an easier time immigrating to the U.S. later.

In giving you this suggestion, I still believe our next step should be maturely and soberly thought through. You should also not view it as a reproach, as I know how often you have put your abilities at someone's disposal only to be turned away. I only want you to know what my latest thoughts have been, and that for me happiness doesn't depend entirely on material comfort.

I am glad your depression is gone. I think it may have arisen because you discovered that your three colleagues already had positions. But you must not let that worry you, as your path will be determined soon. You need to maintain your strength of will, we both need to. And above all, you should not force matters. Everything will

---
125 Matthew 6:31
126 Matthew 6:11 (a line from the Lord's Prayer)

work out by itself. If it happens now, or in month or two, it doesn't really matter. You should recognize that you cannot dictate your own fate. You know the saying: "Things always turn out differently than we think!" But you might write up all the pros and cons of east vs. west in your next letter. Maybe that will help us figure out the best course, and we can discuss it when we next meet. Either way, there will be some risk.

If you can gain some advantage at the ETH, then that is good, but I find it meaningless to work just to pass tests. Our correspondence is probably good for your soul. Therefore, we should not restrict it, but pursue and deepen it.

I am very tired now and will go to sleep. Sleep well, my dear Bobussja.

Anneli

LETTER B34

Zurich

[Saturday] June 23, 1945

My dear Anneli,

I thank you for your letter. I would like to answer it this morning. But first I must share something with you. Yesterday I was invited to the Scandinavian Club by Mrs. von Schoulz. It was a very exclusive party at a hotel at Seestrasse no. 125. About fifty Swedes, Norwegians, Danes, and Finns gathered there, including the General Consul, other consuls, and ladies in their national costumes. I was glad I could attend, not only because it was the "Scandinavian Club," but also because I knew I would have the opportunity to meet Dr. Bloom, who is half Norwegian, and his family. National songs were sung. People there were dancing the latest, most fashionable dances in which the distance between the gentlemen and ladies was about fifty cm(!),[127] so no impropriety was possible, or if there was any, it would be easily seen by all. Some people think dancing is indiscreet, even evil. For me dance is artful and elegant. Of course, it depends on the style of dance. It should be a symphony of bodily movement, as with ballet.

Dr. Bloom is sixty years old, his wife about twenty-five. Accompanying them were his son and daughter. They are in their mid-twenties, so I assume they are from his first marriage. The whole family made an excellent impression on me. Mrs. Bloom is an artist and a sculptress, and she loves to learn languages, including Russian, which she is currently studying. She studied English in England. I don't find her exceptionally good looking, but interesting, intelligent, and artistically talented. Despite their large age difference, Dr. and Mrs. Bloom seem well suited to each other. He is a world traveler and has a bearing one might describe as aristocratic and distinguished. A youthful looking man for his age, he seems to be in good condition physically.

---

127 About twenty inches

Dr. Bloom is one of the most interesting professors I have had at the ETH. Only Prof. Niggli makes a more solidly learned impression, although as a person he is less refined. The Blooms want to travel to England so Dr. Bloom can give a series of lectures. Afterwards, they will go to Italy to study art.

I find our age difference, the only issue brought up by your father that is legitimate, to be no hindrance for us. The Blooms' marriage is evidence that such a relationship can work well. Yet the conditions must be such that we can, on our own and with the help of external experiences, develop and grow. Every living creature must bloom and thrive, otherwise depression and other destructive tendencies could surface. On the other hand, if development exists, neither of us will be tormented with depression.

There were five single women nearby with whom I could have danced. But I tried to resist as much as I politely could, for your sake. I very much regret that you could not attend the party, as I would have been proud to have you at my side. I would have been happy to have you converse and dance with others and would have been proud to show off my sweetheart and my jewel. My dear, we must have complete confidence in each other and be proud of each other. If there are things you do not like about me, please have patience. We are both continually moving to a higher, more refined level. My work is also going better, and I am working in a more systematic and goal-conscious way. Lately, I have been going to the ETH every day to try to get ahead so that I can understand the material as well as anyone else working in the industry. I must make up for lost time.

I may have mentioned this to you before in the strictest confidence: I have found a wife. She lives by Lake Thun, but that shouldn't concern you.

And now to your letter!

What must we both strive for? To find a place on this earth where we both can find a way to develop and be productive, and where our capabilities, knowledge, abilities, and talents can best help and serve our fellow man. I believe the U.S. and Russia would be the best places to do that. In other countries I would have to make many adjustments and might not be able to reach the same heights professionally. Maybe I might eventually, but only after many years.

What are the pros and cons with Russia?

Pro: Compared with other countries, it is in Russia and the United States where a person's ability is most highly valued. The Russian Revolution resulted in a breakthrough in the development of all people who were previously hindered in every way by a relatively small group of people from the upper classes (aristocrats, church, and bourgeoise). All revolutionaries were banished to Siberia in former times. That is why Siberia is not a land of criminals. Quite on the contrary, like the United States, it is populated by courageous, freedom-loving people. In Russia, the state's only interest (which it passionately pursues) is to force its citizens to be productive and to be of service to their fellow citizens. Russia is the most idealistic country in the world, where the development of all its people is easily achieved. Education, school, health care (doctors, hospitals, health spas) are available to all for free. Every person is a credit to his community, and the community takes good care of him.[128]

However, I would have doubts about Russia if the direction of this development (mental and spiritual) is false, or if instead of encouraging each person to serve his fellow citizens, its goal becomes the legal exploitation of the populace by and for the sake of the state. Observing current trends worldwide, one finds aspects of every country (maybe in Russia most of all) that make one uneasy. But if one looks at the end goal and thinks about it as a realist and idealist would, then Russia may be the most compelling. The final goal is the development of creativity itself. If you recall my lecture on the purpose of life, I address conservation, perfection, and lastly, creation.

I find the Communists have many Christ-like ideals and can sometimes realize them more readily than Christians do themselves.

---

128 It seems astonishing that Boris would have this rosy opinion of communism after experiencing persecution in Siberia, where he and his family were considered enemies of the people because they had been capitalists prior to the revolution. In many ways Boris continued to view his homeland in a positive light, just as he had during his childhood.

What I don't like is that Russia holds up materialism as an ideal, and this batters a person psychologically in that one is in danger of viewing people as machines without souls. Human beings are devalued thereby. The main objective is for citizens to work hard and develop their talents to be of service to the state. It is this work that is most highly valued. In this way one steps a bit closer to the Christian ideal of serving one's fellow man despite everything, yet the current tone of this in Russia is mechanical, technical, industrial, and rationalistic (that is, soulless = heartless = loveless = godless).

The situation can become dangerous if one distances oneself too far from God. Our job as Christians is to understand Christ as a human being, but one who has reached the divine. He is a person, not a fantasy. Christ's aim is to save and develop mankind, and to create strong people. Yet they must be real people, not machines, people who believe that a human being is the noblest, greatest [creature] on earth. To minimize conflict, people must strive to emulate God in developing their ideal conception of perfection. Then all differences will disappear (race, religion, nationality, class), particularly those differences that people have created themselves. So, if one really wishes to focus on creating a better future for mankind, one must address the education of the soul, with no thought about becoming rich, or building oneself a fabulous villa, and the like.

What dangers could I face in Russia?

The living standard in Russia is lower than in Europe even though the main goal of the state is to attain a good living standard for everyone. In the last few years much has been accomplished, and in the next few years even more will be, so the living standard in Russia may soon equal or even exceed that of Europe. The only thing I could be reproached for is that I worked for the Germans until 1939, although I had no choice. I was compelled to accept my situation and remain there. I had tried to emigrate many times, but no other country would accept me. I doubt it will really come into question. But if it does, the consequences could be very grave. Here are the main concerns I have:

In the United States if one has knowledge and luck one can become a rich and completely independent man. If one works for one company or another, then one focuses only on oneself and not on high-minded goals. One has complete freedom of thought and speech. With luck, life in the United States would be much more comfortable, freer, and less dangerous, even though the people are more egotistical. If one wants to work for the betterment of mankind, then one might get involved with Christian organizations to help the persecuted, the poor, and other such groups in need. But then you would be helping specific groups of people, rather than all of mankind.

If one is an idealist, one ought to go to Russia. Of course, one can do good in the United States and all over the world too. But in Russia your value is determined by the yardstick of the state; that is why so much progress has been made there in many areas. If I were certain I would suffer no grave consequences because of my past (there would be no grudges held against me) in Russia, I would go to the United States first for a few years to further my professional experience. Then afterwards I would put myself one hundred percent in the service of Russia. Perhaps Russia will become more transparent eventually. It is possible I might be offered a choice of a dozen positions there and may be called upon to share my scientific and mining expertise with Russian engineers. With that might come the possibility of travel abroad, assuming I can win their trust. If the United States denies me entry outright now, I might opt for Russia instead and try to get to the United States later as a Russian citizen.

Another advantage Russia has over all other European countries is that its power, influence, and world position will always be more significant. It is more comfortable to live in a powerful country than in one that is subservient to other, greater powers, which may subject it to dangerous political winds and compel it to change direction against its will.

As you can see, this is a really difficult question. When we are together again, we will discuss it further. I think a steamboat ride on Lake Thun would offer us such an opportunity.

And finally, I would like to thank you for wanting to share these problems with me and help me solve them. You cannot imagine how much that means to me and what a burden you lift from my shoulders in this way. I don't want to overpraise us, but I believe that we are very well matched. All we need now is patience.

Our conception of God will gradually become more unified too. Everyone believes in something, and everyone has his or her own God. Even Stalin has his beliefs and his own picture of perfection.

About Germany: It is important for you to know that I do not want to live in Germany again under any circumstances. My hope is that if my U.S. immigration visa comes through, I might have the opportunity to become a naturalized citizen there. Otherwise, I would have to try to get to the United States on a tourist visa and once there, hand over my doctoral work to contacts at various universities. But this is all just guesswork right now.

I have an irresistible longing to tell you that you mean an awful lot to me, that I know you can make me happy, and that I will only be able to find complete happiness when I can make you happy too.

I kiss you and stroke you very tenderly,

My dear Anneli,

Your loving Boris

LETTER A47

GWATT

[Saturday] June 30, 1945

My dear Boris,

I would like to write you a quick note for your Sunday. My heart is so full, yet I find it difficult to put words together. I think my brain is too tired. Your last letter* did me good. It is comforting to know there is someone in the world who wishes you well. I find it wonderful that you are so cheerful now. Go ahead and keep being that way, good things will come of it. Also, if you want to give those two women a few Russian lessons, I would not object. You would probably enjoy it too, as it is creative work.

Boris, you should not be dissatisfied with yourself because you cannot use your God-given gifts fully right now. You lived through a difficult period and did not willingly put on those chains. They were laid upon you to purify and deepen your faith. Wear them thankfully while keeping your eye on your goal of serving people and humanity. Work toward it at every possible opportunity.

A few days ago, I saw a man on the street. He was wearing a stocking cap with a red star and a golden sickle. I thought to myself, "Aha, he looks like a Soviet citizen!" The man did not give me a bad impression. Afterwards, I suddenly thought, "If only Boris would never have to regret that he could not return to Russia!"

You may have also read that a commission (which included some Russians) came to Switzerland to study the plight of mishandled Russian citizens. Could this perhaps bring you some opportunities?

Now I need to tell you a few other things. I came back once again to the novella by C.F. Meyer (he is one of Switzerland's most important authors) entitled *The Saint*. It is the story of Thomas Becket. You can imagine how I plunged into this book. It is terribly interesting, and when I am finished with it, I will tell you all about it. I have intentionally avoided reading the other book about Henry VIII because I don't want to just read through it, I want to really understand it. But I am not quite up to it right now. That is why I started reading this novella, which seems a bit lighter.

In the next few months, I will have to fulfill a three-week assignment for the National Service,[129] but at this point I don't know the exact date. I look forward to it as a break from my current routine. The daily drill here is so repetitive, I want to get out of Gwatt and out of school for a while.

I will say goodnight now because I am very tired. I wish you a pleasant Sunday. Relax, go outside in the sun for a bit, dear. I kiss you very gently, your eyes, your cheeks, and your mouth.

My Bobussja,

Your Anneli

---

[129] All Swiss youth, both boys and girls, were required to complete a few weeks of *Landdienst* (national agricultural service) during World War II. See Franziska Wick, "Landdienst: A Swiss Tradition," *Little Zurich Kitchen*, 2016, https://www.littlezurichkitchen.ch/landdienst/.

LETTER A48[130]

GWATT

[Sunday] July 15, 1945

Good evening, my dear Boris,

I tried to write during the day, but it was so terribly hot, I just couldn't concentrate. Good that the lake is so close by, it kept things a bit cooler.

I thank you for your letter and the two art postcards. Here are my thoughts about them. I found the woman's head excellent; it has something so clean about it, with slightly defiant, but sincere eyes. It is interesting to compare it with the head of the *Mona Lisa*. I don't know, but I increasingly find the latter just a bit demonic.

On first impression, I find the figures in Michelangelo's *Creation* good too. I think Adam and Eve are especially wonderful. But I have trouble delving into it deeply, as I am put off by every depiction of God. I also don't understand why people talk about God as they would a person. As I discovered this past winter, a sea of errors and superstition is hidden behind such representations.

I am also of the opinion that shortsightedness is what keeps people from knowing God; that is, their self-love makes them blind. If only your ideal, that all people might become one with creation and treat each other like brothers, could be realized! But I must say that the world looks dreadful to me right now. On a small scale, life seems to be nothing but conflict and discord, and on a large scale, it seems narrow and full of worry. When I hear about the awful turmoil and complicated circumstances all around us, I fear things will never improve, and that a life under those conditions is not worth living.

---

130 The following text (John 14:6) written by Anna at a later date appears at the top of this letter: "Christ said, 'I am the way, and the truth, and the life; no one comes to the Father, but through me.'" N.B. This letter reveals a real breakthrough in Anna's thinking on Christianity, the path to which she describes as "a new little door."

Imagine for a moment, if the kingdom of God were to break into this world, into mine and yours, do you think all your difficulties would suddenly disappear? I don't believe it. While people still live on this earth, natural people, there will always be conflict.

But I believe if equality is attained, these conflicts will no longer be unbridgeable. You said in one of your last letters that Christ was faithful and obedient until the end. That showed me a new little door, and now I see it very clearly: Truth resides *in the world of the spirit.* Truth is *the* way, and the world must ultimately go the way of truth, whether it wants to or not. Truth stands *rock solid*; it is unshakeable. Christ is the embodiment of this truth. Maybe, as you say, Christ was the first person to fully recognize it. The prophets made a start. That is why Christ said: "*I am the way, and the truth.*" And that is why Christ's resurrection was inevitable. Whether it was a spiritual or physical resurrection is not so important. Truth is the godly principle, and it is as permanent and strong as any of nature's laws, but one cannot grasp it by seeing it, but only with one's spirit. Isn't it true you are convinced the creative spirit (love) will be victorious in the end? That is why we can go confidently forward into the future. We are only two little specks of dust within a huge cycle. If our lives were full of misfortune and pain, that, too, would be part of creation within the realm of God.

In taking this new view of Christ today I have unexpectedly gotten closer to understanding a lot of things. How strange! I am happy because the two of us are working through these issues together. Also, I would be so glad if you could come to Gwatt soon. It has been so long since we last saw each other, and I still feel so far away from you sometimes. Come soon, dear. I have been chattering a long time now; it is already midnight, and I must go to sleep. I hope you had a good Sunday. I will respond to the second half of your letter in my next letter.

A quick tender kiss for you, my Bobussja,

Your Anneli

LETTER B35

[Monday] July 16, 1945

My dear Anneli,

On Saturday and Sunday afternoon it was horribly hot, so I went swimming. Today we are getting a fearsome rainstorm.

I got two letters from you today[131] and I thank you for them, and for the flowers and the pears too.

Anneli, I must see you again very soon. It seems like all the uncertainties about our future are spinning around me today and I am feeling particularly frazzled. My situation is frustrating. There is no one here with whom I can discuss my problems. I had placed great hopes in Prof. Freudenberg, particularly after I heard him lecture in Bern. But I was disappointed when I went to see him, even though it was certainly my own fault. But perhaps I idealized him too much.

I am happy your apprenticeship is finally coming to an end, slowly but surely. Your work sounds quite demanding, so in the end you will value your achievement even more. Anyone can learn if they have enthusiasm, but with little enthusiasm it becomes much more difficult.

My semester is almost over. Up until Saturday I worked very hard. Today I slept in late. I wonder if the weather or the upcoming trip is to blame.

I do not want to write much today, as my thoughts are very disorganized. Besides that, I need to leave soon and will likely not get back until after 9 p.m., well past my usual bedtime! Please don't be upset about this short letter.

---

131 One of the two letters is probably Letter A48, which appears above. The other letter has been lost.

I would just like to add that your thoughts about religion and your world viewpoint are continually getting closer to mine. They may soon be quite similar. That is desirable for us, despite the other differences that must remain (or our life together might become boring!).

I wish you a very good day. I miss you terribly and kiss you tenderly.

My Anneli,

Your Boris

LETTER B36

[Wednesday] July 25, 1945
7:30 p.m.

My dear Anneli,

I thank you so very much for your letter.* I received all the enclosures. I will take the money you offer on the assumption that we will both make use of it the next time we meet. But promise me one thing: The next time you are short on funds, write me immediately. I always keep Fr. 200[132] in reserve for emergencies. In any case, I thank you for this gift. It reveals the depth of your love, as an offering of money is a sacrifice for us both.

Today I happened to meet a man from Marseille who has no blood relatives in the U.S., but despite that he will be receiving his visa in two weeks and will be hired there as a scientist. He remarked that it is crazy how difficult the authorities make it to immigrate. He also said that starting in mid-July all decisions will be based on affidavits (from guarantors in the U.S.) dependent on local consuls. That means it will be like it was before the war, and that is much better for me, as I can mobilize all my connections and friends to help me. Assuming this, all my supporting documents should be at the American consulate in Zurich within two to four months. I am glad some opportunities are at hand and that several people are working on my behalf. I have guarantors and even distant relatives in the United States. The cost of my trip will be covered either by Switzerland or by the United States. So, everything really should work out.

I just need to be patient and not make any sudden, ill-considered moves. European countries are a lot closer, and if I decide to stay in Europe, there would be no rush. But I do not want to miss any good opportunities. Right now, Germany may even be worth considering, even though it is under allied control. I imagine if I were to join the

---

132 Equal to about $50 in 1945

allied effort in Germany and apply for U.S. immigration there, I could get U.S. citizenship eventually.

Here is another idea: If everything goes wrong, I could try to get permission from Switzerland to go to Belgium and France and dig up my documents which are still buried there.[133] This would guarantee my return trip to Switzerland. It might also give me the opportunity to put everything in order. The Swiss committee for refugees would certainly provide me with travel money. Also, this way I would have a chance to communicate with the Russian legation.

Anneli, my dearest, how I would like to emphatically declare my love for you, but I am holding back because you have asked me to be less emotional. But at least I don't feel that I am all alone anymore. I feel as if I really do have you. You help me more than you know. I am sure that once we are together for good it will be easier to achieve balance and satisfaction, and to create joy in our lives. We will have everything we need to be happy.

In hope of that future, I embrace and kiss you tenderly and firmly.

My dear Anneli,

Your Bobussja

---

133 It is unknown which documents Boris is referring to here, or whether he ever went back and retrieved them. In 1940, while living in Belgium, he had agreed to work as a coal miner which allowed him to receive official identity papers from the Belgian government. He may have buried them there before his hurried departure for France when Germany invaded in May of 1940. He entered France a few days later, just as the French government was falling to the Germans. He eventually obtained false papers from the French Resistance and was even able to get official identification papers from the German-controlled regime, but only by using a false name. Three sets of his false French identification papers survive, but it is unknown whether any of them were buried in France (see *Lenin, Hitler, and Me*, pp.183-185). See also Letter B24.

LETTER A49[134]

GWATT

[Wednesday] August 1, 1945

My dear Boris,

It is too bad that you were not able to stay here an extra day. I had the whole day free. In the early morning I worked on English vocabulary which I enjoy a lot. I think if I worked hard, I could pick up English quickly, as I really like the language an awful lot.

In the afternoon I sat in on a Bible study class and we discussed the prophet Jonah. This book shows that the Jews had no knowledge of God's forgiving love yet. Only through Christ did it become known.

Again, the question surfaced whether God's voice comes from without or within. As you know, the theological community here refutes the idea that faith is dependent on an inner voice with the justification that psychologists have discovered that these inner voices (i.e., the subconscious) may vary in accordance with the disposition or secret desires of the individual. Truly, I also find that if one relies too heavily on one's emotions it could well lead to a frustrating muddle. As for myself, I believe that both are necessary: an outside trigger followed by inner development. From this, a new realization is born: If one is led toward love, is that not the voice of God?

They also discussed whether Christianity is tolerant or intolerant. Consider Christ's words: "I am the way, the truth, and the life. No one can come to the Father except through me." Taking this to an extreme, we can see the many mistakes the Church has made throughout its history: "If you don't want to be my brother, I will crush your skull."

Do we now agree on this point, Boris? You said one should not be too narrow in one's interpretation of Christianity. But we also agree that it needs to be supported by a strong framework. That is likely why God is so often personified in the Bible.

---

134 From this letter we learn that Boris visited Anna in Gwatt on Sunday, July 29.

This afternoon I had visitors. Dr. Fraenkel brought a cake and I made tea and we invited Dr. Roniger from Basel and Miss Voellung to join us. The tea and cake were good, otherwise it was not so interesting.

Now to your letter.* I enjoyed last Sunday much more than the previous Sunday, despite the little irritations, which didn't bother me at all in the end. It is exactly moments like these that clearly show how deep and serious our relationship has become. If we are to spend our lives together, we will surely experience some clashes and misunderstandings until we have worn down each other's little horns. You must realize that you are a forty-year-old bachelor and that I have a very stubborn nature; it will not be easy for us to live together.

Dearest, you need not be overly thankful toward me. It goes without saying that I will always give you as much as I can, just as you do for me. You know I treasure your honey so much because it was you who gave it to me, and because I know how much you enjoy eating it yourself.

Last Sunday I was mostly angry with myself, mainly because I was jealous again (about the swimming pool and Mrs. von Schoulz). But I know that jealousy only destroys and creates pain for us both. It keeps you from being open with me and trusting me completely when you happen to find another woman attractive. Please don't think badly of me; I am really going to try to become more sensible about this.

Boris, I think about you a lot. Your character is becoming more strongly defined in my eyes. I understand better and better how you view things, and the better I understand you, the more I can help you. I would so like to help you with all my strength, and not just by stroking you, rather with a serious word or a helpful criticism at the right moment. I only want what is best for you; I do not want to nag you. But I am young and still have a lot to learn, so excuse me if I sometimes make mistakes.

You complain that you have lost your sense of security because of the difficult years you had since 1939. But think this over carefully: Wasn't that sense of security you had when you thought nothing could happen to you really a fallacy? You must learn from that experience that bad things can happen in any situation. No matter how many precautions you take or how much willpower you have, one cannot escape the will of God or fate.

Boris, you must wake up now. You must build again, not upon yourself, but upon the security of truth (the resurrection of Christ), or the godly principle, more succinctly, on the victory of love. You must become stronger and more decisive. You are a good, decent man, and for that reason you should freely be who you are and leave your timidity behind. Please understand that I am not reproaching you for being timid, as I can see and understand your whole situation firsthand. But trust in God completely. We know he is not just fantasy, but that he lives. Do not become mired in doubt concerning your future, but strive to move forward in a creative direction, always doing what you can. God can ask no more of you. You must learn to be patient and to perfect and strengthen yourself spiritually.

I hope your work is going smoothly again. When you see that things are moving forward, you will have more courage.

I would like to come back to our discussion about Russia. I don't see why you feel you must return to Russia if you are a pure idealist. No nationalistic country understands or appreciates purely creative work. You want to work for the benefit of mankind, not for the benefit of a single nationalist power. Russia is and remains a big question mark in that one cannot really tell whether its politics and policies will benefit or harm its people. In any case, its acts of power are not ethical, and neither is its propaganda. Boris, you taught me that life must be protected above all else. If you are against Christians who kill people because they would not convert to Christianity, how can you now support Stalin who kills people for political reasons? Where does he get the right do this? He is only a human being.[135]

I am enclosing an article about Pablo Casals so you can learn a little about him. It is worth reading, as Casals is one of the greatest

---

135 After Anna voices her strong misgivings about Russia in this letter, the idea of going there is dropped entirely.

musicians of our time. I hope one day we might be able to hear him play. Please send the article back to me; I would like to keep it in my music scrapbook. I am also enclosing the art postcard so you can exchange it.

I hope you understand what I have written here, and I hope you have found renewed courage. My free day is over now; I am going to sleep. I was so shaken up during the August celebration[136] that I am feeling a bit down, so that is why I am going right to bed. I kiss you very sweetly and tenderly, dear Boris, and I look forward to your next letter and even more to our next meeting.

Your Anneli

---

136 August 1 is Switzerland's national holiday.

LETTER A50[137]

WINTERTHUR

[Tuesday] August 21, 1945

My dear Boris,

Those were beautiful days we spent together in Weggis, weren't they? I thank you from the bottom of my heart for all the love and tenderness you showed me. Because you are so good to me, it is a doubly heavy burden for me to bear when I get irritable and intolerant toward you so easily.

I just received your letter.* The effect of it was like a sunbeam. I would so much like to throw out all the bad things in me and put down my heavy burden, but I don't know where to find the strength.

Dear, you did well by deciding to go to Geneva Monday; a lot of things became clearer as a result. Things are moving forward, Boris.

How is it that you have connections to the American consulate in Zurich?!

I read an announcement yesterday that the Americans are seeking Swiss people to go to Germany. I wanted to send you the article today. I believe the offer might apply to you too. The salaries they are offering are not at all bad. Maybe it would be easier to take this route to the United States, rather than a direct one?

My thoughts are with you, and I wonder how things will turn out for you. Please write to me soon. Here in Winterthur everything is quite nice. You know, I used to be the center of attention in my family; now I am merely tolerated, and that only because I happen to be here. This is probably partly my fault because I bear too little love for my parents.

About the chocolate that accompanied the pears, everything was alright; I brought them inside. I wish you much success this week and that both you and the mine can profit from it.

---

137 Three weeks have passed since Anna's last letter. She writes of a vacation she and Boris have taken together in Weggis, a small scenic town on Lake Lucerne. She is writing from Winterthur, so she is visiting her parents during her summer break from school.

Now I kiss you very tenderly,

My Bobussja,

Your Anneli

Anna and Boris walking in Weggis (Summer 1945)

LETTER B37

August 31, 1945
8 p.m.

My dear Anneli,

I arrived at the mine at 6 p.m. and then washed up and ate dinner. Now I am sitting by the window looking at Mont Blanc, which is less than forty kilometers away. It has just turned part pink-purple and part blue-white, and I feel totally with you in my thoughts. I was so sorry that I could not find the time to write you a few reasonable words during the mad rush of these past few days. But I thought of you continually and am anxious to know how you are doing. National Service will probably be a nice change for you, but I worry you will over-exhaust yourself and not get good food. But at least it will all be over in two weeks.

When I came up here today, I was surprised to find no letter from you, but I expect that is because you don't have my exact address. Also, you wrote out your address so unclearly that I am not sure you received my letters.

My address here is:

Boris Kochanowsky, Mining Engineer
Dorénaz Anthracite Mine
La Meronnaz, Dorénaz
Valais

Please let me know if I can reach you by telephone. My telephone number here is 6.58.59.

And now goodnight.

P.S. I would be grateful if you could correct a letter for me that will go to Dr. Oppenheim in Geneva.

Sunday, September 2, 1945

My dear Anneli,

This is the third letter I have written you, yet I have not received a single letter from you. Please write me as soon as possible, as I am very concerned about you.

Last night I finally got enough sleep, though I still feel sleepy today. Tomorrow the work will begin.

It is a gorgeous day today. Two years ago, I was in Chamonix, just fifty kilometers[138] from here.

I wonder when we will see each other again.

In Zurich I did not buy myself a Klepper coat,[139] as the merchant I spoke with felt they were of very poor quality. All he had were leftover war supplies. I will probably buy myself a gabardine coat in one or two months. My old one has been washed and mended, so it still looks presentable.

I wish you a good day and kiss you tenderly,

My Anneli,

Your Boris

---

138 About thirty miles
139 A kind of lightweight raincoat used extensively by the German military

LETTER B38

[Tuesday] September 4, 1945

My dear Anneli,

At last, I received your dear letter* and package. I was relieved to receive them, as I had not heard from you for so long. Thank you for the cup, the cake, the flowers, and the dictionary. If possible, please send me flowers once a week, as there aren't any around here at all. This is a very comfortless, lonely place, especially when there is no work to do. There are only loud mountain folk and two old ladies in the cantina. Yet the work itself is very engaging because I have been given an interesting assignment: to rationalize the mine, in other words, to reorganize the mine sensibly. I must make sure the right work and extraction methods are being used and try to reduce production costs while increasing actual production. I hope to have some success.

A whole year has gone by since we met, and an awful lot has happened. I wonder how things will stand for us a year from now. We should celebrate our first-year anniversary when we next meet. I would be in favor of taking a trip to Zermatt[140] in three weeks. Fall is really the most beautiful time to visit the mountains. We can meet in Lausanne later. If I need to stay in Valais much longer, maybe we should celebrate our anniversary in Lausanne?

In today's newspaper I read an announcement put out by the American Legation in Bern that all laws concerning the possible employment of Swiss citizens in Germany are invalid, as the bureau that handles this has not yet been established. It will only be set up in the coming weeks when they are able to find appropriate personnel for this department. So, I guess I have not yet missed this opportunity, although I feared I had.

I can easily imagine that your National Service work is very taxing, but fortunately it is not as hot now as it would have been in

---
140 The location of the famous Matterhorn

mid-summer. Can you use the sunglasses I sent you? I bought them for you because I knew you would be working in the fields. Later we will buy you a more attractive pair. It is good that you now have the chance to become acquainted with simple country folk. One should experience the world from all sides.

It is beautiful up here in the mountains; the air is wonderful and so is the light.

I have a big room and the food is plentiful, and so I am well taken care of. We get the following monthly rations:

200 grams [about 1 cup] of sugar
600 grams [about 20 ounces] of jam
2,000 grams [more than 4 pounds] of cheese
900 grams [2 pounds] of fat
350 grams [12 ounces] of butter
6,400 grams [14 pounds] of meat & sausage
520 grams [about 18 ounces] per day of bread

How are your meals? Until now I have been over-indulging. From now on I will try to eat more sensibly. While I am here, I will surely gain weight, as I have good food, good sleep, and good air, and climbing around all day in the mine is good exercise.

I will close my letter now. I wish you all the best and kiss you very tenderly.

My Anneli,

Your Bobussja

P.S. Did I by chance leave my English textbook with you in Gwatt? I can't find it anymore!

LETTER A51[141]

Gwatt

[Wednesday] October 3, 1945

My dear Boris,

I want to write you another short letter so that you will receive it this week. As I was typing a letter for you, I realized that I would need to practice a lot more to get really good at typing.

Dear, I would like to get closer to you, to sneak right inside you, not to discover your secrets, but to see your heart better and get to know it as well as my own. You don't know how sorry I feel when I am mean to you. It lies like a millstone around my neck when I think about my reckless, surging character burning through me. Only one thing comforts me: that you love me, and forgive me, and want to help me do better.

I think all human love is permeated by a recurring tendency to distance oneself from God (God's love) due to human frailty. The opposite of that is what Jesus calls doing penance. This act of doing penance is one of the most productive things a human being can do.

You shouldn't have any concerns about money, Boris. I will not set my heart on it. I am standing in the light of truth, and this truth says that man, and only man, is the most important thing on earth.

You laughed at me last Sunday when I told you that I would like to serve in a small way. You shouldn't laugh. I will give you my reasons: I would like to see as much of the world as possible and get a broad overview unencumbered by details. But I am not the kind of person who can carry a large burden for the sake of mankind. Why should I waste my time? Wouldn't it be better for me to be a good wife to you, a good mother to our children, and try to help poor people a little? I would like to try to bring joy where I can, rather than expend

---

141 A month has passed, and some intervening correspondence has been lost. From this letter we learn that Anna and Boris spent the previous weekend together.

all my energy trying to do something that is too overwhelming for me to manage, wearing myself out while neglecting everything else.

Dearest, I am sorry I have not been more confiding lately. But you are a bit to blame for it too, through your silence. But I should have known I could rely on you. Where there is no trust, no love can grow.

We should write to each other more. Before you go to sleep try to briefly tell me your thoughts and what is in your heart. I will try to do the same. It doesn't have to be long, but this will increase and encourage our contact.

I will say goodnight now. Write to me soon. I eagerly await your letters.

Take a loving little kiss from me. I wish you much courage and success in your work.

My Bobussja,

Your Anneli

LETTER A52

[Thursday] October 4, 1945
Evening

My dear Boris,

I'd like to give you a quick goodnight kiss. Today it really hit me that the drone of everyday life dulls the senses. What a battle it is for the spirit to free itself from the prison of details and rise above it to the heights of the ideal. But I must remember what you said to my mother: "A life without cares? There is no life without struggle!" I must also think of what Jesus said: "I have not come to bring you peace, but rather the sword."[142] By this he is referring to this very fight. I think of Beethoven too, who became so great through struggle. So, now I will give you another little kiss and go to bed.

[Sunday] October 7, 1945

Dear,

It is already Sunday evening. I had wanted to do a lot of work today, and yet I have done nothing. A colleague of mine was on vacation and came to visit me. We played some piano music for four hands, we sang, we listened to recordings, and later we went to church together. Then the day was over. But I feel I have profited from our time together. I realized that if one really wants to play the piano well, one must play completely, with one's whole being, not just with the hands and the ears, but with the heart and by simply being totally aware. Then all the difficulties resolve themselves. My courage is renewed. This girl told me I have talent and that I should take more lessons. You know, I felt completely present today with

---

142 Matthew 10:34

her. It wasn't like when you and I play together, because then I am always afraid you will get bored.

I am a little uneasy because you didn't call today. I hope I will hear from you tomorrow.

The letter to the professor is clear and I will type it as soon as possible. You know that I work for you gladly, but it does take me a long time.

I am happy you have taken on a second mining job because the greater and more current your work experience, the easier it will be for you later.

Now I will give you a little kiss and send you my heartfelt greetings,

My Bobusschen!

Your Anneli

LETTER A53

[Saturday] October 20, 1945

My dear Boris,

It is already late, but I want to add a few words to the little package I am sending you.

I am feeling quite stable emotionally and have suddenly become so awake that I can see things much more clearly and freshly now. In the last couple of days, I have been thinking about us, about Christianity, and about the world, and I am grateful for the sobriety I have suddenly found within myself to do this. I know you are a bit afraid of this sobriety, but you needn't be because it comes out of my love for you.

I have thought over whether our two characters are well-suited enough for us to maintain and continue our mutual love. Something became very clear to me in thinking this over: It all depends on our mutual understanding. "Understanding everything means forgiving everything."[143] This is the basis upon which one can build a lasting relationship. It is in this way we will be able to overcome all the difficulties that naturally arise between two people. Is it not true, Boris, that a few aspects of our separate views on Christianity still need to be ironed out between us?

I need to stop now, or I will fall asleep. So, good night dear. Here is a long--------------kiss from me.

---

143 *"Alles verstehen heisst alles verzeihen."* Madame Anne Louise Germaine de Staël (1766-1817) was a French writer and political theorist. See also Letter A57.

[Sunday, October 21, 1945]

Good day my Boris,

Is there any way you could manage to send me more letters? I would really like to take part in your life, but I can't if you hardly ever write to me.

I have thought over this clothing refund opportunity in Belgium.[144] It really seems like a questionable thing. Of course, it is easy to say that Germany was the cause of this loss. But the most you could get would be replacement costs. If I were you, I would not dwell on this or be upset about it. The main thing is that you were rescued. Material things can be replaced.

Take another long...............kiss from me.

My Bobussja,

Your Anneli

---

144 Apparently Anna and Boris had discussed some opportunity Boris might have to receive reparations from Germany for property (particularly clothing) that Boris lost when the Germans invaded Belgium.

LETTER A54

Gwatt

[Thursday] November 1, 1945

My dear Boris,

I got your package and I thank you very much for it. It is very dear of you to take care of me so faithfully. The cheese is really first-rate, even Dr. Strupp thought so, even though he is not much for cheese in general.

I got another package from you that really surprised me! The *Lebkuchen*[145] is so beautiful and wonderful that I could not bear to take even one bite of it. For all this lavish attention you will get a particularly long, loving kiss from me. Yesterday I was able to purchase a space heater for my room and I am very happy with it and very thankful to you for it. I paid exactly Fr. 51.65,[146] and so you see that the money you gave me sufficed. The space heater has 1,200 watts and warms up my room wonderfully. I am feeling much better again, and this afternoon I will go to work.

It would be lovely if we could see each other somewhere on Sunday; we would have a lot to talk about. I will await your call on Friday evening. Until then take a tender greeting and kiss from me, and again my thanks for all the loving things you do for me.

My Bobussja,

Your Anneli

---

145 A traditional kind of gingerbread which is often decorated
146 Equal to about $12 in 1945

LETTER A55

[Tuesday] November 6, 1945

My dear Boris,

I hope you arrived well in Meronnaz and found everything in order. One thing that really pleases me about you is how hard you can focus on your work, and how, after such a long disruption to your career, you can be so industrious. On the other hand, I find it a shame how isolated and one-sided your life has become, such that you can no longer pursue your interest in helping the rest of the world. I know you will suffer under these circumstances eventually. It might be a good idea for you to buy yourself a radio. Try to take some time off as soon as you can, you need a few days' rest.

Today I thought a bit more about our discussion concerning the woman who murdered the German officer. It is a difficult case, but I cannot condemn this woman for her deed. If I try to look at it realistically, it is just horrible that this simple, ordinary woman could have the strength to do it simply out of desperation. Imagine, she is part of an oppressed population and there, in front of her, stands one of her husband's murderers who wants her love (that is, her friendship and kind words). She has pity for the boy, but he murdered her husband! Just think how you would react if you were confronted with my murderer, a murderer who holds you captive. If she were good to him, her peers would consider her a traitor or collaborator. No, I find her deed was done out of desperation. But she is just a link in the chain of activism that has made Norway so famous in the last few years, and for which we have the greatest respect, the underground resistance.

Boris, you yourself know that war forces men to alter their standards, but even then, it is possible to be Christ-like. I just cannot accept a Christianity that calls on us all to become pious brothers who say "yes" and "Amen" to everything and endure all kinds of abuse without defending ourselves. Christianity grants us the freedom to love unconditionally. Yet all people are different, so they must have the freedom to love differently too. Gotthelf said the following: "Christ with his symbol [the cross] does not want to hover above our heads, rather he wishes to reside inside each of us. Every heart should be his cradle. He is always the same Savior, and yet he also desires to be each person's own, special Savior, just as each person is a unique, special sinner."[147] Christ would make humans out of us, not angels.

I must end this letter as it is already quite late. I enclose the meat and bread coupons I was able to exchange. Take a tender greeting and kiss from me.

My Bobussja,

Your Anneli

---

147 Jeremias Gotthelf, *Erlebnisse eines Schuldenbauers* (Berlin: Julius Springer Verlag, 1853), p. 121

LETTER B39

[Monday] November 19, 1945

My dear heart!

I ate some of the fruit you sent while I read your letter.* I thank you for both most heartily. You edited the letter to Grassmück[148] very well. I think you will be a wonderful secretary. In time you will realize how important your contribution will be to our future. You already know you will be a good wife.

As I told you on the telephone, I received a telegram from Mr. Grassmück. He writes, "Glad I found you. Please cable me if interested in mining position in Argentina or need money, await airmail." He also paid in advance for a thirty-word reply. I wrote back to him: "Very thankful for your trouble. I am interested in the position in Argentine mine. Please share with me the requirements, possibilities, and naturalization. I do not need money."

Today I received a letter from the American Friends Service Committee (an American Quaker organization in Geneva). They write they have received a report [about me] from the Tolstoy Foundation and that they were able to find me a guarantor in the U.S. who can assist me financially. They asked how I plan to pay for my ticket. I wonder why they asked this, as it should be covered by the Swiss refugee committee. But if I work for two more months, I should be able to pay for it myself. So, what do you say to this?

Maybe we should commence high-level negotiations?! As seats on steamships bound for the U.S. are booked up six to eight months in advance, we still have plenty of time to prepare for the journey. Yet surely there will be even more steamships going in the coming months, and probably also airplanes, so one could arrange to travel

---

148 Gerhard Grassmück, a fellow mining engineer, was an old school comrade from his Freiberg days, 1923-1929. (See *Lenin, Hitler, and Me,* pp. 77-78, 81, 209, 216, 221.) This letter to Grassmück was not just a friendly correspondence, but an application for a job in Argentina, so Boris felt the need for Anna's editing.

with a delay of only three or four months. I am sure we can get your visa in that amount of time. I would really like you to finish your schooling first, however. I doubt we will be able to leave before May.

I hope to visit you at the end of this week. First, it is very important that we speak about all this in person, and secondly, I feel I really need to take some time off to relax. All my work is going very well, so I can easily take a couple of days off. I hope this time our plans will succeed. I am eagerly looking forward to it. I will set aside at least four to six days, as I would also like to visit Lausanne, Zurich, and maybe Lugano. I already have my travel authorization in hand.

I am sure this news will excite you, but you must try to digest it well (your expression!) before my arrival. I believe naturalization in the U.S. or in Argentina will not be a problem. After a five-year residence one can become an American citizen.

By the way, according to the new laws, naturalization in France is quite easy, as you can see from the enclosed brochure. But I doubt France will come into question for me right now.

So, my little dear heart, everything has come to pass as we planned. The end of the war, the solution to our immigration problems and naturalization, all will be resolved without much effort on our part. Only patience and determination are necessary.

We will speak about all these possibilities in person. Until then, patience! I will go to bed now; it is very late. I wish you a good night.

With a kiss,

My Anneli,

Your Bobussja

LETTER B40

Hotel Victoria
In front of the Trient Gorge
Vernayaz (Valais)
Fam. E. Bochatay-Carraux, propr.

[Wednesday] November 28, 1945
9:30 p.m.

My dear little heart,

I am back in Valais in Vernayaz,[149] where I am staying the night. Tomorrow morning at 7 a.m. the ascent will begin. I am not looking forward to it, as it is physically strenuous and if one always takes the same route, it is also quite boring. But there is nothing to be done about it; it is a necessary evil.

I thought again about our last meeting. I think our love is continually becoming more tender, more beautiful, and more refined. Don't you agree? I was especially pleased with how much your piano playing has improved. I think here, too, your love for me is the cause of it. You make the extra effort on my account. I am convinced that in the same way, out of love for me, you will be able to do much more. But I, too, do a lot of things for you. I hope we will continue to influence each other in a positive way both inwardly and outwardly.

I think time is passing quickly, and it brings us ever closer to each other. But when will that moment arrive when we may be together forever?

I sent some letters off to Argentina today via airmail. I am anxiously awaiting word.

I plan to do everything I can in the mine in the coming weeks without any thought of the bonus I was promised (which I doubt I will get anyway).

---

149 A village close to Dorenaz, where Boris has been working. He was living in a mining camp up in the mountains. One had to climb to the camp on foot from the village in the valley below.

I enclose Fr. 20[150] so you won't have to use any of your money when you mail me packages. But please do not send me any more with treats. I just gobble them up all at once. It would be best to send me a pound of nuts, a banana, a pear, and two apples. Try to send me a package on Friday or Saturday, so that I will get it on Sunday.

And finally, I would like to thank you for all you do for me. You are a dear person. Every time we meet, I feel renewed and armed with new energy and courage. Your tenderness does my soul good, but I hope I mean as much to you and that I help dispel your loneliness. I would do more if I could.

Tomorrow the work begins. Please don't be angry if my letters are infrequent. I will try to write as often as I can.

Now I kiss you very, very tenderly,

My Anneli,

Your Boris

---

150 About $5 in 1945

LETTER B41

[Saturday] December 1, 1945

My dear heart,

I received an airmail letter yesterday from Grassmück. He says:

"Please send me an account of your plans by airmail and let me know how I can be of help to you. I can find you a suitable mining position in Argentina at any time and you would be, of course, my guest until you can learn the language and get used to the new living situation here. The only difficulty you will encounter is actually getting here, as this country is hermetically sealed off to immigrants, but for you I expect it will not be such a big problem because your case will be evaluated by higher authorities. When you are finally here, I am sure you will be able to begin a new life under very favorable circumstances. Argentina is a very beautiful, vibrant, and hospitable country, offering unrestricted possibilities in the mining industry (of which my company is taking the lead, along with others). It would be of great satisfaction to me to help you create a secure life here in the coming months. Please share with me your exact personal information, passport number, etc. assuming you are on board with the idea of coming to Argentina." He continues, saying that he is now an Argentine citizen and believes he won't leave the country, as he feels a strong debt of gratitude toward it and admires its beauties.[151]

So, what do you say to that? I have decided that even if I were to get a U.S. visa now, I would still go to Argentina first. I am eager to go, not only because of the prospect of a tempting job offer, but also because it will force me to learn another language.

It seems that until I learn Spanish, I will not be able to work and would have to remain Grassmück's guest. For that reason, I think it would be best for me to travel there as soon as possible. If all goes well, my Spanish will be in good shape in a couple of months. Today

---

151 Grassmück eventually moved to Canada with his wife and daughter.

I will write to Bern to ask that my Nansen passport[152] be reissued. I must prove that I had one before, so I will probably have to send an inquiry to Belgium where my last Nansen passport was issued.

I will send a telegram to Grassmück to see if my immigration application can be accelerated. Grassmück has always been a very dynamic individual, even when I knew him in Germany. I believe he will see that I get all the necessary paperwork within a month.

In the newspaper I read that in December Soviet ships will be departing for South America four times as often as they did in November. Surely in January and February even more will go. Besides that, far fewer people travel to South American than to North America. So, I think I will certainly be able to get a boat ticket for a February departure easily. Today I wrote to Geneva asking whether my travel expenses can be covered by the Swiss refugee committee. I hope to spend my last month with you in Gwatt.

From the above it appears that the plan is for me to depart alone. But the final decision still rests with *both* of us. I am suggesting this plan because I would like you to finish your schooling and to have a chance to relax a little afterwards. That means you would have to wait until July to travel. Also, it would be a bit rude to ask Grassmück to put up two guests, instead of one.

If I can be ready to begin my job in two months, that is if I could at least have command of the technical language by then, I could start earning money. Surely, I will be able to assist Grassmück with his work even sooner.

Now I will turn to your letter.* You write, "Of course there will be crises, tests, and pain in our marriage, but we want to learn from those things too, as we know that through them our souls will be refined and deepened." I disagree, I don't believe that we will have any

---

152 Nansen passports, first issued to stateless refugees by the League of Nations, were internationally recognized refugee travel documents from 1922 to 1938. They were named after their promoter, the statesman and polar explorer Fridtjof Nansen. By 1945, Nansen passports were no longer being issued, so Boris is using outdated terminology, but other forms of travel documents for refugees were obtainable by then.

crises or pain in our marriage. I cannot imagine it. We are both much too kind and dear to cause each other any pain. I doubt I could hold out for more than a couple of minutes before I would try to soothe you, and neither would you. If you are impatient and irritable for a half an hour, like you were in Weggis and earlier in Gwatt, then I will have to deal with those "crises" and patiently wait until the clouds pass and the sun shines again. As you have much sunshine in your heart, I know I will never have to wait long.

The only thing that might upset me is if you slack off in learning the skills you will need, particularly studying new languages. But at present you speak German and French much better than I do. You seem to have a talent for languages and much more time to devote to learning them than I, so you will undoubtedly speak Spanish and English much better than I as well. And because you are still so young, you can comfortably sit on the school bench and study up on all the subjects you neglected in your youth. It is my dearest wish that you grow and develop and learn much, including languages, typing, piano, singing, dancing, how to drive a car and more. Perhaps, in a year or so, we will take an auto tour of South and North America and with luck I will be able to introduce my discoveries to important people in the United States. But even if we stay conservative in our expectations, we will hardly have a bad time of it, as Grassmück suggests. One can really rely on him.

I am still enjoying my work here very much, but the atmosphere is souring on me. As far as money goes, the job doesn't really pay well enough to make it worthwhile for me to stay much longer. What keeps me here is not the bonus I was promised, but my gratitude toward Switzerland and its hospitality. There are many small-minded, hateful people here, but they do not bother me personally. But the overall atmosphere is poisoned by their nasty gossip. I will lose both of my unpaid trainees in the next few days. Together they cost the mine Fr. 400,[153] while the poorly paid workmen get Fr. 450 a month. As I can no longer do any in-depth research here [without the help of

---

153 Less than $100 in 1945

the two trainees] and must run the mine based on estimation only, I will not be able to bring it up to the highest modern standards. That means a loss of Fr. 100,000 a year, all because, as some of the workers here would have you believe, the two trainees are eating too much! I find it childish. But despite this unpleasantness, I will not lose my courage and I will try to do my best. It is always best not to focus exclusively on your own advantage or comfort, but to handle the situation by following your wisdom and conscience.

It has gotten late, so I will end here. I would like to stress again that the final decision about how we get to Argentina rests with you. So, think everything over carefully. I agree that you view everything too bleakly. But maybe that is because you are still so young and do not know the world yet. When you have seen South and North America you will feel more secure, and your decisions will come more easily.

So, my dear little heart, let things go well with you and please write as soon as you can. Your letters bring me much joy and strength.

I kiss you, my dear Anneli,

Your Bobussja

P.S. Today I spoke with Dr. Oppenheim in Geneva. He told me that he noticed my voice no longer has any depressive quality in it (which refugees are at times afflicted with). I am happy about that. I also find that my step has become surer.

P.P.S. Please send me some Nestle coffee.

LETTER B42[154]

GWATT

[Tuesday] December 25, 1945

My dear little heart,

I am sitting all alone in your room at the Heimstätte right now. I am angry with myself because it seems like nothing is improving and my resulting ill humor may be infecting you. My only comfort is the hope that next Christmas may be a real Christmas for us. You know, in Russia the holidays have much more meaning and are experienced on a deeper level. One prepares for weeks ahead of time and then when the holiday arrives, it is a real celebration. Here in Europe holidays seem to be more of a formality. The main thing is that the associated rituals have been fulfilled, for example the Christmas tree has been lit, the Christmas songs are sung, and the Christmas *Stollen*[155] has been tasted, and so on, regardless of when these events occur. This complaint, too, proves my ponderous and sentimental nature. No wonder, I was raised in bear country!

Tomorrow the grind will begin again, and I must continue to be courageous and brave. I should be content with whatever happens, especially because I have you! You are a wonderful person and I look forward to when we can be together forever. It looks as if time is working in our favor now, and all we need do is to wait patiently until the earth has rotated enough times around its axis.

I hope everything is going well for you in Winterthur and that you get back to Gwatt in good health.

I enclose here the letter and telegram from Grassmück and ask that you order copies of them soon and send them back to me, especially the documents I have enclosed with this letter.

---

154 More than three weeks have passed, and some intervening correspondence has almost certainly been lost. It is Christmas day. Anna has left for Winterthur to spend the holidays with her parents, but arrangements have been made for Boris to stay alone in Anna's room for a few days.

155 A traditional kind of Christmas cake

Please buy yourself a beautiful brooch. Write and tell me what the brooch and the photocopying cost so I can send you the right amount.

I kiss you very tenderly,

My Anncli,

Your Boris

P.S. Please read my letter to Mr. Grassmück. If you find the style good and the handwriting readable, then you can send it just as it is. Otherwise, type it up as soon as possible and send it back to me so I can sign it. I left some airmail paper for you on the table.

I also left you twenty coupons and money to compensate you for my stay in Gwatt. I slept there five nights and ate four lunches and four dinners and had Christmas *Stollen* with tea. Besides that, I made two telephone calls for Fr. 1.80 and Fr. 1.40 (Fr. 3.20 total). I am leaving you Fr. 50.[156] The rest you can use for your brooch. This way you will at least have your Christmas present.

Now good-bye my dear little heart! Let things go well with you.

---

156 One dollar was worth about Fr. 4.30 in 1945.

1946

LETTER B43

[Saturday] January 5, 1946

Little heart,

Many thanks for your little package. But please be more frugal and don't send me so much next time. We must both try to save, as we may soon need the money. I just received a letter from Grassmück. He wants me to send him my personal information immediately so he can move ahead with my immigration application.

The situation is quite tense as my visa may come through within the month. If that happens, I will have to leave my current post. Because your parents are unlikely to cover your trip, I would have to go alone and try to establish myself professionally as quickly as possible. If my immigration takes longer, other possibilities might come into play. Grassmück has now asked whether I will be coming alone or with family. The answer to that rests entirely with you. I think we still have a little time to work this out. But difficulties with your father might prevent your departure. When we meet next time, we should discuss this. I hope you will take some time to think all this over carefully before then.

Your short letter* brought me much joy, especially your remark that Gwatt seems empty without me, and that you are mine and I am yours. I hope you will also remain at my side if I encounter bad luck or financial hardship. We both must take our marriage very seriously, and see it as a mutual freewill union so it will survive both hard times and good. Otherwise, it is not worth much. But I think we are both idealistic and realistic enough to understand the depth and seriousness, as well as the beauty, of marriage.

When I returned to the mine, I hardly recognized it. It will take me a week to bring it back to normal. Hopefully, I can reach the required production levels by the end of the month. Please cross your fingers for me, otherwise I will have difficulties with my supervisor. I will be glad when this job is over.

I kiss you most tenderly,

My Anneli,

Your Bobussja

LETTER B44

[Sunday] January 6, 1946

Little heart,

There are several pressing things I must ask you to do. Please take care of them as soon as possible as each day lost could create problems for us. Here is the list:

1. Order two copies of my passport and driver's license.

2. Read through my letter to Mr. Grassmück and if you find it good, type it on airmail paper and make a carbon copy for me. Send everything (the letter and copies) back to me express in a good, strong envelope so that it won't get crumpled or dirty when it goes on the coal cable train. I will sign the letter and mail it back to you so you can send it on. Because it will take extra time to send it back and forth, I ask that you please hurry with this. Make note of all your expenses.

3. Please make four copies of my curriculum vitae on airmail paper. But you need not rush with this, as I still have two copies left. You can type them next Sunday. I want to write a letter to the Tolstoy Foundation and would like to enclose them.

That is all for now. You can see how important it is that you are able to type well. Typewriting and languages are crucial skills to have if you want to be of help me. The more you can help me, the more productive I will be, and the greater your advantages will be too.

I kiss you,

Your Bobussja

Enclosures:

1. Passport
2. Driver's license
3. Letter from Grassmück
4. Curriculum vitae
5. My letter to Grassmück

P.S. A quick thought: Your parents could prevent our marriage because I am a refugee right now. Should I become an Argentine or American citizen, I would then no longer be a refugee, but a foreigner. From that moment on the legal situation would be different. As far as I know, the existing laws concern stateless refugees only, not foreigners. But I am not quite sure. I would have to research it in more depth.

LETTER B45

[Sunday] January 20, 1946

My dear Anneli,

Please pardon me for not answering the questions you posed in your letter* yesterday. But I was terribly tired, as I usually am on Saturday evenings, and could only wish you a good night. But today I will try to answer your letter.

Before I do, I want to tell you about a strange dream I had. As you know, I dream very rarely. Since my arrival here I think I have dreamt only twice. Both times you were in my dream. Last night I dreamed you had twins!

Now to your letter! As far as typing mistakes and foreign languages go, I must tell you I will not be lax with this. You must be able to type well. You must also be able to speak and write well in different languages, especially Spanish and English. You must work hard at this, otherwise you will be a hindrance to me, rather than a help. Unfortunately, my talents in language are limited, and my wandering imagination sometimes lends me to laziness. You must try to inspire and spur me on in this with your youthful vigor and strength.

I am hoping to find a professorship somewhere, even if it brings in less money. This is because I would rather reside in a large town or city and because of my strong interest in scientific pursuits. I believe this is your inclination too, as you love worldly things (art, clothes, jewelry, music, etc.). We both also relish theater and meeting interesting people. So, let us strive to move in this direction. However, for the next three or four years we will have to live in a mining community of some kind. But even there we can try to create a favorable environment for ourselves.

We both need to undergo a maturing process, and part of that process is healing. We have been damaged, but we are not damaged beyond repair. Our psychological wounds must be healed with the best existing remedy: love. Your recurring depression is the result of your psychological wounds. I, too, have psychological wounds that I must take great pains to address. I am counting on your help. For my part, I will do everything I can to help you be what you want to be.

Here is another fundamental question we must consider: You claim I have Christianity only in my head, not in my soul. Maybe a third party unacquainted with either of us could render a more objective verdict? Strangely, at a point in my life when I considered myself a resolute agnostic (and admitted it to anyone who asked), Mutti[157] described me as a "deeply religious person." It seems that my soul has a religious string inside it that will play when struck properly. During my life I rarely had any opportunity to practice religion. I lived under communism from age fourteen to seventeen. From then until I was thirty-four, I was an atheist and narcissist. Only later in France was I introduced to the foundation of Christianity by Protestants and Catholics. You must understand this clearly and be aware of the times we live in.

I agree with you that my earlier world view and disposition is only useful for strong people. What foundation would serve weaker people then? That is hard to say. As I have told you before, I am strongly drawn to Jesus as I see in him the salvation of the individual and all of mankind, but I know that every epoch represents him in a different way. I believe that our epoch, too, has not fully comprehended him. As Tolstoy says, biblical history is strongly influenced by romanticism, superstitious imagination, and a mythology created by people who lived two thousand years ago. Your understanding of Christianity and Jesus is much deeper than mine. I would gladly learn from you.

I doubt you will find my comments here satisfactory. But I think it would be even harder for me to express my thoughts on the telephone. We must let these questions rest for a time; perhaps the answers may come more readily in the future.

In three days, you will be an adult, and then you will be able to determine your own fate. The moment is fast approaching when

---

157 Mrs. Wunderwald, whom Boris affectionately called Mom (*Mutti*), was his landlady in Freiberg, Germany. See *Lenin, Hitler and Me*, pp. 95-96, 108, 130-131.

you must make a crucial decision! For your birthday I wish you a healthy, happy, and long life. Also, I wish you a good, loving man. Hopefully, you have found one already! You already know what my birthday present is. I hope the money will be in your hands in time. Buy whatever will bring you happiness.

I hope we can see each other again in the next week or two. The dull environment here is really bringing me down, and I think a break would do me good. It probably would not harm you either. I miss you too.

I kiss you very tenderly,

My dear little heart,

Your Bobussja

LETTER A56

Gwatt

[Sunday] January 20, 1946

My dear Boris,

I would like to discuss something very serious with you today. Our focus on idealism may have led us to overlook reality. By chance, I came into a discussion with Dr. Strupp about our future. He told me he would strongly discourage us from leaving Switzerland without any means of support. We may be fooling ourselves in thinking we will have an easy time adjusting to our new life. We may encounter circumstances that could turn a young wife into a huge burden for her husband. He added that things could get quite unpleasant for a young married couple without any means of support. Dr. Strupp is an intelligent man. I believe we would do well to listen to what he has to say.

I have thought it over. There is another reason which favors your traveling first and establishing at least a small basis for our living. I know if we decide to leave together in May or June it would create tremendous upheaval for me at home. That might mean I would have to leave my parents in a state of great disappointment, and we would get nothing from them for our wedding. It would be much better if I could calmly and slowly prepare them, then maybe my parents would gradually come around. Also, I think it would be better if we stay apart right now, so each of us can think things over calmly. We must clearly understand that our marriage might pose some risks, not just to our lives and happiness, but also to our children. How children suffer when their parents are in an unhappy marriage! Our children will be our legacy and our posterity, and we should try to leave behind the best possible legacy. We must not simply follow our instincts and emotions; we must consider everything carefully.

Dear, I hope you understand what I mean. You should realize that a true friend is not someone who just caresses you and says pretty words; a good friend is someone who tells the truth, even when you don't want to hear it.

Now a little bit about my birthday gift. Dear, I forbid you to make big expenditures; now is not the right moment for that. If you want to bring me joy, I would like to have the book entitled *Art History of the World*.[158] It costs about Fr. 15-16.

Now my dear, carefully think over all I have said.

I kiss you tenderly,

Your Anneli

---

158 This is probably *Kunstgeschichte der Welt* by Hermann Leicht, first published by Orell Füssli in 1945.

LETTER A57

GWATT

[Sunday] January 27, 1946

My dear Boris,

Instead of continuing our earlier discussion on Christianity and morality, I would like to discuss something else that concerns both of us. But first, I want to ask something of you. Please do not read my letter quickly through, lay it to the side, and say "Yes, yes, you are right." You see, it takes a lot of effort for me to put my soul and everything that moves me into words. I am speaking to your soul, and I would like to receive a response from your soul.

Today I was suddenly struck by the enormous difficulties we are facing in making decisions about our future, and I would like you to recognize those difficulties too. Dear, do you clearly realize that if you marry a much younger wife, you will have to adapt yourself? You will have to take care of yourself so that you can stay young, both physically and mentally. Here is an excellent saying I found about this that I want to share with you:

"The most important spiritual aid to staying young in old age is always to be learning something new, to interest yourself in everything, and always to have something to look forward to."[159]

You must become more active mentally and start looking at things more thoroughly, rather than passing over them superficially. Do not simply put aside new things you do not understand, but study them carefully.

You must also realize that I will not remain the young girl I am today. I will change. Do you think that if you stay as childish as you are now, and I become a mature woman, there won't be any conflicts?

---

159 Anna quotes Carl Hilty (1833-1909), a Swiss philosopher, writer, and lawyer.

I have put enormous effort into deepening and improving my knowledge, and I would like you to strive for that as well.

As you also know, Boris, after our marriage you will have to take responsibility for me, your wife, and later for your children too. As the man in the family, you will have to protect us.

There is something else that lies heavily on my heart. You must make a clean breast of your past and be completely open with me. Boris, I firmly believe that you are a clean and honest fellow in your heart, no matter what you did in the past, or what you will do in the future. But I believe a person should stand by their words, as well as their deeds, whether they are good or bad. I think you know as well as I that a stable marriage cannot be founded on secrets. Look to yourself, Boris!

One more important thing: Our respective relationship must evolve and become deeper. We have been occupying ourselves an awful lot with superficialities lately, but spiritual contact, which is the most important thing in any relationship, has diminished between with us. You wrote in your last letter that you would like to help me and stand by me, but you did not know how to do it. I would like to explain something to you. The biggest help that one person can be to another is to give understanding to the other. "Understanding everything is forgiving everything."[160] Pay attention to these words; they are true. Boris, understanding someone means being able to put yourself in his place and grasp his true nature. Because when you understand him, then you will know when he is in need, when to give a strong word, when to remain silent, when tenderness is needed, and when to give advice. You see, putting your soul into the soul of another is the most beautiful result of a happy union between a man and woman. Dear, this help of one soul to another is more valuable than a hundred gifts.

Now I would like to add how happy I am to hear about your work in the mine. I hope that you can go even further and improve on your achievements. I believe everything you tell me. I believe you

---

160 See Letter A53.

can do what you promise. I trust you blindly, without proof. Can you imagine how great my joy would be if I were to see you try to do what I ask?

Please take some time to properly digest my words and send me a thoughtful reply. I wish you a good week and a successful close to the month.

I kiss you very tenderly and lovingly,

Your Anneli

LETTER B46

[Tuesday] January 29, 1946

My dear Anneli,

I was so joyful when I read your wonderful letter, especially because I sensed your soul was speaking directly to mine. The tone of our last few letters has become quite businesslike, and the sincere contact we had at the beginning of our correspondence has been lacking. Also, we have been writing to each other less often than we used to. The reason is easy to understand. We are overly preoccupied with our work. That is why I was so glad to read your lines: "I put my soul and everything that moves me into words, and I say them to your soul and want your soul to give me an answer." I found these words so wonderful that I could not hold back and just had to call you. I suddenly had a great desire to speak with you, to hear your voice in which I can sense your soul.

I will answer you in turn. The decision about our future, which is in our hands alone, is truly not easy.

I am fully conscious that I am marrying a young woman. You are certainly very young, but I believe a much older woman would not be a good match for me.

You write: "You must become more active mentally and start looking at things more thoroughly, rather than passing over them superficially. Do not simply put aside new things that you do not understand, but study them carefully."

I completely disagree with your accusation as I believe I have researched many problems in depth. Just think, in France my thirst for knowledge was so great that I traveled widely to visit many people (including Reverend du Purry, Reverend Eberhardt, and Prof. Peretti) to consult with them on many topics, despite the Gestapo ID inspectors on the train who might have discovered that my papers were false and that I was not really a Frenchman. In Zurich, why did I seek out Prof. Brunner and go to his lectures? And at the refugee camp, why did I put so much effort into preparing a lecture on a topic as challenging as "The Meaning of Life," giving it in French, a language I don't know well at all?

I do not push things aside and I do not look at things superficially. But there are certain problems and questions that cannot be clearly answered. And if one occupies oneself with these questions, then it is no surprise that some of them may not be answerable in the end.

When you say that all your efforts are going toward achieving a deeper and better understanding, that makes me very happy. In the future we can work toward this together. But you must not think that the deep understanding of the wisest people on earth is so very easy to grasp. There are many tough nuts to chew on. I can imagine us sitting together in the evenings in a comfortable room in front of a piano, while we read interesting books together. And when we play pieces on the piano, we will not play them through quickly as we do now, but we will first thoroughly study the psychological foundation of the piece and try to recreate it when we play. Only then will we create art that will bring joy. You must learn much more, so we can work fruitfully together. Of course, it brings me much joy to help you and to see your progress. I think of you as a gold mine that I must work to bring all your talents and good qualities out from deep within you to the light of day.

It has gotten late. I must go to bed and will answer the rest of your letter tomorrow.

[Wednesday] January 30, 1946

I am glad that you take pleasure in my accomplishments. But unfortunately, I cannot realize my full capacity here because my boss does not fully trust me. Also, his methods and his way of managing the workers really do not sit well with me.

I eagerly look forward to the day I will have saved enough money to put my wardrobe in order, as I always have placed a lot of importance on looking my best. Unfortunately, for many years I have had to give up on that and lower my standards. You shouldn't worry that I appear a bit shabby now. This is only a money problem that will soon be remedied.

Finally, I would like you to know that I have been completely open and have kept no secrets from you. Doing so would only bring us pain in the future and would be a detriment to our relationship. So, in this area too, you need not have any worries.

I seek in you a complete woman and I want to be a complete man for you. These are challenging goals, but we must both strive for them with all our might, as our happiness depends on it.

And now, good night. I kiss you tenderly.

My dear Anneli,

Your Bobussja

P.S. I am also enclosing my watches. They are full of coal dust and don't work anymore. Please have them cleaned and repaired and buy simple leather watchbands for them. For the moment, I am keeping my alarm clock in my pocket!

LETTER A58

Gwatt

[Sunday] February 3, 1946

My dear Boris,

Let me explain. I would like to examine our relationship in a clear and serious way with my letters. The decisions we make now will affect our entire lives, and many of them have nothing to do with your career. The question is whether our characters mesh well or not. Boris, we must hold back our emotions a bit, and think through these issues rationally. If we do not do it now, it will be too late.

You say if our love is real and true and of the until-death-do-us-part variety, everything will turn out well. Love unto death is a concept, one that poets use in their dramatic verses, but in ordinary day-to-day life it has a bit of a different face. I, too, believe that there are people who devote themselves to each other exclusively, but how many inner struggles, tears, and how much suffering are hidden behind it all? It is not as easy as you imagine. A marriage is not a seventh heaven, a marriage is a struggle, just as life is a struggle. How conditional is human love? If one of us hurts the other, or is unkind, where would our love be then? You see, in marriage the readiness to make sacrifices can never be so great that it destroys the one who offers to make those sacrifices. Therefore, because human love is bound to one's character, we must discover whether our characters can fulfill the promises and sacrifices we are requiring of each other in our marriage.[161]

These ideas are not easy to understand, but please try, as they are extremely important. You see, Boris, it is not wise of you to quickly dis-

---

161 The issues Anna brings up in this paragraph and in the ones that follow are crucial to the success of their relationship and show that she is much more of a realist than Boris is. His unwillingness to seriously confront her reservations and his inability to understand Anna's inner struggles now and throughout their marriage would indeed lead to future crises.

pute what I have to say. These are not accusations; they are suggestions from someone who has your best interests at heart. You should treasure them. I don't know what you were like before I knew you, but I see how you are now. I see how you, in a childish sort of way, see problems where sensible people would not find any, and I see how poorly you understand the inner soul of other people. Sometimes I would like to tell you a little story about something I experienced that touched my heart, but I can't, because I know, even before I begin, that you won't take the trouble to understand what I'm saying and will simply brush it aside with an indifferent remark. These are small details, but extremely important ones. What do the fabulous earth-shattering deeds we will do together matter, if there is no true spiritual connection between us? For example, you maintain that my periods of depression are outward phenomena. That is the clearest sign that you don't really understand me, because otherwise you would see that my depression belongs to me, just as my nose does. That is how I arrive at my greatest and deepest realizations which make me a richer and more mature person. Without them, I would be a frivolous and superficial creature.

When you have immersed yourself deeply in Christianity, what then? There are thousands upon thousands of problems and questions that can be discussed and researched. Didn't you yourself tell me once long ago, "I am always too lazy to study things in depth."

Also, Boris, you burden me with far more responsibilities than what is reasonable. I am responsible for what you will do in the future and for your spiritual condition. I must also care for your physical well-being, study English, Spanish, and French, and practice the piano. I should study art and history, and further I should learn how to type and take shorthand, and if possible, I should also earn money and take care of your correspondence. But Boris, I am not a horse, I am a woman. I would gladly help you, and will do as much as my strength allows, but this is too much. And you must be clearly aware of this: I work very slowly, and when I am emotionally unstable, I can only do only half as much. And why should I study art if later, when I want to discuss it with you, you say to me, "Oh, I don't understand a thing about art."

An understanding of art, or any other topic for that matter, will not fall into your mouth like ripened grapes, one must work hard at it.

You write in your letter that you hope to give me what I seek. Now I ask you: What do you think I seek?

We both must try hard to establish a deep relationship. When I ask you to become more active and take more of an interest in my world, it is not good of you to say, "Oh, I am active enough." Dear, I don't say these things because it brings me joy to nag you, I say it because I need it.[162]

I am sending along a small book with this letter for you to read. You should try to read more, Boris. You will certainly like this little story. It is about the Nordic spirit which you have often told me about. I find the story charming and moving, but I would have preferred something more open-minded and big-hearted. I would lose my mind and suffocate in the tightly controlled, intolerant atmosphere described in this book. I love people with high ideals, but only those with a broad-minded, noble heart, with the ability to understand and forgive human frailties. With them there is freedom; with all others life would be a perpetual prison filled with drudgery.[163]

I will include here a poem by Carl Spitteler:

You don't need laws,
They come from within you.
All of wisdom says:
Look and reflect upon yourself.[164]

---

162 This demand seems quite "modern" coming from a twenty-year-old girl in 1946, years before the rise of the Women's Liberation Movement.
163 These last two sentences, in a nutshell, eerily point to the probable cause of the ultimate failure of their relationship. Anna had a tremendous capacity for seeing and understanding the subtle inner workings of other human beings, while Boris tended to project his own opinions and ethic sensibilities onto other people, especially those he admired. Boris had high ideals, but little tolerance for failures and mistakes. This would often lead to disappointment, disillusionment, or sometimes something close to a righteous indignation, something Anna would experience firsthand in the last years of her marriage to Boris and which she prophetically describes here as "a perpetual prison filled with drudgery."
164 Swiss poet Carl Friedrich Georg Spitteler (1845-1924) was awarded the Nobel Prize for Literature in 1919.

These words are not easy to understand. I did not understand them myself at first. But I kept coming back to them and thought about them again and again until suddenly they stood up strong and clear in front of me.

Here is another wise saying by Gottfried Keller. (Spitteler and Keller are two important Swiss authors):

"It is strange how even the best human being must have some bad characteristics, like a proud sailing ship that needs ballast below, without which a good, safe journey would be difficult."[165]

That is all for today. Think carefully about all I have written, and only then answer me, all right?

In the meantime, I have received my birthday present from you, and I thank you very much for it. But I will delay opening it until I see you.

Now take a loving kiss from me,

Your Anneli

---

165   From the diary of Swiss poet and author Gottfried Keller (1819-1890), September 15, 1847

LETTER A59[166]

Gwatt

[Tuesday] February 26, 1946

My dear Boris,

To be a good example to you, I will write you a few words now so you will receive this note when you get back to Zurich. You don't need to make any more excuses about being too lazy to write. It seems like this is probably a bit of apathy, like you showed this morning. If you had not been too lazy to bring a shaver along when you were visiting me, you could have shaved here. Then we would have been able to say a few words to each other. But let's drop this; apathy has no place in a marriage. And learning to type is just a trifling thing when you know that by doing so you can bring joy to another. If I spend just two minutes thinking about what I did today and what I want to tell you, then I can always find something to write about. You know, Boris, I don't think you really are as lazy as you claim to be because your head is full of good ideas and thoughts. You have energy and zest for life; you are simply lethargic sometimes. As soon as your toe feels better,[167] you should exercise and tone up your muscles. I, too, would like to get myself going in this direction.

So, now I will be very good and go to bed. I kiss you very tenderly and lovingly.

Your Anneli

---

166 Three weeks have passed. Some intervening correspondence has been lost. Boris has just visited Anna in Gwatt and is on his way back to Zurich.
167 For many years Boris suffered toe pain due to an old skiing injury.

LETTER B47

[Thursday] February 28, 1946
10:20 p.m.

Anneli,

I was just sitting in the train station waiting for my suitcase when I suddenly got the urge to write to you. But I don't know if I will succeed in clearly expressing my thoughts in this letter. Please forgive me from the outset!

You know, we both are a bit messed up. Surely, each of us has many talents and good qualities, but we also have a few negative traits that constrain us significantly. I feel as if I have been chained up for years and am only now able to begin moving again. While I was a refugee, I lost much of my morally clean and courageous attitude. Now I feel as though I am ascending but have a swamp underfoot and must exert myself mightily to get myself out of it. Part of this "swamp" is also, as you rightly state, my laziness and inertia. Surely, I must have inherited this trait, yet my mind clearly tells me I must either collect all my courage and energy to maintain a stricter attitude, or I will suffocate in my own laziness.

I don't wish to accuse you of laziness or inertia, yet your archenemy, your depression, consumes you and holds you back. You must free yourself from the idea that your depression belongs to you as much as your nose does. That is a terrible and dangerous notion. The reasons behind your depression can be explained by the following:

1. You are compelled to live without parental love and a proper homelife. You sought a good homelife but could not find one in your surroundings (at home or at the Heimstätte). Of course, this will make you feel depressed.

2. You are not completely satisfied with your career.

3. Your extremely long apprenticeship undermines your energy. In the evenings you feel exhausted physically and spiritually.

4. Your past, even though it is forgotten and renounced, does not bring you satisfaction, even when you try to look at it in a positive light.

5. Without a doubt you have had a very unfortunate upbringing.

6. Your surroundings, including the current one in Gwatt, have too many negative components. You have no good role models before you.

Against all these negative influences you have a crucial advantage which lies more in your subconsciousness than your consciousness: your zest for life. You are a creation of God who has endowed you with creative strength. The greatest threat to that strength resides within us: laziness, inertia, greediness, and the resulting self-satisfaction, idleness, and false illusions.

If we want to be courageous, moral people, we must exert ourselves powerfully. We must energetically push away everything that holds us back, including negativity and all other influences that impede our life. We must avoid them and keep cynicism from flowing through our beings and souls. If a person's ear and eye can tolerate the destruction of the most perfect and wonderful, then he becomes an ordinary, vulgar being. Protect yourself from that.

Yes dearest, it won't be easy for us to reach our ideal, but that should be our goal. If we can both make it to America, it will be easier for us, as the world of the Anglo-Saxons[168] is significantly nobler than the rest of the world. Only in the highest circles does one encounter high-minded natures; elsewhere one finds only crude farmers and cynical types.

Shall we agree to forge ahead and encourage each other to have pure and courageous hearts? During our last few months in Europe,

---

168 Here Boris is referring to the United States as an "Anglo-Saxon" country.

we should consciously use our time well. A completely new life awaits us in America.

I would like to give you another piece of advice: You should prize and observe the strength of a love that is built upon feeling and sensibility. I find you are too sober in your thinking, and in fact so sober, I sometimes cannot tell if you really love [me] or not.[169] It is possible that I am mistaken and am the one lacking in healthy sobriety. Perhaps it would be best to have a third party make that judgment.

I will end my letter now. I wish you a pleasant Sunday. Be sure to rest well. You need it!

I kiss you firmly,

Your Bobussja

---

169 Anna has become so guarded emotionally that Boris wonders whether she really loves him. Could it be she is having second thoughts? Two of Anna's recent letters (A57 and A58) show that she is having some reservations.

LETTER B48

Monday, March [no date], 1946

My dear heart,

I am very much looking forward to our next meeting on April 6-7. Until then I will try to leave you alone as much as possible. It is probably better if I write to you less often too, so you will not be distracted. You need to work hard and concentrate. So, work efficiently, with the understanding that you should not over-exert yourself.[170] And please buy yourself some nourishing food! Don't save money on this; put it all on my school account. Above all eat oranges, apples, nuts, and in the mornings eat muesli with sugar. This is not just a request, but a command, as you are already mine, and you have sworn to obey, understand!? Above all, your nerves must be in good shape. The person who can maintain the greatest calmness is the winner. The one who loses his head loses everything.

My work at the mine is moving forward nicely. Today I spoke with Mr. Gehring at last. He approved everything, even though it will cost over Fr. 100,000. All my suggestions were taken, including my proposal that the workers get a twenty percent wage increase.

I will end here so as not to excite you too much. I will write less often. But you should still know that there is someone close to you who is crossing his fingers for you. So, break a leg!

I kiss you very firmly,

Your Boris

---

170 Anna is preparing for her final examination.

LETTER A60
GWATT

[Tuesday] March 19, 1946

Good evening, Boris,

First, I would like to thank you for all the love you continue to show me and because you always take such good care of me. And most particularly, I would like to thank you for believing in me and for giving me courage. These are my weakest points, so this where I need your help the most.

I have been thinking over our debate about whether to go to the United States or Argentina. Argentina really attracts me. It would be nice to be rich and have everything one wants, but at the same time I believe wealth alone does not constitute happiness. True happiness comes from within. We must let all this take its course and wait and see how these two options present themselves.

I hope you arrived well at the mine and found everything in order. I am anxious to find out whether you will succeed there. I would be glad to hear all your news.

I am so happy about us, as I believe the decision to live our lives together is solidifying in us. And when this decision becomes final, I am certain we will have the strength to overcome any hindrances we may face.

I wish you success, a strong working spirit, happiness, and joyful courage. Everything will work out fine!

Here is a tender kiss from me,

Your Anneli

LETTER B49

FRUTIGEN, CANTON BERN[171]

Sunday, March [no date], 1946

Thank you for the little package. I am happy you will take your examination on April 4; then at least we can see each other on the weekend. It is "cruelty to animals" to be so close and yet not be able to see each other.

You must concentrate on studying these last few days. But the main thing is to get a lot of rest. Sleep well and eat well. Don't spare any expense. You cannot succumb to depression now, so use all possible means to combat it (e.g., cold showers, etc.). You are doing the right thing when you encourage yourself by saying: "If others can do it, so can I!" But realize the result of this examination will have no influence on my judgment of you. But the better you do, the more satisfaction you will have. These kinds of tests depend a lot on one's attitude and luck.

I am doing well here at the mine. I am quite satisfied with my colleagues and am also well-respected by them. I will be able to make many improvements here eventually, but first I must get approval for doing some measured investigations. Production is not going very well right now because we don't have enough workers, and many of the newest ones have left because they prefer outdoor work in good weather, for which they are also generally better paid.

I have a good typewriter here at my disposal, but still no telephone. When I get one, I will call you, so you will know.

My room is in the new barracks and is quite pretty, yet I do not wish to live here much longer. The medical orderly is a masseur. He has offered to give me a daily massage. Maybe he can help my toe?

The view from here is magnificent. The air is wonderful, and the personal relationships I have are much better than those I had

---

171 Frutigen, a village near the mine where Boris is working (Kandergrund), is less than ten miles south of Gwatt.

in Valais. As I have financial backing, I am quite calm while I await news from America. I ask that you, too, be inwardly calm.

Here is a kiss for you,

Your Boris

P.S. I have not yet gotten my passport back from Dorénaz. Please send my letter to Dorénaz from Thun, as I do not want them to know I am working at this mine.

Boris at the Kandergrund mine (Spring 1946)

LETTER B50[172]

[Friday] May 3, 1946
9:20 p.m.

My dear Anneli,

I would like to thank you for your visit and the wonderful birthday gifts. I always think I am not nice enough to you and probably wear you out talking about silly things. But you know me well enough to know that nothing I say is meanly meant.

I got back to the cable car right on time. If I had arrived five minutes later, I would have had to sleep at the bottom of the mountain.

I want to go to sleep right away as I must get up at 5:30 a.m. tomorrow.

So, goodnight!

Boris

---

172 Six weeks have passed, and any intervening correspondence has been lost. Anna has visited Boris in Frutigen.

LETTER B51

[Sunday] May 19, 1946

My dear Anneli,

I thank you for the little package you sent. I am happy to hear that Cortot's[173] concert was a wonderful experience for you. Please go to concerts and plays often. You can readily rely on my financial help for this. I am also glad you bought yourself a new coat; I am sure it looks wonderful on you. If you can be patient, wait with your other purchases until we are together again. It would bring me much joy to be with you when you go shopping!

All day yesterday I rode around with Mr. Gehring in his Ford. We were in Solothurn and Neuchatel.[174] I must say my old Mercedes drove a lot smoother, as it had swing axles.[175] Also, I was disappointed with the Swiss roads; they are in bad condition. The roads in Germany, Spain, and Italy are much better.

Today I climbed the mountain and so I am very tired now. The view was obscured. I picked some flowers for you; I hope they will still be fresh when they reach Winterthur. I am also enclosing a piece of butter for you to have with your morning coffee. I hope it will still be good by the time you get it.

I, too, think it would be better to postpone our trip to the Jungfraujoch.[176] It is still cold, and the air is not clear enough. The best time would be in fall. Another reason I would like to hold off is I have already spent a lot this month. Maybe we could go next month?

I congratulate you on your visit to the dentist!

What does your long ball dress look like?

I would like you to set up a meeting for me with your father as soon as possible. Naturally, you should wait for an opportune

---

173 Alfred Denis Cortot (1877-1962) was a French-Swiss pianist and conductor.
174 Two locations near Bern, north of Gwatt
175 This was a type of independent rear suspension. Mercedes was one of the earliest adopters of this technology.
176 A scenic tourist destination in the Swiss Alps

moment to bring it up with him. Should the answer only be apparent on Thursday or later and next Sunday becomes a possibility, please send me a telegram. Calling won't be easy now, as it takes at least six minutes for me to get to the phone. Good luck!

You said in your last letter that I needn't have any fear on your account. What joy that brought me! I must confess I have absolutely none. You have become more mature, and I know I can trust you completely.

I kiss you,

Your Bobussja

LETTER A61[177]

WINTERTHUR

[Friday] May 31, 1946

Dear Boris,

I received your dear letter and thank you for the news. Although we are under a lot of pressure right now, we must be smart and not overwhelm my father with too much information. When you meet with him, please do not pressure him for the quickest possible response just so you can reply to Grassmück sooner. You could spoil everything that way. Take some time and quietly think everything over carefully so you will be able to find the right way to say what needs to be said, relying on your knowledge of people and your forty years of maturity. In the end, it is your place to ask for my hand. I cannot do it. So, I will leave it to you; hopefully everything will work out fine.

A thousand loving greetings,

Your Anneli

---

177 Anna has completed her final examination and has left Gwatt permanently. She is now residing at home in Winterthur with her parents.

LETTER B52

[Saturday] June 1, 1946

Anneli,

I am writing on the train. I hope you can read my handwriting. So, your father prefers that we marry prior to my departure. Hmmm... should I, or shouldn't I?

But seriously, if this wedding can take place in the next two or three weeks, then let us go ahead with it. Otherwise, we can draw up a formal promise to marry before a notary (without a public announcement, so your relatives are not spooked), which would suffice for you to obtain the visa.

I think the first scenario is the only one that is practical.

But you must know that I will only marry you under the following conditions!

1. You must always eat breakfast.

2. You must wear your hair the way you used to.

I want you to take good care of yourself and not do such silly things! You could lose all your teeth or have a heart attack or lung problems, or the like. The body is like a machine. If it is not properly cared for (if it gets inferior fuel, e.g.), it will not work well. An elephant might be big and strong, but if he doesn't get enough food, he will get sick. On top of that, you yourself say that you don't have much resistance. No wonder! In conclusion, I want to have a healthy wife, not one with false teeth or a sour stomach, understand?[178]

Here is a big kiss from me,

Your Bobussja

---

178 It is unclear what Boris is complaining about. Perhaps he discovered that Anna was smoking?

LETTER A62

ZURICH

[Monday] June 3, 1946

My dear Boris,

I miss you very much; we are so far apart and live in such different worlds. After having lived in the countryside for four years, I have settled in well here and am enjoying city life. In fact, I like it very much. But you need not worry; in time I will get my fill of it and look forward to living in a more peaceful place again.

Next Thursday I will go hear a French symphony orchestra play a concert with pieces by Dukas, Franck, Debussy, and Ravel. I am looking forward to it. Later there will be concerts given by Arturo Benedetti[179] and Louis Kentner.[180] Can you tell me who Yehudi Menuhin is?[181] His first concert is completely sold out. He will play Bach, Mozart, and Franck.

What are you doing and thinking? We know so little of each other. It's a pity that we are both a bit lazy with our writing.

Regarding my parents, I am going to leave it all in your hands. That is the man's role, as you should know. I will, however, give you some advice. It is the same advice Mr. Grassmück gave you. The more simply and straightforwardly you can represent our situation, the easier it will be. Do not let my father know how rushed we are and that we need to send Grassmück our answer soon. Let him have some time to think about what you have to say, otherwise it could ruin everything.

---

179 Italian pianist Arturo Benedetti Michelangeli (1920-1995)
180 Hungarian pianist Louis Philip Kentner (1905-1987) moved to England in 1935 and specialized in the works of Liszt and Chopin.
181 Yehudi Menuhin (1916-1999), an American of Lithuanian extraction, was one of the most highly regarded violinists of the twentieth century.

Your plan to visit my parents in Winterthur at Pentecost[182] may depend on the weather. If the weather is good my parents will want to drive to the Engadin.[183] You should leave the day and time of your visit completely up to them. So dear, I hope to hear from you soon.

I kiss you very tenderly,

Anneli

---

182 In 1946, Pentecost was on June 9.
183 A scenic region in southeastern Switzerland

LETTER A63

WINTERTHUR

[Wednesday] June 5, 1946

Dear Boris,

You have made a complicated mess for me again! You cannot simply set up a meeting with Mr. Stauffacher without letting me know. You have no idea whether I can come or not. Also, your letter* to my father was very unfortunate. You are not coming to see him to do some horse trading, you are coming to get to know my father better and gradually get him to agree to our marriage. You shouldn't plan the meeting date yourself; you will come when you are invited.

You must not rush these things. Don't let yourself be pressured continually by Grassmück. He will just have to be patient. He has no idea what your situation is.

My parents will be visiting the Engadin on Saturday, Sunday, and Monday, and they want to take me with them. You can imagine how inconvenient your new plan for us to meet with Mr. Stauffacher is for me.

Listen carefully! I asked my father if I could invite you along on this trip, which then led to a long, complex discussion. Well, I can tell you the situation is much more difficult than you can imagine. I think it would be best if you, as the man, would take the situation in hand. If you want to marry me, you will have to do more than just a little here and there at your leisure. You need to approach it with full understanding and wisdom. I do not want my father to accuse me of pushing this marriage. That would be an insult to me, as a woman.

My father has the following objections to our marriage: 1) our age difference 2) your statelessness 3) that we have no money and no livelihood and 4) that I want to go to the other end of the world. That simply is not what a good Swiss would do, he says. I must say, I didn't expect him to be quite so petty and narrow-minded. Well, there is nothing we can do to change him, and that is not the most important thing anyway. We have our goal in front of us and we must keep our eyes on it. My father did not come to a definitive decision as to whether he would invite you along on the trip or not. We will leave Zurich Saturday at about noon. Of course, if the weather is bad, we will not go. Better not plan anything for the moment and wait for further news from me. It would also be good if you would telephone Mr. Stauffacher, apologize, and explain to him that I am going to be traveling with my parents. I will contact you Friday, at the latest.

Dear, please don't be too angry with me because I am a bit upset about this confusion.

Take a loving kiss from me,

Your Anneli

LETTER B53

MINING ENGINEER B. KOCHANOWSKY
KANDERGRUND MINING COMPANY
KANDERGRUND, CANTON BERN

[Monday] June 10, 1946

Very honored Mr. Stahel:

Two years ago, I met your daughter in Gwatt. It would be a great honor for me to make your acquaintance too, and I would be extremely grateful if you would allow me to visit you for this purpose.

In anticipation of your eagerly awaited reply,

I remain yours,

With the highest respect,

Boris Kochanowsky

LETTER A64

WINTERTHUR

[Wednesday] June 12, 1946

My dear Boris,

A thousand thanks for your dear letter;* it brought sunshine to my heart. I would like to quickly tell you my reaction to all that you said.

Dear, I understand exactly that as your wife I would be your helpmate first and foremost, but you will certainly understand that you must ask for my hand in marriage. It is impossible for me to do that. It would be a risk for me if later you were to claim you only married me because I insisted upon it. You understand, that would be horrible for me.

Now listen, I want to give you some instructions. I have prepared my father. He has read the letter from Mr. Grassmück and, as you know, I had a discussion with him. He said that he just can't imagine such a thing, but that at the minimum he would insist you prove that taking this job in Argentina is really the right thing to do. So, in other words, he would like you to go alone, and if all goes well, I would follow a year or so later.

To my surprise, I was very calm while discussing this with my father. I didn't contradict anything he said, but to each of his reservations I explained my argument in favor very calmly, and I got the feeling that I did somehow make an impression.

He wants you to travel alone. But I want to go with you. We must be very clever with our next move. We must put together some very valid reasons why I must travel with you. Most especially, do not tell him you want me to accompany you because the beautiful trip would be much more gratifying if we travel together. My father would laugh right in your face! You must try to make clear that there is no risk involved, that you need me, that you would not let me travel alone, and that within a year there might be another war. Bring along the new letters you received from Mr. Grassmück, but don't show them to him right away. Wait until there is a good opportunity to do it.

Boris, you must not threaten my father, just stay strong and unyielding.

Here is a loving kiss from me,

Your Anneli

P.S. Don't be shocked when you come to visit. I went to the hairdresser!

LETTER B54

[Thursday] June 13, 1946

Little heart!

I advise you to prepare all your documents and photographs right away. Then we can send them off quickly and ask Grassmück to take care of your visa as soon as possible. Please try to go to an excellent photographer this time and see if he can make lots of copies for Fr. 5-6. You will find a shop on Bahnhofstrasse and another one on Limmatquai. Please put up your hair the way I like it, understand? Then hold your little nose in all different directions, one pose after the other, all right?

I got some information this morning about the possibility of flying to South America via England, and I can share the following with you:

1. You could fly from Geneva to Gothenburg [Sweden] and from there board a Swedish steamship and sail directly to Buenos Aires.

2. You could fly from Geneva to London and from there fly with an English airline to Argentina. This option would be cheaper: Geneva to London for Fr. 240. London to Buenos Aires for Fr. 3,500.

Between June 15 and June 20 will there be a change in the British military rules affecting passenger ships. Let us hope the restrictions will be lifted soon, so you can leave from Liverpool.

As soon as I have more news, I will write you right away. If you want to travel by way of Sweden, you should take the necessary steps immediately.

Also, please abstain from accusing me of being so wishy-washy about getting married and introducing you as my fiancée. Do you think that I am some sort of marriage swindler? Do you think I would risk embarrassing myself in front of Dr. Kurz, Grassmück, and all my acquaintances here in Switzerland and my future acquaintances in Argentina? You should lay all your misgivings aside and make sure we can get through to your father as soon as possible. Time is flying, and the pressure is mounting. We dare not take any unnecessary steps, otherwise we will lose time, and I might have to travel by myself.

As far as money goes, we are both big spenders and somewhat wasteful with money We must try to change that tendency, otherwise we will never amount to much. Luckily, food is dirt cheap in Argentina.

We must be strict and critical of ourselves if we want to establish a life together. More seriously, and most importantly, we must channel all our efforts into developing a creative life together and not bicker, which I really cannot abide.[184] All of life's power is reduced to nothing that way. Many people live like that, but we don't want any part of it.

Your Boris

---

184 During the last few months of their courtship, Boris becomes increasingly disturbed by Anna's short temper. Tensions are mounting with her parents and Anna is feeling the effects of that discord more keenly than when she was living in Gwatt. The next letter (B55) also shows Boris' growing uneasiness with Anna's easily aroused anger.

LETTER B55

[Monday] June 17, 1946

Anneli,

Today I expected to receive the photos you ordered, yet the postman had nothing for me. I assume that means you have not gotten them yet. I had to call two photo shops in Bern and ask them to contact the Zurich shop to request that they send them to me as soon as possible. I am quite upset over this because I have not yet been able to send Grassmück the items he requested.

Yesterday I sent out all three letters (to Grassmück, Stauffacher, and Gamble). I have an enormous amount to accomplish here.

While I was in transit, I thought a lot about you. I had trouble shaking off a nagging uneasiness, as we have been quarreling a lot lately. Each time we try to put the blame something else: overwork, nervousness, a temporary stressful situation, etc. The actual reasons probably lie much deeper, and we must scrutinize ourselves. I think it is simple pig-headedness (I'm right, you're wrong) and poor self-control. If this is just a passing problem, then it is probably not too serious. Should it become constant, my patience would eventually come to an end (even little drops of water continually falling on stone can make a hole), and then there could be suffering, crises, and catastrophes in our marriage, as you say. I don't want to undergo suffering and crises because of mounting trifles.

The purpose of these words is not to shock you, but to make you aware of the seriousness of the problem. I cannot bear it when you suddenly explode in my face; that can lead to terrible arguments. One must distinguish the big things from the little things, and at least be broad-minded about the little things.

Pardon me if I speak plainly here, but I think I need to do so. I know you are facing a lot of pressure right now. Maybe it is the toughest time of your life, and I want to be considerate of your situation. But fighting does not sit well with my psyche. I am the sort of person who never starts or puts up a fight with anyone, and I do not want to start doing it with my own wife. Don't upset yourself about this too much, but in the future please try to control yourself better. I think our future depends on it.

I kiss and embrace you,

Your Bobussja

LETTER A65

Winterthur

[Monday] June 17, 1946

My dear Bobussja man,

I have taken care of everything today! The photos were at the post office by evening. I find the ones marked XX best and I advise you to have more copies of those made. I don't find the ones in profile particularly favorable. Don't use them for the passport or other official documents. Also, I would like you to send me a good photo of yourself please!

At the travel bureau I learned the following:

1. Right now, it is unknown when travel by British ocean liner will be possible.

2. Neither Swedish nor Dutch boats may land in England.

3. Boats and planes are always completely booked two months ahead.

4. The boats that go to South America (that means Buenos Aires too) land in Brazil or Uruguay first.

5. Prices: The cheap tickets (not the cheapest) are Fr. 1,400 (with several people staying in the same cabin). A bit higher class (good), again with several people staying in the same cabin goes for Fr. 2,300. An even higher class ticket which includes two cabins goes for Fr. 3,500-4,000.

So that's it. The man there was very nice and told me if I needed further information I should come back.

But it seems we have something of a dilemma. Hopefully, things will turn out for the best.

I much regretted that I couldn't give you a good-bye kiss today. I hope instead to give you a welcome kiss next Sunday.

Did you survive the trip and get back home in one piece? Did you have success, or not? Tell me a bit about it.

My tooth has left me in peace up until now. I hope it was only a temporary pain. I will keep my fingers crossed for you this week when your hour at the dentist in the beautiful villa arrives.

Enough for today, my dear Bobsche! Now I send you a thousand dear little greetings and kisses.

Your Anneli

LETTER B56

[Thursday] June 20, 1946

Dear Anneli,

I received letters from you and Grassmück today. As a result, we must meet again next weekend.

Grassmück writes:

"Our new general director at the mine, Rene Addor (a Swiss), says you are to come as soon as possible. Get a seat on an airplane and get here as soon as you can. Because your marital status is uncertain, a postponement of the approval of your immigrant status may result. So, it may be best for you to arrive alone now as a bachelor. Your bride could then follow soon, and you could be married here [in Argentina]. Maybe inquire at the Argentine consulate and ask them what would be best."

Can you let me know whether your father can see me next Sunday? Then call Mr. Stauffacher and set up a meeting with him for Saturday or Sunday. I need to meet with him because I need help filling out some forms I received from Argentina that are in Spanish.

I regret now that we delayed sending your father my letter and lost so much time. You must listen to me next time, as I have more experience.

I kiss you,

Your Bobussja

LETTER A66

WINTERTHUR

June 1946 [No date]

My dear Boris,

It is Sunday afternoon. I have thought our situation over carefully. It really is a bit complicated, but we shouldn't make it any more complicated than it is. If I were you, Boris, I would immediately reserve a seat on an airplane and go directly to Argentina. I would not waste time traveling to the U.S. in case your [Argentine] visa is revoked for some stupid reason. We will be able to live frugally at the mine in Mendoza,[185] and you will soon have enough money to get to the U.S. on your own. Go ahead and travel to Argentina now. It is the best way.

Furthermore, we wrote to Grassmück that you will come alone as a bachelor first, and that he should get a visa for me as your future bride. We don't know what Mr. Grassmück will have done about it by the time he receives your next letter. Speak with my father about this and don't give up. There is no sense in threatening to marry. It would make a bad impression on Mr. Grassmück if we change our story and tell him he should do all this in reverse: "I will come married, please get a visa for my wife." We must stop vacillating now, otherwise we will not move forward.

The sooner you leave, the faster you will start earning, the faster things will get better for us. I am not afraid of traveling to Minacar alone. The main thing is that we love each other. Many a young couple would find it wonderful to be able to go live in isolation together. Trust Grassmück, Boris. If he didn't have something good for you, he wouldn't be pressuring you so hard to come.

If you order your ticket now, we could work on getting my travel documents in order before your departure, so that I could be in

---

185 Minacar, the remote mining community where Boris will work, is in the province of Mendoza in western Argentina.

Buenos Aires in a few months. We could take our honeymoon trip there. It would be less difficult and rushed than here in Switzerland.[186]

Please be so good as to call me tomorrow evening at 7 p.m. and let me know how the discussion went. If my parents are at home, I will answer your "How are you?" with "So-so." Then you will know that I cannot speak freely. Please give me your telephone number so I can call you at any time.

I am with you very firmly in my thoughts and kiss you very tenderly,

My dear Boris,

Your Anneli

---

[186] As it turned out, they married and honeymooned in Switzerland just prior to Boris' departure for Argentina on August 9.

Boris (July 1946)

Anna (July 1946)

Postscript

In 2020, during the COVID-19 pandemic, a cousin in Switzerland contacted me. She was working on a genealogy project and asked if I could supply her with photos of some of my Swiss ancestors. As I was rummaging around in my basement in search of the photos, I stumbled upon some of the other papers that had been in my mother's box. I had long since finished translating the letters that had been in the uppermost folder, but had not investigated the rest of the contents very carefully. To my surprise, I discovered a binder containing additional letters my parents had written after their marriage, from the day my father left Switzerland up through and beyond their divorce in 1970. More than twenty of them were written in 1946 during their three-month post-wedding separation.

In a rush to get to his new post, my father had boarded a flight for Argentina in August; my mother did not follow until the middle of November. Their letters during this period focus on some of the more mundane details of travel: bookings, visas, last-minute purchases, and the like. Yet there is much of interest, too, that continues and enhances the story of the newly married couple preparing for a new life in the wilds of the Andes Mountains. I have freely omitted some of the more mundane passages in the translation that follows, choosing to focus instead on material that reveals the course of their relationship and their evolving attitudes about the world and Argentina in particular.

It seems that Anna and Boris had some heated arguments during their honeymoon and parted less than amicably. At least part of their disagreement was about money. Both were unsettled by the experience and address their concerns in their letters.[187]

---

187 However, in his memoirs Boris recalls their parting in very loving terms: "Thus, after only a brief ten-day honeymoon, was I forced to leave my dear wife behind. Separating was heartbreaking for both of us. She cried when I left her, but she showed unwavering courage, which only increased my admiration for her." See *Lenin Hitler, and Me*, p. 215.

Having completed her training in Thun earlier in the year, Anna is still living at home with her parents. To Anna's deep regret she still finds her relationship with them strained and loveless. Boris encourages her to find it in her heart to forgive them their deficiencies, as they undoubtedly mean well.

Also of interest are my father's descriptions of Minacar, the remote asphaltite mining community where he worked for more than two years after his arrival in Argentina. He describes it as a paradise. His words and the few pictures I still have of the area conjure up a fascinating, otherworldly realm, one which I imagine few tourists have experienced. The tiny community of about 1,000 persons was quite self-sufficient, having its own doctor, school, and security personnel. The closest town, San Rafael, was about 300 kilometers away. Yet from the start, my father felt at ease there, finding the people friendly and interesting. Perhaps he was trying to paint a rosy picture for my mother, but I believe he was sincere in his appreciation of his new home.

During their separation, Anna had to arrange her own passage to Argentina, which was no easy task in 1946. She continued to have doubts about her marriage and about her ability to fulfill Boris' expectations. Her appetite and love for travel awakened after taking a week-long tour of Italy. This fondness for exotic places and her enthusiasm for the people and culture of those places continued and increased throughout her life. The challenges and advantages of married life aside, Anna surely must have looked forward to the adventure of traveling to the New World.

LETTER A67

LAUSANNE

[Friday] August 9, 1946

My dear Boris,

What an experience it was for me today to see you fly off in that silver bird. I don't want to be too sentimental, but I must say, "God be with you!"

Please write soon and tell me how you are doing and about all your impressions.

Dear, we must gather our strength during these months of separation, and when they are over, we must endeavor to begin our life together with strength and courage. Our future depends on us and our good will. I am ready for anything, so long as you are there to help me.

With a loving kiss and my best wishes for your good arrival in Buenos Aires,

Your little wife

LETTER B57

LONDON

[Saturday] August 10, 1946

My dear heart,

I arrived yesterday an hour earlier than the travel agency in Lausanne predicted. The confusion lay in the fact that they gave me the estimated arrival time based on Belgian time, rather than Swiss or English time (they are the same).

The flight to London went very well. I flew over the exact area where I crossed the Swiss border in 1943 and the Belgian mine where I worked in 1940.

On Tuesday morning I will leave London, so I won't have time to do any touring. Many people here are still experiencing deprivation because of the war.

Mr. Griffith[188] recommends that if you travel by boat you take a Swedish ship, rather than an English one, because the food will be much better. But in the end, it will be your choice.

Here are some words of Pestalozzi:[189] "What you become depends on you." So, think about yourself and try to discover your faults and try to rid yourself of them. At the same time, do not think of yourself as worthless. All people make mistakes. But one must always try to develop one's talents and rigorously uproot one's faults. We can help each other with this, and we will and must do it. We must establish a good marriage. Fights, lack of principles, and laziness will lead to crises. We must both strive to become fine, strong, educated people. You have the same goal as I in this respect, so you must strive for it too. It will lead to a deepening of our love, and we will achieve a higher regard for each other. Otherwise, we

---

188 Boris' host in England
189 Johann Heinrich Pestalozzi (1746-1827) was a Swiss pedagogue and educational reformer.

will continue to fight constantly over nothing, like we did during the last few weeks we were together. Our marriage bond will weaken and dissolve quickly. So, let us both strive industriously to repair our relationship for the sake of our happiness.

I send you many kisses,

Your Bobussja

LETTER B58

LISBON

[Tuesday] August 13, 1946

5:30 pm

Little heart,

In a few minutes I shall fly from Lisbon to Africa. The flight to Bathurst[190] will last six hours. The flight from London to the Spanish coast was not so interesting. Only when we were over Spain and Portugal was it worthwhile. The plane made some grinding noises right before it landed. I am sitting in the airport now having tea and a piece of cake made of very white flour.

I feel strange leaving Europe. I first arrived on February 13, 1923, and left today, on August 13. I will arrive in South America on August 14. We will see if I have better luck with the number 14. I will arrive in Buenos Aires on August 15.[191]

Your Bobussja

---

190 In Sierra Leone
191 On his way to Buenos Aires, Boris made stops in Natal and Rio de Janeiro.

LETTER B59

Rio de Janeiro

[Thursday] August 15, 1946
7:15 a.m.

Little heart,

We landed in Rio last night. Everything seems expensive here. I am impressed with everything I have seen in Rio so far: the buildings, the climate, and the exotic looking men and women. I am more impressed with Rio than I was with London. But I do not know what London was like before the war.

The flight was very exhausting. Imagine leaving London at 11 a.m. and then being in the air almost constantly for thirty-four hours. It was hard to sleep because we had to stay in our seats the whole time and it was horribly noisy. The small airplane I took from Switzerland to London was far less noisy than the larger one I had for the trans-Atlantic flight. I wrapped cloth around my ears, but it made little difference. I also had to endure the constant shaking and heaving of the plane as it went up or down and when we hit air pockets or went through clouds. Today my flight to Buenos Aires will last only seven hours.

I freely and completely admit that I should not have been so stingy during our honeymoon, so please forgive me for that. But you must correct your attitude toward money as we cannot spend a lot of money on everything. One would have to be a millionaire to do that, and I am not one. Fortunately, we will be able to live very cheaply in Argentina. Maybe that will solve most of our problems.

Your Boris

LETTER A68

WINTERTHUR

[Friday] August 16, 1946

Dear Boris,

I have decided that I would rather travel by boat than airplane, and I would like to leave no later than November.

My neuralgia[192] is no better. The doctor prescribed me some pills, but they did not help.

I am just back from a two-hour English lesson. My teacher is from England, and she only speaks English with me. I am making good progress.

Oh Boris, let us forget all the ugly things we said to each other, and let us begin a new life in a new land, among new people. We must not begin where we left off. We should start anew, with Christ.

Boris, I have done you wrong, and I want to ask your pardon from the bottom of my heart. I am full of regret. Dear, please try to create an atmosphere of peace around me with your calm strength. That is what I need. Please believe that despite all the hateful things I said, at heart I am still the good, honest girl you knew in the summer of 1944. Even if I am sometimes exasperated with you, in my heart I know you are the best and the dearest person in the world. I would never have wanted to marry a different man.

You are right when you say our fate rests entirely with us. It is up to us to make it a reality. We should cease lecturing each other; we should act!

Do you remember when, in earlier days, we discussed Christianity at length? I said then that everything depends on the spirit and the word. You said that the most important thing is what one does. You said, "I judge a man by his actions, not his words." But now we see that both are equally important (the golden mean). Even when

---

192 Neuralgia is a stabbing, burning, and often severe pain caused by an irritated, damaged, or infected nerve.

I was stubborn and said nasty things, I still listened to you. Every day I encounter situations in which I feel I need advice. Then all at once I hear a little voice in my heart saying, "Boris would say to do it this way."

I kiss you tenderly. My thoughts are always with you.

Anneli

LETTER B60

BUENOS AIRES

[Friday] August 16, 1946

My little heart,

Our landing in Buenos Aires yesterday evening was difficult. Visibility was poor, and the pilot made multiple attempts to land at two different airports. Finally, he landed at a military airport, something that has never occurred here before. So, my arrival was much delayed. But Gerhard Grassmück and his wife Karin picked me up and gave me a wonderful welcome. Now I can finally sleep well again.

Karin told me that she has had neuralgia too. Fortunately, it cleared up completely. Her doctor told her to go to Minacar because the climate there is so much better than in Buenos Aires.

Six kilometers from Minacar there is a ravine with a river. I am told that from the mine one can see a distance of a hundred kilometers. I will probably get there in about two weeks. I hear it is still quite cold in the mountains now.[193]

Your Bobussja

---

193 August is wintertime in Argentina and Minacar is at a high elevation.

LETTER B61

BUENOS AIRES

[Monday] August 19, 1946

My dear little wife,

Dearest, you must forgive me that I was so nasty and mean to you before my departure. You must realize that in marrying you, I took on a great responsibility. At the time of our marriage my earnings had ceased, and my expenditures were increasing dramatically. On top of that, I was unsure how things would turn out in Argentina. I was very uneasy. Now things are much better. I have been so well received by Grassmück and his associates that I think things will go well for us here. I will have to see how the people in Minacar are, but I am told they are friendly. When I start earning again, I will have the means to spoil you. So just have a little patience now, and you will get what you have always dreamed of, a man who will love you forever. Be careful with your expenses now, but do not spare anything on your health. You must take good care of yourself.

I suggest, especially as you are not completely over your neuralgia, that you travel by boat rather than by plane. My experience with flying was quite frightening, despite my strong nerves. Sometimes planes fall suddenly when there are air pockets. Takeoff and landing can be troublesome. You might want to get a doctor's opinion about this.

I learned that the company's administrative director at Minacar and his wife are Swiss (Mr. & Mrs. Gerstberger). Minacar has its own doctor. There is good skiing in the area and a lot of people own riding horses. Horses cost 50-100 pesos.[194]

Your Bobussja

---

194   100 pesos equaled about $25 in 1946.

LETTER B62

BUENOS AIRES

[Thursday] August 22, 1946

My dear little heart,

I am told that airfare from London to Buenos Aires is about 3,000 pesos now. One would not save as much as I had thought. Making the trip by boat will take about eighteen days.

Next week I will travel to Minacar. Currently I am working and eating a lot. One can eat better here than a European king and do so very reasonably. Clothes, underwear, and leather goods are also much cheaper than in Europe. The directors of the mine own land in San Rafael and drive there twice a week. A lot of English people live in San Rafael and in Buenos Aires, and they are much loved, unlike the Americans. At Minacar the climate is terrific. On Sundays, many of the workers go riding. Often, they picnic at a lake close by that sits at an elevation 200 meters above the mine, or they go fishing in the river valley below.

Your Bobussja

LETTER B63

BUENOS AIRES

[Sunday] August 25, 1946

My dearest,

Thank you for your letter of August 16. Your words did me good. Sweetheart, if I did not believe in you, I would never have married you. I have great faith in you. It is the foundation of my love and trust in you. But listen to me a little more closely next time (you need not lose your freedom in doing so), and you will see that I am not as bad as I might have seemed when we were last together.

Be at peace. All the bad blood between us will remain behind in Europe. The great ocean will wash it clean. We will start a new life here. We must strive to look for only the best in each other.

Gerhard has gone out of his way to help me. He will help us both make a good start. It will seem like paradise to you. We will have a little furnished house built in the farmhouse style[195] surrounded by fabulous, towering mountains. The air quality is splendid. It is very sunny, and you will see fabulous colors everywhere, in the sky and in the surrounding terrain. The area is ideal for skiing in winter.

The mine has hired and retained excellent employees. All those who have not passed muster have been dismissed. You will meet and probably befriend two young women here. One is the schoolteacher; she teaches in the school every day. She will be able to give us Spanish lessons. Her husband speaks English exceptionally well. He is fifty years old and works in the mine office. The other woman, Mrs. Addor, is Parisian. She will surely invite you to her home. She and her husband have land in San Rafael. It takes six hours to get there by car. She goes riding often. There are a lot of riding horses around at the mine. There are also many dogs here. Minacar has two policemen and several watchmen. The mine hires

---

195 *Bauernstil*

a doctor to serve the miners and the entire community. Everything is well organized.

Food is so inexpensive it would make no sense to try to save money on it. You can learn a lot about setting up a household from Karin. She is a splendid housewife, and I am sure she would be delighted to explain things to you. She even has a Russian cookbook written in German. The Grassmücks and all their friends send you their greetings and are awaiting your arrival with tremendous eagerness. I have shown them your picture, and they find you very charming.

When you arrive in Buenos Aires, you should take three days to rest and shop for all the things you will need here, including boots, riding pants, long pants, and a leather jacket.[196] Leather apparel is cheap. A leather jacket costs about 120 pesos, much less than you would pay in Switzerland. You should be sure to bring all your sweaters along. The nights in Minacar are cool.

The Argentines here have very white skin and either black or red hair. All of them have thick, healthy hair, probably due to the wonderful climate and nutrition. Karin says she has much more hair now than when she arrived here seven years ago.[197]

Your Bobussja

---

196 The leather jackets my parents purchased in Argentina are still in my possession.
197 From this we can assume that Gerhard and Karin arrived in Argentina in 1939, prior to the start of World War II.

LETTER A69

WINTERTHUR

[Sunday] August 25, 1946

My dearest Boris,

I received your letter about your trip and the one from Buenos Aires written on August 19. Both made me happy.

Boris, I will no longer make excuses for myself. Last month I was nasty and cold toward you, and it is perfectly right that you should object when your wife treats you so poorly. I must admit that you are right in much of what you said in your letter. I do so want to be a real lady, but so often I still seem to be a thick-headed, defiant child, just as you often are still a rascal despite your forty years.

Dearest, I am glad we are separated now; it will allow us to reflect on our relationship more objectively. A few weeks ago, we peered into a terrible abyss. But now we can gather the strength to push ourselves away from the precipice and get back on the right path. Without a doubt we were on the wrong path because we lacked true understanding, as you also noted in your last letter.

Do you agree that our relationship has become more superficial lately? We are always occupied with external things, and thereby we forget our souls. What do I know of Bobussja's heart, and what do you know of mine? Do you know that my heart has become stubborn and hard? Do you know I was so caught up in myself that I forgot that I married you to help you, to make your burdens lighter, and to make you happy? Yes, I had forgotten all those things. Moreover, I forgot that I pledged myself to you and agreed to be led by you. My wishes became uppermost in my mind. I forgot that the souls of others are delicate and must be shown consideration. Love between two people should not be trampled upon. Even if that love is very great, it is still delicate and breakable. This is a terrible self-accusation I lay before you; I feel terribly guilty. The sense of my own powerlessness depresses me so much, I want to cry. But I will not because I know it will not help us. We must learn to understand each other again, to understand that you are mine and I am yours. The only way to do that is through Christ. I do not desire, as I did in earlier days, to become a fanatical Christian. But I see that people need the spirit of Christ to love each other truly and to look forward together into the future. It makes us free and allows us to be creative, which gives our hearts courage, hope and love, and shows us that other people are human beings too, made of the same flesh and blood, and in need of love as much as we are.

Boris, I would like to repeat a prayer here that I included in my letter to you on October 27, 1944:[198]

"Father, let us lay everything, everything in your hands—our love and our future. You lead your children, and so it is you who has brought us together. Let our understanding grow and strengthen our common mission: to save ourselves for you. Father, we are nothing without you. Make us strong. Grant us your blessing, your spirit, and your light, *so that we may serve you.* You know our hearts best; if it is your will, let us find each other and become one soul in your presence. Amen."

Don't these words apply to us even now?

We should not expect everything to change all at once. We must begin afresh, from the ground up, slowly building up one stone at a time so the house will not collapse in the future. We both have wounds in need of healing. These wounds are still fresh, and therefore we must protect each other at every turn, even while we go about our work.

Dearest, I know you have many important things to think about now, but I believe it is necessary that we confront these serious problems. You said yourself that if things between us are not right, you cannot work well.

---

198 No letter from Anneli survives from that date. This prayer does not appear in any other letter.

You wrote in your last letter that you want me to forgive you for being so stingy during our honeymoon. I do not think you are a stingy person at heart. I understand full well that you were somewhat fearful right before your departure, as our funds were dwindling away so quickly.

I want to apologize for something I did not do but should have. It pleased me so much that you bought me some fruit and sweets just before you left. I am sorry I did not thank you for them at the time.

Boris, I must tell you something. You know how much I enjoy beautiful clothes and beautiful things, and how glad I would be not to have any money troubles. But there are other things that are even more important to me. What use is the prettiest house and the most expensive fur coat if one is unhappy? I would be a thousand times more content to have only life's barest necessities along with the strength to make you happy.

Do you feel you have left your chains behind now and that you are your own master again? How do you like Buenos Aires? How do you like the people? Do you feel you can trust them? I wish you much success as you begin your work in Minacar. I hope you find your co-workers excellent.

I hope you are not too lonely; I am all alone too. I do not feel comfortable at home anymore. I find no love here, even though I need it badly. After I leave, you will be all I have in the whole world. I can never return here.

Anneli

LETTER B64

BUENOS AIRES

September 2, 1946

My dear heart,

Your letter of August 25 just arrived, and reading it did me a world of good. I miss you so. I see how much you regret your actions before my departure, and that true regret will be met with my true forgiveness. I steadfastly believe in your honesty and decency. My faith in you and my love for you is built upon that belief.

It pained me to read what you said about your parents, that you are uncomfortable with them and feel you can never return home after you leave Switzerland. All people can make mistakes, even our own parents. One must learn to forgive all those who wrong us, but especially our parents. When we are together again, we will try to win them over, not because we fear them, but because we want to show them that love is stronger than hate, arrogance, avarice, or pettiness. I do not want you to lose your father because of me. You should continue being a good daughter to him. Be grateful to him for wanting the best for you in his own way. He may be wrong, but do not condemn him for his mistake! Think about your relationship with him, and let Christ's love guide you.

I will be traveling to Minacar in the next couple of days. You may not receive my next letter very soon; it takes mail a whole week just to get to Buenos Aires from Minacar.

Try to get here as soon as you can. I am missing you terribly and cannot wait to see you.

I kiss you tenderly,

Your Bobussja

LETTER A70

WINTERTHUR

[Tuesday] September 3, 1946

My dear Boris,

How happy your letters have made me! You have opened the door to my heart again with your loving heart. First, I must tell you a few things that I know will bring you much joy. My English lessons are going very well and that makes me happy, especially because I know my progress will please you. Also, last night I had the pleasure of listening to Beethoven's *Pastoral Symphony* on the radio. I thought of you all the while. How grateful I am to you for showing me the beauties of classical music.

Thank you for the photos of Minacar. I find them extremely beautiful. You are there by now, and I hope it will be a paradise for you, too, and that you will be happy in your work. I believe we will spend many happy hours there. I thank you for your faithfulness; you may believe in mine. I want to give you exactly what you give to me.

Take a tender kiss from me, and another, another, and yet another....and another.

Your Anneli

LETTER B65[199]

MINACAR

[Saturday] September 7, 1946

My dear little heart,

At 7 p.m. Grassmück and I took the train from Buenos Aires and arrived in San Rafael the next evening. We traveled the 1,000 kilometer stretch in a sleeping car. It was interesting to see the unfamiliar landscape. There were areas of uninteresting barren wasteland, but for the most part we saw farms and livestock ranches.

In San Rafael we were met by Mrs. Addor. We had dinner with her. She hails from Paris and is a friendly, cheerful woman. She and her husband have a nice estate with an attractive house here.

Later we went to see Mrs. Gerstberger, the wife of the business manager at Minacar. They also have an estate in San Rafael.

After staying the night in a hotel, Gerhard and I left at 9 a.m. the next day and traveled by car to Minacar. For the first fifty kilometers we drove over flat land, then we ascended to a high plateau of about 1,000 meters. We then drove 150 kilometers west until we reached the high mountains. The road then goes south along the mountains until you reach the last train station at Malargue. From there one must continue over the mountains for another hundred kilometers or more. For the last forty kilometers the road follows the river.[200] The road to Minacar diverges from the river about twelve kilometers from Minacar and this is where Mr. Addor's little house stands. I believe his house is at an elevation of 1,500 meters, while the mine itself is at 2,200 meters.

From the mine you can view a vast, magnificent panorama, including the valley with the river I mentioned earlier. The surrounding mountains are between 3,500 and 4,000 meters high.

---

199 In this letter Boris recounts his journey to Minacar and his first impressions of it. I have included it in its entirety.
200 The Rio Grande (Argentine)

These are mostly flat-topped mountains where one can comfortably take hikes, ride horses, or ski in the winter. The landscape has magnificent colors, as the mountains are either covered with green grass or littered with different kinds of stones which lend the surroundings their amazing colors. Even the sky has many beautiful colors. The tops of the higher mountains are covered with snow throughout the year.

The weather here is splendid; there is little rain. It is almost always sunny and quite windy (like in the Engadin), which makes the heat of summer quite bearable. In the winter it is supposed to be cold (down to minus 20° Celsius at night). Everyone wears furs, which are available in all price ranges. You will have to buy one for yourself.

The mine employs between 300-800 workers. It is the largest coal mine in Argentina. The mine has its own doctor (they are currently searching for a new one), pharmacist, hairdresser, and security police (state police, as well as policemen hired by the mine itself). It is like a small independent settlement. The houses are much stronger and better built than at Swiss mines. The business manager's house, where Grassmück and I have been staying as guests, is magnificent. We will have a smaller one.

Mr. Gerstberger owns a beautiful horse. He lets the mine workers ride it on Sundays. You can ride it too if you wish, especially on workdays. Gerstberger and his wife have been in Argentina since 1930. He is very personable and about forty years of age. In February Grassmück will also be forty.

There are many other intelligent, kind employees here. You will be able to take lessons in Spanish, English, and even French from a couple I met here. The wife, Argentine by birth, is a schoolteacher. Her husband speaks many languages, including perfect English. They ask me frequently when I would like to start lessons. I have no time for it right now because of my workload. But once you are here, we will study English together. Addor, Grassmück, and Gerstberger are extremely kind, which makes my work environment much better than what I encountered in Switzerland.

I am quite content here. I hope you will be too. You will enjoy the wonderful climate and the beautiful surroundings. You will have your own little house with which you may do what you like. The conditions are such that I think you will be able to make a good recovery from your current illness. As far as I am concerned, you need not work too much. You can easily hire a housekeeper, then you can put more effort into learning languages. The only thing you may miss is the city. But I am prepared to take you to Buenos Aires, or another city, for a month two or three times per year. When you arrive in Buenos Aires, I will pick you up and we will purchase all the clothes you will need here. We can also buy a radio, a record player, and records. You may want to bring your own linens.

Almost all the people at Minacar are Caucasian. There are few Indians and I have seen no Negroes at all. Even the simplest people are intelligent and clean. Because of good nutrition and an excellent climate everyone here is healthy. The people look like they get a daily shot of vitamins.

The only disadvantage here is one must be very self-reliant. One can get rich quickly, but one can also get into a lot of trouble easily too, as there is no Frau Dr. Kurz, Freudenberg, or social security. At most, you can count on good friends. But I believe this "pressure" of potential danger will be good for us. We must rely on our good health and ability to absorb the language quickly, using and increasing our talents. If we do this, our life will not be boring, but exciting. This is especially important for you, because I will be working at the mine many hours each day, and you must find ways to occupy yourself.

[Friday] September 13, 1946

Bring only paper money with you, no coins. Also bring an alarm clock, your electric cooker and roaster, and the bill for your trip.

Try to get yourself well while you are still in Switzerland, as there are no specialists here.

I feel in excellent health right now. The work at the mine is not too taxing. It is easy to get around. My Spanish is getting better, and I am conversing with people more. Everyone is very polite. If you make language mistakes, they are patient and try hard to be of help.

Do you remember what happened on this date two years ago? We have made much progress since then. You see, I did manage to turn your head!

I am quite sure we will be able to understand each other much better here than we did in Europe, and I hope we will soon succeed in becoming a single droplet.

Your Boris

P.S. I just found out that a plane belonging to the airline I took to South America crashed after takeoff in Africa. (It was not the plane that I flew.) All the passengers perished.

LETTER A71

Winterthur

[Monday] September 9, 1946

My dear Boris,

I received your dear letter of September 2. I thank you for your kind words of encouragement. Do not worry, I am trying to be nice to my parents, even though it often hurts me to realize that they do not love me as much as parents should. Despite that, I am still trying to bring them joy.

Dear, please do not be impatient with me. You know yourself how difficult it was to get a plane ticket. A boat ticket is even more difficult to obtain. On top of that you are forty and a seasoned traveler, whereas I am only twenty and have hardly stuck my nose over the Swiss border. Have no fear, I will do what I must to get a ticket.

The doctor says he can do no more and that my neuralgia is due to mental stress. I must find myself an orderly, peaceful way of life and avoid getting overly excited.

Air France tickets cost Fr. 1,300 to fly from Paris to Buenos Aires. But I would never sign on to fly because I want to arrive in Buenos Aires in one piece. In the last few weeks two Air France airplanes crashed. Mr. Stauffacher tells me they have bad engines.

If I feel better, I will take a trip to Italy. There is a tour leaving on September 22.

I send you my most loving kisses my dear, dear Boris,

Your Anneli

LETTER A72

WINTERTHUR

[Tuesday] September 17, 1946

My dear, dear Boris,

I received a letter from Mrs. Grassmück this week in which she tells me you spent some pleasant days together and that you have been able to recover from the fatigue of your trip. She says you are learning Spanish quickly and enthusiastically. You are so brave, Boris. I can see you very lifelike before my eyes, how you are using all your strength and energy to prepare yourself for your new job which will be the cornerstone of our life together. I long for you and feel that I belong to you more each day. It is clear to me now that I must give up my prior life completely and begin again, living with and for you. Others have done it before us; we can do it too.

I have signed up for a week-long Italian tour beginning September 22. I will visit Milan, Genoa, Rome, Florence, and Bologna. I am looking forward to it greatly and hope the weather will be good. In a week I will be able to pick up my visa in Geneva. As you can see from the enclosed photo, I have gained three kilograms.[201] I still have no boat ticket. I have been in touch with three different travel agencies and am told I can do nothing but wait, wait, wait. If nothing comes of this, I may end up flying after all.

Anneli

---

201 Even in neutral Switzerland food was rationed during World War II. Anna did not go hungry during the war, but some food items were unavailable or difficult to find. Three kilograms is about 6.5 pounds.

LETTER B66

MINACAR

[Sunday] September 22, 1946

My dear Anneli,

I have been in Minacar for three weeks. Grassmück and Addor left a week ago. Now I live in a two-room apartment and eat with the workers in the canteen.

Here is a typical day for me:

I get up at 7 a.m. and eat breakfast at 7:30. We have coffee with milk, bread, cheese, and marmalade. Then I work from 7:50 until noon. Lunch is at 12:30 p.m. We get soup, two different meat dishes, oranges, and more bread, cheese, marmalade, and coffee. We can eat all we want. Then we work from 2-6:20 p.m. Tea is always available at the mine. Dinner is served at 8:30 p.m. It is much like lunch as far as the food goes. Red wine is available at lunch and dinner. Board costs 2.50 pesos per day.[202]

We will get coal to heat our house and free electric lighting. You can hire a maid to help you with the housework. Our house (the one they plan to give us) is still occupied. We will have three bedrooms, a kitchen, a bathroom, and a gorgeous view! They will renovate it for us. It will come with some basic furniture (table, chairs, beds, cabinets), but everything else we will need to supply. We can buy sheepskins to cover the chairs, but I will leave the decorating to you.

I learned that the mine was founded in 1941.

I strongly suggest that you travel by boat, not plane. Crashes are just too prevalent. The airline I took lost one of its planes in a crash on September 8. I had hair-raising experiences on my trip. We had motor problems three times. It was so noisy I could not sleep. Traveling by ship is much more relaxing and for that reason better for you.

---

202 A little less than $1 a day

It was stupid and cowardly of me to be so foolish during our honeymoon. Please forgive me. But understand that it takes a lot of courage to marry a young woman and to go to the other side of the world with almost no money and lacking language skills. We must lay our fate in God's hands with trust, but we also need to use the talents God has given us to the best of our abilities. That is, we must not be idle, but tackle everything with energy and fight for our happiness. But do not worry, just believe that I love you very much.

Your Bobussja

LETTER B67

MINACAR

[Monday] September 30, 1946

My dear little wife,

It has been two months since our marriage, but we have been together so little!

I understand a lot of Spanish now, but still can only say the simplest things. We had forty students here visiting from one of Argentina's mining schools. There are only two in the whole country. I hope to get a position at one of them someday! I am not bored here, even though this place is at the end of the world. The colors are beautiful, in the sky and all around in nature. It would be a wonderful area to paint. But no one would believe that the paintings are true to life. The cloud formations are very unusual too. The food is excellent. I must hold back so I don't gain too much weight![203]

[Tuesday] October 1, 1946

We still have no doctor. It is important to be healthy when you arrive. Please try to restore yourself to complete health before you leave. One must travel 1,400 kilometers to Buenos Aires to see a specialist. There is a small clinic in San Rafael which is six hours away by car. Doctors are expensive and probably not as good as the ones in Switzerland.

Your Bobussja

P.S. Karin is expecting a baby.

---

203 Boris gained a lot of weight in Argentina. The diet there was very meat-heavy; beef was especially plentiful. At his heaviest he was close to 200 lbs.

LETTER A73

WINTERTHUR

[Sunday] October 6, 1946

My dearest,

I received your letter about your first impressions of Minacar. I also received the photographs Gerhard took. It was a good idea of yours to send me pictures, thank you! But despite that, it all still seems strange and foreign to me. I am having a hard time imagining what it is like there. I can imagine that you are working hard now with great enthusiasm. I am so happy you like the place and that you are satisfied. You need not worry about my needs. I will enjoy living in the mountains. I may miss city life now and again, but that is not so important. I will try to get in a lot of concerts, plays, and operas now. I often go to the movies.

But now I must tell you about my trip to Italy. I am still recovering from it. Switzerland now appeals to me far less than before. Yes, everything here is very well organized, clean, and comfortable, but Swiss people are not as relaxed or cheerful as the people of the south. In short, I am completely excited about my Italian experience. I would like to continue traveling until I have seen the whole world!

My trip was quite exhausting, but wonderful. Because we rode around in a bus, we had a lot of contact with local people. I must say that one often makes poor, false assumptions about the Italians.[204] In truth they are not at all unpleasant. I really liked the Riviera, especially the ocean. I could not get enough of it. I also liked Rome, but to completely grasp it and all its beauties was impossible in the short time we had, only two days. My favorite place was Perugia, a little city between Rome and Florence not far from Assisi. It is built on top of a rock. Too bad that none of the rivers (the Tiber, the Arno, nor

---

[204] Even in the 1960s when I visited Switzerland in the summers, I witnessed the condescending attitude of many Swiss toward Italian guest workers and laborers.

the Po) had any water. I really enjoyed the Italian summer heat and I noticed that it helped my neuralgia. I am glad that when I arrive in Argentina it will be summertime.

The other people on the tour (about twenty-five in all) were mostly Swiss. In Florence we had a tour guide who could speak fluent German, Italian, English, French, and Spanish. At the end of the tour, we asked who our guide had been. Turned out he was Baron Orbinsky, a former Russian aristocrat. It is interesting to see where these people end up and what they are doing.

I send you a thousand loving little greetings and kisses,

Anneli

LETTER B68

MINACAR

[Saturday] October 12, 1946

My dear little wife, my little heart,

I strongly advise you to travel by boat because so many planes have crashed lately. It will be better for your neuralgia, it will be more relaxing and a more interesting experience for you, and it will be Fr. 1,000 cheaper.

Stauffacher told Grassmück that you have only one fault: "You are very beautiful."

Snow fell in Minacar for the second time. But it melts very quickly in the midday heat. Summer nights are cool at this high elevation. Winter daytime temperatures are between -5° and -10° C, and at night about -20° C.[205]

Boris

---

205 Daytime winter temperatures between 23°F and 14°F, nighttime about -4°F.

LETTER A74

Winterthur

[Tuesday] October 15, 1946

My dear, dear Boris,

Thank you for your letter of September 22. I got it last week. I am so happy that you arrived safely in Minacar and that you like it so much. It does sound like a paradise.

I am glad we will have our own house. It would be good if before my arrival you could look through it carefully and write down what we will need.

My parents are willing to lend me some money (Fr. 1,000) for my trip. We can send it back to them after my arrival.

All your talk about riding pants and boots makes me eager to start riding. I will look forward to it, but I am a bit worried because I had a bad experience with a horse once as a child.

I spent some time with my grandmother,[206] helping on her farm. It was very cold. Every Tuesday and Friday I have my English lessons. Tomorrow I will go to Zurich to see an Ibsen play, *Ghosts*.

I would like to thank you for trusting me enough to let me make my own decision about how I will travel to South America. Dearest, we are two very different people, and each of us may decide to do things differently, not incorrectly, just differently. But if we want to live together, we must learn to respect those differences. There are thousands of ways to do something, but everyone thinks only his way is right. In a marriage one must be convinced that one's mate has it right too. That is the end of my sermon. You certainly have a lot of other things to think about right now. But this sermon is not only meant for you, but also for me.

That is all for today. I send you my greetings and a thousand kisses.

Please write again soon!

Your Anneli

---

206 Anna Bertschi

LETTER A75

WINTERTHUR

[Wednesday] October 23, 1946

My dear Boris,

As far as my trip goes, I am still quite frustrated and have nothing definite to report yet. Everyone is having difficulty obtaining tickets for travel. I am not the only one. All one can do is wait and hope for the best. I will let you know as soon as I can by the fastest possible means once I secure my passage.

We have been married for three months, yet I still do not feel married. We have been apart so much. Don't you agree? But we dare not complain because we are at least half to blame for this separation in that we agreed it was the best course for our life together. But I am looking forward to our reunion.

I would like you to explain exactly what you mean by becoming "a single droplet." It is important for me to know because if we are to work together toward a common goal, we must agree on the nature of that goal from the outset. Let me explain how I view this problem. We will always be two people, each with his own character, strengths, and weaknesses. But because each of us loves the other as much as himself (that is, we regard the other as another "I") we devote our lives to each other. Your problems become my problems, your joys become my joys, your life becomes my life. And if our two souls share a life so intimately and have such a great understanding of the other, then nothing, not even the biggest misstep, will separate us. Then we will be like a single droplet. At least this is the way I see it. Please do not forget to answer this question in your next letter. It is very important to me.[207]

I am looking forward to your next letter and all your news. I send you a loving kiss.

Your Anneli

---
207 No written answer to this question from Boris survives.

LETTER A76

WINTERTHUR

[Sunday] October 27, 1946

My dear Boris,

I finally have a ticket on the French ocean liner the *SS Campana* which will leave Marseille for Buenos Aires on November 15. I decided to buy a third-class ticket (saving Fr. 1,000) so that I could share a cabin with a Swiss lady I know. I will leave Zurich on November 9 and travel to Paris via Basel. Then on November 12, I will leave Paris for Marseille, arriving on November 13.

I saw Verdi's *Aida* and I also heard an English pianist, Louis Kentner,[208] who played a whole program of Chopin. I am crazy for Chopin now!

Your Anneli

---

208 Anna also mentions Kentner in her letter of June 3, 1946 (A62).

LETTER A77

ON BOARD THE *SS CAMPANA*

[Wednesday] November 20, 1946

My dear Boris,

We left a whole day late! The boat is over-filled with passengers.[209]

I am on the top level of the rear deck now, the only place on board that is not overly crowded with people. Today I am finally relaxed enough to really enjoy the trip. I can take the time to admire the blue sky, the deep blue sea, and to the right, on the horizon, a beautiful brick-red strip of land, the coast of Africa.

My trip through France went well. My days in Paris were lonely. But Paris itself was wonderful. I did not like Marseille; it was so dirty. But it was interesting to see all the different kinds of people there.

There are about twenty other Swiss people on board with me. I am happy not to be all alone. Some of them have been to Argentina before, and they are telling me a lot of wonderful things about the country! I wish you were here with me now, but we will see and experience many wonderful things together in the years to come. I will see you in two and half weeks!

A thousand loving kisses from

Your little wife

---

209 At this time the *SS Campana's* capacity included 105 passengers in first class, 152 in second class, 230 in third class, and 820 in the steerage section, for a maximum total of 1,307 passengers. This maximum was likely exceeded on this voyage as Anna says the ship was "over-filled." In 1951 the ship's accommodations were reconfigured to accommodate 257 passengers. In 1976 the ship was used in the making of the movie *Voyage of the Damned*, based on the 1939 voyage of the *MS St. Louis* which attempted to transport nearly 1,000 Jewish refugees to Cuba. For pictures and more history about the *SS Campana* see Reuben Goossens' websites at ssmaritime.com/Campana-Irpinia-1.htm and ssmaritime.com/Campana-Irpinia-2.htm.

Mining settlement Minacar, Argentina

Gerhard Grassmück, Anna, and Boris at Minacar (1947)

Epilogue

Other than what little my father says in his memoirs and what appears in the letters they exchanged during the months just after his solo departure for Argentina, there is little information on the state of my parents' relationship during these early years of their marriage. My father was heavily engaged with his work, which he found interesting and challenging, and my mother was intrigued with her new surroundings and its people. After about two years at Minacar, my father received an invitation to teach at an Argentine mining school in the city of San Juan. They decided to build a house there and stayed for four more years, until their U.S. visas were granted. Emigration to the United States was the fulfillment of a dream my father had held since childhood. After so many prior failed attempts, nothing would stop him now. They packed up their most precious belongings and left as soon as possible. They did not even take the time to sell their house. When they finally sold it, they had to take a big loss due to the intervening devaluation of the Argentine currency. But that was of little consequence to them. They arrived in New York City in early January 1953, ready to start life anew again.

Finding a job in the U.S. in the 1950s during the Red Scare proved difficult for my father. He spoke with a thick Russian accent and, at forty-eight, he was no longer a young man. His English was broken and his professional experience in Argentina and before the war in Germany did not seem to carry as much weight as he had hoped it would. Finally, after job hunting for many months, he was offered a professorship in mining engineering at the Pennsylvania State University, a position he gladly accepted. Boris and Anna moved to State College, Pennsylvania in August 1953, quickly fell in love with the town and its surroundings, and remained there for the rest of their lives.

While their new home provided my parents with what they were seeking in terms of a pleasant environment, exposure to the arts, and the possibility for self-improvement, it was here that their marriage ultimately fell apart. It seems that Anna's discontent gradually mounted over the years, but my father was unable to mitigate it, and may not have even been fully aware of it. Frantically trying to build up a fortune in a few short years before his forced retirement from the university at age sixty-five, Boris spent many months away from home in the summers and during his sabbatical semesters. After my birth in 1957, my mother suffered multiple miscarriages, yet still had to manage the household and raise me during my father's absence. I imagine that the stress of those years, along with my father's high expectations and lack of understanding, contributed to Anna's unhappiness. Anna's problems with self-esteem and her fiery temper may also have exacerbated their poor communication. Their differences, already evident in their early love letters, grew in the absence of that necessary understanding and effective communication, and in the end tore them apart.

After their divorce in 1970, my father immediately descended into a state of deep depression, whereas my mother moved on with her life, remarrying within a year. They agreed that I would be shared equally between them, which meant that I would see each of them almost every day and would be provided with two of everything (including pianos) so that I could carry on with my life as before, regardless of whom I was visiting. I had had the benefit of a secure, loving family environment until that point, so at thirteen I was able to accept the situation without too much difficulty. I knew both of my parents loved me deeply and wanted what was best for me, but all the shuttling around quickly grew tiresome. I did not complain, but I resolved to attend college out of state. In four years, I would be free to come and go as I liked.

Despite the little inconveniences I suffered, I knew the divorce had vastly improved my mother's life and state of mind. She seemed almost like a new person. I never begrudged her this decision and felt protective of her when my father railed against her during our conversations. At least at first, he blamed my mother entirely for the divorce. In later years, however, he was able to see that he was partly to blame.

One of my mother's passions had always been traveling. She was able to pursue this interest extensively with her second husband, Charles Hosler, whose professional duties often took him to exotic corners of the globe. Their other shared interests included history, culture, and nature. For thirty years, until Anna's death in 2000, Charlie and Anna seemed to enjoy an ideal marriage.

While it took him a long time to come to terms with the divorce, my father gradually took up his professional life again and even remarried fourteen years later, in 1984. His second wife, Maria Chudobba, had for many years served as a secretary to the director at the Rheinische Kalksteinwerke, the German limestone mining company where my father had worked until 1939. He returned frequently in later years to work as a consultant, and that is where they met. Their marriage turned out to be a good one. Maria was extremely kind and supportive, and she loved my father dearly. She was steadfast to the end and took excellent care of him during his long, debilitating final illness.[210] After his death in late 1992, Maria remained in State College for ten more years, and then returned to Germany in late 2002. I was able to visit her there in 2004, a year before her death.

---

210 To read more about my father's last years, see the Epilogue of *Lenin, Hitler, and Me*.

Afterword

Grandmother's Gift

In November 1999, shortly after returning from a trip to Switzerland, my mother began to experience terrible back pain. She had suffered from back pain for most of her adult life because of early-onset osteoarthritis in her neck and spine, but this was much worse than anything she had experienced before. Suddenly, one of her vertebrae fractured spontaneously, and the pain became intolerable. Her doctor treated her with pain medications. When she went in for tests, the scans showed she had cancerous tumors in her spine. Cancer rarely originates in the spine; it tends to occur when cancer in another part of the body has metastasized. By early January, the doctors had discovered the culprit: lung cancer, stage four.

She had first started smoking as a young person. It was fashionable at the time, during World War II and through the 1950s and 1960s. Smoking was romantically depicted in many Hollywood movies, especially those of the popular *film noir* variety. Who would not want to emulate the most famous movie stars of the day? However, my mother was never a chain smoker; she kept her habit under control. She rarely smoked in my presence, usually waiting until after I had gone to bed, or lighting up at parties I did not attend. Our house never smelled of smoke; she was careful to keep a neat, tidy, fresh-smelling house. Once, when I was seven years old, I happened to see her sitting in the living room smoking a cigarette. I remember thinking this quite unusual, so I sat myself on her lap and started talking to her. I asked if I could try a puff. Surprisingly, she agreed. Of course, after a single inhalation I choked and sputtered horribly. Many years later, I asked her why she had let me have a puff of her cigarette when I was so young. She said it was because she never wanted me to smoke, and she thought the experience would cure me of my curiosity. It did indeed have the desired effect: I never smoked again.

Charlie insisted that she stop smoking once they were married. He even insisted that she throw away all her remaining cigarettes. She did so, reluctantly. For nearly thirty years she had led a smoke-free existence, yet here she was in 1999, suffering and dying from lung cancer, the same disease that had felled her own father thirty years before. Hans, however, had been a chain smoker all his adult life. He was thoroughly addicted and continued to smoke until his death, even after he knew he had lung cancer. He was rarely to be seen, in pictures or in person, without a pipe in his mouth. Indeed, second-hand smoke in her childhood may also have affected my mother's lungs adversely.

My mother's oncologist recommended chemotherapy, and so she resolved to fight the disease. It proved to be a losing battle. The drugs quickly and severely reduced the quality of her life. How difficult it was for me to watch her decline. I was living in Falls Church, Virginia at the time and was caring for my ten-year-old son, Andrew. I called her frequently and visited as often as I could during the school year.

In June 2000, once school was out, I took Andrew up to State College and we remained there for most of the summer. My in-laws, Sybil and Robert Hutton, who lived nearby, kindly watched Andrew during the day so that I could be with my mother as much as possible during the last weeks of her life. My husband, Greg, stayed in Falls Church during the work week, joining us on weekends.

Sometime in early July, my mother experienced a crisis and had to be hospitalized. The doctor decided to halt the chemo treatments at that point. After a week or so, much to her doctor's surprise, she became a bit more stable and went home. The drugs she was taking then were making her more comfortable, but they were also making her sleepy and weak. One day, on the way to the bathroom, she fell and cut her head open on a door jamb. Back to the hospital she went, this time to get her head stitched. Charlie decided that because she was so weak and unsteady now, he could no longer care for her at home. He contacted a continuing care facility close by to see if they might have a room for her. There were no beds available on the regular wing; the only opening they had was upstairs in the Alzheimer's unit. It was the only option, so it would have to do.

Soon after she was settled in her private room overlooking picturesque Mount Nittany, my mother received a visit from a woman on the administrative staff. She had come with her routine set of questions that were asked of all incoming Alzheimer's patients. One of them was: "Do you know why you are here?" My mother startled the questioner with the blunt truthfulness of her reply: "I have come here to die." Another day, someone came in with a medical questionnaire and asked my mother how many times she had been pregnant. She said, "Once." Later, at home, Charlie told me she had lied. She had had several miscarriages and at least two abortions. She had lied to shield me from those painful events in her life.

It was mid-August and Andrew's eleventh birthday[211] was approaching. I mentioned it to the nursing staff, and they suggested we have a party for him in his grandmother's room. They would supply a cake and balloons. My mother was pleased with the idea and asked me to purchase some gifts for Andrew so she could present them to him at the party. I went into town and bought two complex construction sets that were his chief fascination at the time. I wrapped the gifts and took them to her room.

The party was held in the morning, the time of day when my mother was most alert. My husband brought Andrew over at about eleven o'clock. Colorful balloons had already been blown up and hung on the walls. My mother, lying in her hospital bed, gave

---

211 August 21

Andrew a big smile and congratulated him on his birthday. He was going to be a "big boy" of eleven in a couple of days. First, we all sang "Happy Birthday," and then the cake was served. Andrew gobbled down his piece and then excitedly approached the large packages. I told him that these presents were from Grandma Anna. As he quickly tore through the wrapping paper, some inexplicable, unseen force drew my eyes away from my son and fixed them firmly on my mother. The brightness of her face nearly blinded me. Her eyes were wide, and her mouth opened into a huge smile. How greedily she drank in those few seconds of exuberant joy her gifts had brought her grandson! I, in turn, could not have been more grateful to see her at that moment as I, too, savored every second of her happiness.

All too soon, the party was over. I heard Greg urging Andrew to thank Grandma Anna for the gifts, and then they said goodbye. We were going to be returning to Virginia later that day. As they waved and made for the door, my mother waved back at them. Realizing it was the last time she would see her only grandchild, she called out to him, "Andrew—don't ever stop being Andrew!"

I remained in the room with her and Charlie. A few moments later Anna's lunch arrived along with her medications, which included morphine and another strong sedative. I almost stopped the nurse from giving them to her because my mother had seemed so happy and comfortable during the party. I said something, but Anna took the pills anyway, no doubt to please the nurse. I was able to get a few bites of food into her mouth before she became too sleepy to eat or talk. She never regained consciousness. Over the course of the next few days, she gradually ebbed away, dying in the earliest, stillest part of that late August morning.

Her last presents to Andrew were enjoyed by him for a short time, but soon were set aside and supplanted by other interests. Yet those last moments of joy she experienced watching her grandson opening his gifts were of immeasurable value to her, and they remain etched in my memory forever.

Late in her life I had asked my mother about her religious beliefs, as she had never shared them with me. She told me she did not believe in the resurrection of the body.

"Only the spirit can live on," she said, "in the minds and hearts of the people you have loved."

Her religious thinking had undergone a major evolution, thanks primarily to my father. But something of what she had learned from her grandmother long ago had remained with her. For as long as I can remember, she maintained a miraculous equilibrium through all of life's trials and hardships, just as her grandmother had in her day, relying on her strong faith. It was something I had always admired and even envied in my mother. She had it still, even as she struggled with the devastating illness that had killed her father. I never heard a complaint escape her lips. She met the challenge with a fighting spirit and then, when treatment failed, a graceful, calm resignation.

In those last weeks we spent together, I asked her many questions about her past and the people she had known, many of whom were long gone. One day she told me about a neighbor girl she had known while growing up in Switzerland who had hated her. She expressed genuine regret that this girl had not liked her. I thought it strange that she worried about it so long after the fact. I suggested that the girl might have misinterpreted something she had said, or perhaps the girl had not been such a nice person in the first place. My mother thought about it but did not reply. I was willing to place the blame on the other girl; my mother was not.

A day or two after my mother's death, an obituary appeared in the local newspaper. No funeral or memorial was organized, as this was Charlie's preference. Because of this, I decided to include a request for written memories of Anna (see Appendix B) in Anna's death announcement which we sent to close friends and family. Neither Charlie nor Anna belonged to a church, and I did not expect that any gravestone or memorial marker would be erected in her honor.

In keeping with her modest, generous nature, she had decided to leave her body to science. Before the end of the year, I received an envelope from the Penn State College of Medicine in Hershey. In it were directions and the plot number of my mother's gravesite. I decided to try to find it. Early the next year, on a cold Sunday in February, I found myself trudging around the Hershey Cemetery in the snow, searching for the marker with the correct number on it. When I finally found it, I was disappointed to see how tiny it was. It merely marked the location of the cremated remains of all the people who had donated their bodies to the College of Medicine in that year. Toward the back of the area, I found a large sign with a message of gratitude from the medical students to the donors and their families for their generosity in contributing to the advancement of science. There were no names to be seen anywhere. Vaguely dissatisfied, I returned home. I never went back; she was not there.

Whenever I want to remember Anna, I go to the Arboretum at Penn State at the north end of campus. You can go there too. Walk around the large oval central pathway, and at eleven o'clock you will find the "Witness Tree," a large white oak donated and planted by George Biemesderfer, a Penn State alumnus and my stepfather Charlie's cousin. In accordance with arborists' tradition, it was named the "Witness Tree" because it was the very first tree planted in the arboretum and would "witness" all future plantings. George, the owner of a nursery in Lititz, Pennsylvania, was a well-known expert in transplanting large, mature trees. When it arrived in that empty field in March 2005, the oak was about thirty-five years old and thirty-three feet tall. White oaks can live up to 500 years, reach a height of a hundred feet, and boast a trunk diameter of up to four feet at maturity.[212] Assuming it can be kept healthy, the tree will remain there for a long time, overlooking the gardens, the campus, and the surrounding community. George dedicated the tree to his cousin, Charles Hosler, and to the memory of my mother, Anna Rosa Hosler. It is also known as the "Hosler Oak." It was a fitting gift, as it reflected their love and appreciation of nature in its numerous and varied forms.

---

212 See https://www.statecollegemagazine.com/articles/new-plans-take-root/ and https://news.psu.edu/story/186005/2005/03/23/witness-tree-planted-arboretum-penn-state.

Since the Witness Tree was planted, the arboretum has flourished in a grand way. As the tree itself continues to grow taller and broader with each passing year, newer additions—bushes, flowers, other trees, fountains, and especially the popular and creative Children's Garden—have gradually come along. These perhaps command greater attention, as many are more colorful and closer to the ground. Yet I cannot help but feel the benevolent grace of the white oak every time I walk past. It lends a grandeur and quiet beauty to the place. If it were suddenly to disappear, I have no doubt it would be missed.

As much as I have now come to better understand and appreciate both of my parents as distinct individuals, each with troubling flaws as well as formidable strengths, I know that I can never be a clone of my father or a recreation of my mother. I am a separate, new being—a seed planted by them to flourish in a unique way. This is as it should be. But it leads me to wonder what gifts I, too, might leave behind.

Appendix A

Anna's Pearls of Wisdom

A33 (March 6, 1945)

It is a great awakening when one suddenly realizes that one is a living being just like animals and plants. Taking this view, a new question arises: What is the meaning of life? The thought that we only live to die is so hopeless. We must be here for a reason. Invariably other questions follow: Why does an animal live? Why does a plant or a flower live? I find no other answer than just to bring joy to those who see it. What is a tree's purpose? To bear fruit. With that I arrive at the point where you led me before: We live so that we can both enjoy the world as a wondrous creation and live in the service of that creation, not just for ourselves, but *within* that creation. One must shake everything around a bit to really understand this truth. It is the source of much strength.

There is always something in the soul that will remain a mystery to the other, and perhaps this is the most crucial part of the attraction between two people. I am glad that I have no such illusions about marriage anymore. I see quite clearly how terribly difficult living together as a couple can be, and that this difficulty can only be borne successfully by a truly great love.

A35 (April 19, 1945)

I do not want to be a piously religious person, but a sensible one instead. The world interests me more than heaven does.

A39 (May 8, 1945)

It is said that complete love is achieved when I am you and you are me. That makes sense to a certain degree, but it is also true that it is by loving that one discovers the real self (the true "I") for the first time, but in terms of the other.

A48 (July 15, 1945)

Truth resides *in the world of the spirit.* Truth is *the* way, and the world must ultimately go the way of truth, whether it wants to or not. Truth stands *rock solid*; it is unshakeable. Christ is the embodiment of this truth. That is why Christ said: *"I am the way, and the truth."* And that is why Christ's resurrection was inevitable. Whether it was a spiritual or physical resurrection is not so important. Truth is the godly principle, and it is as permanent and strong as any of nature's laws, but one cannot grasp it by seeing it, but only with one's spirit.

A49 (August 1, 1945)

Russia is and remains a big question mark in that one cannot really tell whether its politics and policies will benefit or harm its people. In any case, its acts of power are not ethical, and neither is its propaganda. Boris, you taught me that life must be protected above all else. If you are against Christians who kill people because they would not convert to Christianity, how can you now support Stalin who kills people for political reasons? Where does he get the right do this? He is only a human being.

A52 (October 4, 1945)

If one really wants to play the piano well, one must play completely, with one's whole being, not just with the hands and the ears, but with the heart and by simply being totally aware. Then all the difficulties resolve themselves. My courage is renewed.

A57 (January 27, 1946)

Please do not read my letter quickly through, lay it aside, and say, "Yes, yes, you are right." You see, it takes a lot of effort for me to put my soul and everything that moves me into words. I am speaking to your soul, and I would like to receive a response from your soul.

"Understanding everything is forgiving everything." Pay attention to these words; they are true. Understanding someone means being able to put yourself in his place and grasp his true nature. Because when you understand him, then you will know when he is in need, when to give a strong word, when to remain silent, when tenderness is needed, and when to give advice. You see, putting your soul into the soul of another is the most beautiful result of a happy union between a man and woman. Dear, this help of one soul to another is more valuable than a hundred gifts.

A58 (February 3, 1946)

I love people with high ideals, but only those with a broad-minded, noble heart, with the ability to understand and forgive human frailties. With them there is freedom; with all others life would be a perpetual prison filled with drudgery.

A74 (October 15, 1946)

Dearest, we are two very different people, and each of us may decide to do things differently, not incorrectly, just differently. But if we want to live together, we must learn to respect those differences. There are thousands of ways to do something, but everyone thinks only his way is right. In a marriage one must be convinced that one's mate has it right too.

Appendix B

Remembrances of Anna

Memories of friends and family who knew Anna in Switzerland

September 5, 2000

On the death of Anna Rosa Hosler

We always called her "Anneli," which corresponded to her sensitive nature.

Our paths crossed early on. We lived in the same part of Winterthur, in Veltheim. We had great-grandparents in common and were classmates in my father's classroom for three years in elementary school. At that time, there was no mutual affection between us. Anneli reminded me much later that I used to pull her pigtails very hard in school.

After school ended, ten years went by before we saw each other again in the USA. I was then working in Richmond, Virginia and would visit Anneli in State College, Pennsylvania. We seemed to get along better than when we were schoolmates. A Jass (Swiss card game) evening with Swiss friends rounded out the visit.

Another ten years later the custom of visiting changed again. I had by then returned to Switzerland. Now Anneli came often to Veltheim with Vera to visit her father and his wife Martha. In between, letters about our families filled the gaps. Reading her letters in her particularly clear handwriting was always a real treat.

The longer we knew each other, the deeper our friendship became. Also, with Anneli's second husband, Charlie Hosler, I felt we had an excellent rapport from the beginning. I gladly recall the times we spent together in Pennsylvania and in Switzerland. I was deeply impressed with her understanding of the Amish people and their customs.

About one year ago Anneli visited for the last time to attend a class reunion. She did not shy away from the exertion of what for her was a troublesome trip to show her solidarity with her school friends. It would be the last visit to the place of her youth.

Hans Ott [cousin]

Locarno, September 2000

The sad notice of Anneli's death hit me hard. The sun had passed its zenith this summer when Anneli, on August 24, left this earth. Her last words to me at the class reunion of last October suddenly gained a different meaning. Could she possibly have had a premonition of her approaching death—or did she already know of a fatal illness when she said to me: "This is the last time that we shall be together."

I don't remember exactly when I first became aware of Anna. But it was in first grade of primary school that I first met her. She really was the most attractive of all the girls. Her natural charm was obvious to everybody.

At that time, Anna lived at Bachtelstrasse 12, which runs exactly east to west through Veltheim. North of the street the ground rises towards Wolfensberg where the swimming pool, embedded in the forest, was situated. Walking further north, you will reach Schützenweiher, the scene of many happenings and activities all through our school days, whether in the summertime at the swimming pool, or in wintertime skating or playing on the frozen pond. In summer or winter Anna stood out as the beauty of our class. South of Bachtelstrasse toward the center of town the ground is flat and heavily built-up. Here was the primary school building and further away, that of the secondary school.

These were the years 1932-1941. One gray day, Anna appeared at school dressed in black, and we were told that her mother had died unexpectedly. From that moment on, I felt a deep compassion for her and closed her into my heart.

In secondary school Anna grew up to become a beautiful young lady who, it seemed to me, perhaps would go a little further than the rest of us. She might not have been very ambitious or hardworking; she was just a capable person who did whatever was expected of her. She never seemed to have any difficulties with schoolwork. Her face was oval and distinguished in a way, with dark blond hair, radiant eyes, and a warm smile, a vision of grace and beauty.

After secondary school we lost touch, going our separate ways, although she always remained present in my memory. I even remember which profession she had chosen. About forty years passed before we met again at the class reunion of 1985 in Mörsburg. This happened to be the last time I was able to see Anna, who had in the meantime become a complete lady, with my eyes. I was so happy when she seated herself next to me at my table after dinner and hold me about her family and life in Pennsylvania.

Then, beginning in 1986, I lost my eyesight. It was so nice to be able to correspond with Anneli during my years of blindness.

Ernesto Weber [classmate]

(Translation by Eiler Ohlin)

HAUTERIVE, SWITZERLAND

November 6, 2000

Dear Vera,

Already two months have flown by since you had to say goodbye to your dear mother.

Yes, time goes so fast. In between we celebrated a class reunion on November 2 at the Goldenberg Restaurant. On this occasion I asked those in attendance to gather their memories of Anna. Unfortunately, I had very little success, as the particular people who would have most likely responded were absent due to illness.

I had a personal experience in the middle of September when I was on vacation in Ascona (Tirol) with my wife. I visited Ernst Weber, who lives in Locarno. Ernst was in Anna's class from first grade until the end of school.

Now he calls himself "Ernesto" and since he turned sixty, he has been completely blind because of two unsuccessful eye operations. Ernesto was a painter, and one cannot begin to imagine what that would mean for someone in his profession. Ernesto went to a special school for the blind so that he could better continue his life and career. With an iron will he developed a new way to identify the colors and has become a very admired and famous painter in the intervening time. Of course, now he is an abstract painter, yet he is always pushing the limits and exploring new directions in his paintings. He has an amazing capacity for work. He lives alone with his seeing eye dog and has a devoted friend who stays with him from time to time. A couple of years ago, a book was published about him and his work with a forward written by the then president of Switzerland, Flavio Cotti. He travels alone with his dog and takes part at nearly every class reunion!

And now to the personal experience: When I was visiting Ernesto, I shared with him that Anneli Stahel died. The reaction—it seemed to me that Ernesto was stuck by lightning and his eyes became moist.

As far as I could tell Ernesto had been in love with Anna from early on while they were in school together. The sad news really cut him to the wick.

Your mother was really one of the prettiest and kindest girls in our school class. I hope this little story will bring you some happiness.

I hope that you and your family will overcome this bad stroke of fate. I wish you much courage.

With heartfelt greetings,

Yours,

Werner Held [high school classmate]

Dear Vera,

The beautiful time of our childhood and youth remains unforgettable for me. We loved and enjoyed being together. Therefore, for a long time we used to call each other "little sister." We were sisters in our hearts.

Anneli and I were both only children, just as our two daughters Vera and Madeleine were too. Both of our fathers were serving together in the military. Both of our mothers were from Winterthur, and they too loved each other.

Aunt Rosie (as I called her) got sick and died at an early age. Anneli, the poor child, was still only a child herself. This time was a very difficult one for your dear mother.

Anneli came to visit me often in Vevey and we saw each other with great pleasure; but saying good-bye each time was difficult. I also enjoyed visiting her in Winterthur at Bachtelstrasse where we frequently got together and had a lot of fun. We also had serious discussions. For your mother during these early years, it was very hard to be without a mother. Your grandfather worked a lot and was often absent. For this reason, Angelina, the housekeeper, was hired. I think that your mother and she got along well. But no one can replace a loving mother, even less a stepmother.

In our youth we would often take our vacations together at "les Moulins" at the Chateau d'Oex. These were unforgettable vacations. Wherever we were, we enjoyed being with each other.

Later when we were both married, I had a daughter named Madeleine and Anneli had a daughter, whom she loved above all else, whose name was Vera. She was so happy and proud of her baby, the pretty little daughter, the sweet teenager she so loved.

Dear Vera, you brought your mother great joy and love. Vera married, made music, worked hard, and had a son of her own, and

Anneli became a happy grandmother overnight—her pride and joy. Often Anneli would say, "Vera is coming on the weekend." Or, "Vera will visit for a few days." Thank you, Vera, for making your mother so happy.

With loving regards,

Betti Michoud [childhood friend]

August 31, 2000

Dear Charles, Vera and family,

We were very sorry to hear about the passing away of Anna and send you our heartfelt condolences.

In retrospect, we are glad that we saw each other last year and could drive her around to see places of interest to her, particularly to Uhwiesen, to see "Rebhof." We thought then that she was frail but did not think it was cancer. At this sad time, the only consolation is that she does not suffer pain and discomfort anymore.

Regarding Vera's request for any memories of Anna, Richard can only remember the few times she came to Uhwiesen on visits, and that his godfather Hans and Anna's mother and subsequently Martha, were our main contacts. Anna moved to your country when Richard was a teenager. As a schoolboy, Richard once spent a week's holiday at Bachtelstrasse in Winterthur.

We renewed our contact with Anna during our trip to Japan when we were traveling through the USA, and since then we corresponded with her at Christmas and saw her whenever she was in Switzerland. She was very proud, Vera, of you and your family and often talked about her grandson. She sent us photographs of her home and family.

It is possible that Hanni Bänzinger-Witzig, who was in closer touch with Anna, would remember more.

With kindest regards to you all,

In sympathy,

Margaret Schenk [wife of cousin, Richard Schenk]

Urdorf, Switzerland

September 4, 2000

My sister Alice and I sat together trying to gather our remembrances of Anneli. As children we visited a few times in Winterthur during vacations. We played with Anneli and rode bicycles. One time we were permitted to go to a dance party with piano accompaniment. Aunt Rosa, Anneli's mother, found us all beautiful clothes to wear on this occasion and even arranged for us to get some lessons with a dance instructor. For many years we (the Bertschi family from Uster) would come and celebrate Christmas Eve in Winterthur at Anneli's house. Our grandmother from Uhwiesen was also there usually. We always so looked forward to spending Christmas with Anneli and her parents.

Later, when Anneli married and moved to Argentina, our contact was limited to letters, until she again began to visit Switzerland. We always were very happy to see her every time she visited.

Lisebeth Krieg and Alice Bertschi [cousins]

August 31, 2000

Anneli and I were playmates, and how I looked up to her! I was only a half a year younger. Aunt Rosa of Winterthur came often with Anneli to our mutual grandmother's (Anna Bertschi) house. We both felt at home at "Rebhof" in Uhwiesen. Grandma had lost her husband when she was forty-five years old and had four children to bring up all alone: Elise (my mother), Albert (of Kilchberg—father of Max and Hilde), Emil (of Uster—father of Lisebeth and Alice), and Rosa. The pastor of Laufen helped her financially so that Albert could complete his teacher's training.

Grandma had fields of grapes and much fruit. Her nine big cherry trees were a source of pleasure for us children. Of course, my father and mother helped her out. My father would pick all the cherries, and both my mother and grandmother walked 1½ hours to the market in Schaffhausen three times per week. I had the most fun when the grapes were harvested. Then all the relatives would come. Anneli was most often our leader when in the evenings we were permitted to go to the playground. One time we played "wild panther" because one had just escaped from the zoo.

Unfortunately, Rosa had a hard life because Uncle Hans was a Jass addict and often did not come home at night. Anneli's mother died young at age thirty-seven. A nasty blow for Anneli, especially since she was so attached to her mother. I was terribly sorry for her at the time. At thirteen one is still a child and has one's whole life ahead without any motherly support.

Yes, and now her life is over. My tears flow as I write. Anneli gave me a lot. Anneli loved my older sister Elsi (nine years my senior), the Diakonissin sister, very much. She died last year.

Our grandmother baked and sent Anneli Basler "Lackerli" (cookies) one week before she died. By the time they arrived, she was dead. She loved Anneli more than anyone. And Anneli was very attached to her grandmother too.

Now, she too is gone, and soon it will be our turn to say goodbye.

I send you, your husband and son our heartfelt condolences. My husband and I live in a condominium right across from the Wolfhalden church, in case you would like to visit sometime. We would be very happy to see you.

Hanni Bänziger-Witzig [cousin]

September 2, 2000

I spent my childhood in Anneli's immediate neighborhood. My parents' house was at Bachtelstrasse 10 in Veltheim, next door to that of the Stahel family at Bachtelstrasse 12. We were both born in 1926 and spent a lot of our free time together. Unfortunately, we were not in the same class because I was born later in the year, in November, and had to enter school one year later. Despite that, we enjoyed a lot of things together.

Unforgettable were also Anneli's parents, Hans and Rosa Stahel-Bertschi, in whose home I was always welcome. When father Hans poured over his copious stamp collection, he always had a few samples left over for us children.

Anneli, who was a very bright child, always had good ideas. We were never bored and when we were playing, Anna was always the leader. Once when nothing interesting was happening on our street, we "infested" a nearby neighborhood, and then we went to more distant neighborhoods. Finally, we lost our way home, and our worried parents had to look for us. The memory of a vacation spent together at Grandmother Bertschi's home in Uhwiesen remains unforgettable to me. There was little space on hand, so we were allowed to sleep at a relative's house in a four-post bed.

Then came the sad time of the illness and early death of Anneli's mother Rosa Stahel. Anneli had to learn how to fend for herself at an early age. Because Hans Stahel was in the military during the war years, she had to rely on herself a great deal. She developed into a beautiful teenager, who was always an example to me. Then came the time in Gwatt and her training in Thun. I had to help with our family's bakery business and our close relationship suffered a long interruption. I heard from Martha Stahel of her marriage to Boris and their move to the United States.

How happy I was when Anneli came to see me years later with little Vera. From then on, we cultivated a regular letter exchange and whenever she visited Switzerland we would arrange to meet. The last time was in October 1999.

Anneli, it is good that there was you!

Marteli Schmid-Hotz [Winterthur neighbor and childhood friend]

Memories of those who knew Anna in the United States

Thoughts of a dear friend, Anna Hosler

On a shelf above my kitchen sink is a wooden Springerle cookie mold, hand carved, with two mice having a pleasant chat. Anna gave it to me shortly after I met her. We had spent many happy hours together planning decorations for the wedding party of our children, Vera and Greg. We had such a good time shopping for flowers, Christmas tree decorations, candles, and holders, and relaxing over a cup of tea or going for lunch at the Waffle Shop. When she gave the mold to me, she said the two mice having a discussion reminded her of us. Since then, every time I look at it, which is often, I think of her. She was one of the loveliest persons that I have ever known, and such a wonderful friend to me. How I shall miss her!

Sybil Hutton [mother of Anna's son-in-law]

Memories of Anna Hosler and
Home-Cooked Meals
December 31, 2000

I still remember the very first time I sat down at the dining table with Anna and Charlie Hosler. That was fourteen years ago in August of 1986. I was twenty-three years old and had just arrived from China to attend a graduate program at Penn State University. Charlie Hosler at that time was Dean of Graduate Studies at Penn State, and through his friendship with my mother and grandfather, had offered to let me stay with them for the first week.

Having just flown twenty-two hours over the Atlantic Ocean, spent two days in New York City, and then taken a ten-hour Greyhound bus to State College, I was both exhausted and nervous when I sat down at their dinner table for my first American home-cooked meal. It was a very hot August evening, the air conditioning was humming gently in the house, and on the dining table there was a bowl of freshly picked flowers from Anna's garden. The house was spacious and beautifully decorated, reflecting the care the hostess had taken to arrange it. Anna wore a white jacket with a beige colored flower printed skirt, and her gentle voice and warm smile had an immediate calming effect on me.

That night Anna made rice, steamed vegetables and some stir fired chicken. She kept apologizing to me that her rice probably was not as good as what my mother would make, and we talked about food in China and food here in the United States. For dessert we had ice cream, and Anna brought out a few different kinds of cookies. She noticed that I particularly liked one kind of cookie that had strawberry filling. After that, Anna always had that kind of cookie ready whenever I came to dinner.

Since that time, I have eaten many home-cooked meals at Charlie and Anna's table. There were birthday dinners, graduations, engagement, then a wedding. When I graduated and left State College, I came back for Thanksgiving and Christmas. Over the years the guests that I have brought to her dinner table also kept growing. First there was my husband John, then my daughter Debbie, and then my son Justin. I have also grown from a single Chinese girl to a professional woman, a wife and then a mother. I began to appreciate more and more the special qualities Anna had, her gentleness, her beauty, and her caring for her husband, friends, and guests. John once said to me after staying with the Hosler's for a weekend, that Anna was the best, most thoughtful hostess he had ever met, and he challenged me to do better, to be more like her. Our dinner table conversation also has grown in subjects, and we shared thoughts on how to cope with all kinds of issues and challenges facing women today.

The last home-cooked meal I had at Anna's table was in June 2000. The only difference this time was I was the one who cooked the meal for her in her kitchen. Anna had been diagnosed with cancer and was undergoing chemotherapy. She had lost a lot of weight because of the reaction to her treatment, and she couldn't eat very well. When she greeted me at the door her warm and gentle smile beamed through her frail body, and my heart was aching when I saw her. I could empathize with her pain.

As I chopped up celery and carrots in the kitchen and boiled water to cook the noodles, Anna brought over a chair and sat down on the other side of the counter. Even though her illness was at the top of my mind, it was a very difficult subject for me to carry on a conversation about. So, we talked about food, I mentioned the healing power of ginger and garlic, and the nutritious value of carrots. When my chicken noodle soup was ready, Anna insisted on setting the table herself.

That night we sat down at Anna's table again, Charlie, Anna, and me, just like fourteen years ago, and ate a normal dinner under very unusual circumstances. Anna ate her first bowl of soup and she then asked for seconds. We talked about my job, the kids, and school. How I wished that the dinner could have gone on forever. I felt that as long as I could keep Anna eating, she would fight the cancer and survive.

As I sat at the dinner table, I also realized how much I have grown in fourteen years, not only in age, but also in my perspective on life, and how much I appreciated her friendship, her love, and her care.

That night when I left her house, Charlie and Anna stood at the door of their balcony and waved to me as I pulled my car out of their driveway. That was the last time I saw Anna.

Stella Si [a PSU student from China whom Anna and Charlie hosted]

September 14, 2000

To Anna's Family,

It is hard to believe Anna is no longer with us. She was a very special person, and now she has quietly slipped away. All her friends will miss her sweet smile and concern for others.

I never knew Anna really well. She had a reserve which some believe is a Swiss characteristic. Yet she was always warm, friendly, and gracious to all.

After the sad memories of her last painful illness have faded, I hope we can all keep within our hearts the memory of dear Anna enjoying her garden, music, and the company of family and friends.

With sympathy and affection,

Nancy Panofsky [wife of PSU faculty member Hans Panofsky]

Thursday, August 31, 2000

We were fortunate to meet Anna and Charles in June 1992 during a trip to Alaska and Siberia. We had a wonderful time—many pleasant memories. The friendship continued after the trip and has grown over the years.

We were captivated by Anna's warm, quiet charm, wonderful smile, and perky attitude. In her home, Anna was a genuinely gracious hostess; she had a way of making you feel special and comfortable.

Through the years we never lacked in conversation. We talked about everything, exchanging thoughts and ideas, and enjoying each other's company and conversations—about everything, including health problems, good and bad. Anna carried her health burden with great dignity. Truly a fine lady.

In celebration of Anna's life, we give thanks for being a part of it. We loved her. Anna will remain in our hearts forever along with many very happy memories.

May she rest in peace.

Ken & Louise Buckwalter [PSU faculty member and wife]

September 4, 2000

Dear Ms. Kochanowsky,

Thank you for informing me of your mother's death. I looked forward to seeing her each year at the American Meteorological Society meetings and will miss her very much.

In her quiet, unassuming way, she was truly a remarkable person. When my husband died, Anna's thoughtful note was really comforting. Her responses to my messages after I learned of her illness were incredible. Although I knew that she was suffering excruciating pain, her notes were always cheerful, and she never failed to inquire about me.

Anna Hosler was one of the most courageous and compassionate people I have ever known. Your loss is shared by all of us who knew her.

Sincerely,

Shirley Baum [PSU faculty wife]

Memories of Anna

I remember Anna for:
   Her gracious self
   Her lovely appearance
   The elegant meals she served
   Our experiences together in China, at AMS[213] meetings, roaming through museums and art galleries, discussion of books read, music enjoyed, places and people visited.

Our first real bonding occurred in June 1979 on our trip to China with the AMS presidents. Anna prepared herself for the trip by taking a course at Penn State on the Chinese language. During a stop at one museum, she thanked the director in Chinese. Surprised and delighted, he turned around and broke off a beautiful big red hibiscus bloom for each of us. At West Lake in Hangzhou, we each had a wild ride in a motorcycle sidecar driven by a young Chinese hot-rodder.

Many such reminiscences made for joyous conversations back home in State College. In fact, she and I presented a program to the Faculty Women's Club French Group describing our adventures in China. Speaking in French was more effortless for Anna than it was for me.

Shortly after our return, Penn State's Department of Meteorology hosted a visit by a group of Chinese meteorologists. Anna served dessert to them in the Hosler home. On the following day they were scheduled to fly back to Washington DC very early in the morning, before the Nittany Lion Inn's food service opened. So, Anna and I served breakfast in the Inn's lobby. She brought fruit and a big jug of tea. I provided an urn of coffee and muffins. Dr. Hsieh, bringing me his cup still half full of tea and asking me to fill the cup with coffee said, "American cocktail!" We often laughed over our hurried exit to the airport, for we left banana skins, apple cores, and crumbs on the coffee tables. It was an experience!

213 American Meteorological Society

I shall never forget:
How I loved to be with her
How I loved to talk to her
How I simply liked to look at her.

I never heard her speak an unkind word about another person. Though she was often in pain, she never complained. A friend like Anna rarely comes in one's lifetime. I shall always be grateful that her life touched mine. She will be sorely missed.

Betty Blackadar [wife of PSU professor Al Blackadar]

September 2000

We came to Penn State in the summer of 1958. For the first few weeks we were pretty miserable with everything new and so many unknowns. Then, the wife of Ernie's department head, Peggy Larson, took me to the fall reception of the Faculty Women's Club. There, I met a Swiss compatriot, Anna Kochanowsky, who was signing up new members for the French Conversation Group. I joined the group, and that was the beginning of a long and deep friendship. Anneli and I met regularly at meetings and occasionally in between. I often sought advice from her; she had such a wonderfully clear mind and always gave me the right advice. I always cherished her thoughts and her judgment, and I'll always keep a special spot in my heart for Anneli. I miss her very much.

Alice Bergman [wife of PSU faculty member Ernest L. Bergman]

August 29, 2000

Dear Vera,

First of all, let me say how saddened we were to read the news of Anneli's death. Even though one knows there is no hope left, nevertheless the stark reality of her being no longer in our midst is felt very keenly. Our thoughts and prayers are with you and Charlie at this most difficult of all times.

I first met Anneli when George and I came to State College back in 1962, and she invited me to a faculty wives' function at her home. You were probably about six years old then.

It was mainly through the Faculty Wives' French Group that the acquaintance continued. Anneli's French accent was delightful. I most remember her as a gentle, considerate person, never loud or argumentative, and always a *lady*.

She spoke of you so often and she was so proud of your accomplishments (and your motherhood!). George and I were in Reno when you gave a harpsichord recital there, and we spoke to you afterward.

Anneli will be remembered with regret at her short life, and with affection by all who had the privilege of knowing her.

With our sympathy,

Jane Schenck [wife of PSU faculty member George Schenck]

August 28, 2000

My memories of Anneli began when she first came to State College. I was then a teenager. Anneli, a lovely, young, sweet Swiss woman, was a new member of my parents' Swiss Group.

The Swiss Group was so important during my childhood, not only because the Swiss people were so important to my parents, but also because they were like an extended family to me and my sister since we had no relatives outside of Switzerland except for Mom and Vati. I so fondly remember gatherings at our house and going on summer picnics, for some reason especially at Black Moshannon.

I remember Anneli's joy when Vera was born and from then on Vera was central to her life.

After leaving State College, I always was updated on Anneli and Vera's lives by my mother and whenever possible when I returned home, I joined Mom at a Swiss Group function or a French Group meeting.

In recent years, Anneli, along with the other Swiss women, regularly visited Mom at Foxdale. This dedication has been most touching to me since I live so far away in California.

I am proud to have known Anneli and I treasure the memories I have of her.

With loving thoughts of Anneli,

Karin (Meyer) Petersen [daughter of Elsi Ackerman, close friend to Anna]

September 2000

Anneli and I first met in the fall of 1953. I remember our first visit in her first apartment where she introduced her first husband as "my Siberian husband."

The Swiss Group, founded shortly afterwards, consisted of Elsi and Arthur Meier, their good friends, Flora and Is Sheffer, Anneli, Boris, Werner, and me. We met at each other's homes every weekend for about twenty years. Lots of good talks! Lots of good food! The Bergmans and Bleulers joined the circle later. Anneli was always a gracious hostess, an excellent cook, a careful and neat homemaker. What stand out most, I feel, were her tact and diplomacy. Always friendly and even-tempered, she also had a lot of good common sense, as well as a strong character. She knew what she wanted and achieved it with diplomacy and perseverance. Boris was quite unique—a bright, big, impressive man with big plans. We heard much about his adventurous past and his ideas for the future. He loved and adored his wife (twenty years his junior). Their age difference didn't seem to matter, not for a time.

Vera was her parents' pride and joy! Her father would have bought the stars for his daughter, but her mom put her foot down. She did NOT want a spoiled child.

I remember the first concert Vera gave at the Music Academy! Her mom and I went to hear her and enjoyed her playing. Vera not only displayed her musical talent (inherited from her father), but also looked very lovely in the blue dress her mom had made herself.

A new life started for Anneli after she married Charlie—a new love, a new house. And, as the wife of Dean Hosler, Anneli encountered many new challenges, and different social obligations. I also encountered her on Christmas with her four stepchildren! It took all the diplomacy and perseverance, all the caring Anneli could muster, to make friends with them.

As our lives changed, I saw less of Anneli. Still, we remained friends. After my divorce, some of my other friends looked the other way. Anneli did not. I appreciated her friendship and her loyalty. While I was at college in Syracuse, NY, Anneli and Charlie invited me to their lovely home for visits. Thank you both! Thank you for your support when my new husband Charlie had a heart attack. When I was attending college after my divorce, I remember fascinating courses, my great friends there, Willy and Tom Evans, lots of tuna fish sandwiches, and a care package Anneli sent after hearing that I broke a bone. The delicacies were wonderful, chosen with great care. But what really touched my heart was that Anneli cared.

We all will miss her.

Olgi Draper [close friend, also Swiss]

October 10, 2000

Dear family of Anna Rosa Hosler,

Ever since I received your invitation to write to you about my experiences with Anna, I have been thinking about how to express to you what a special person she was to me.

I was not a close friend of Anna's, but she always made me feel special. I met her in 1972, after Dean Hosler hired my husband into the faculty of the College of Earth and Mineral Sciences. She was the Dean's wife, and I was a young faculty member's wife. She was warm and sincere and genuinely interested in me. Every interaction with her over the ensuing years was the same.

Anna always remembered my name, always greeted me with warmth, and was always interested in my family and my activities.

I grew to respect her for her smile, her graciousness and poise, no matter what the setting.

Over the last several years we had lunch together with a group of women from the University Women's Club. At these luncheons recently, Anna began to share stories from her childhood and young adulthood. I was so impressed with the richness of her life, her experiences, and her humbleness. It was obvious that she loved her husband, loved her family, and enjoyed her life.

Anna was a person that we all respected and that I will try to emulate.

I am so saddened by her death. We spoke to each other about a month after her diagnosis as only fellow cancer patients can. I knew then that she was ready to fight her disease. I know that she left you with positive lessons about life and death. I will always remember Anna with the utmost affection and respect.

Fondly,

Sue Tressler [wife of PSU faculty member Richard Tressler]

Made in the USA
Middletown, DE
30 October 2022